Heather Jensen

I0608384

# MARY THOMAS'S DICTIONARY OF
# EMBROIDERY STITCHES

# MARY THOMAS'S DICTIONARY OF
# EMBROIDERY STITCHES

Revised, full-color edition of this classic
book, with over 100 new stitches

## NEW EDITION BY JAN EATON

Trafalgar Square Books

# FOREWORD

MARY THOMAS, author of the original edition of this book, was born in Wantage, Berkshire. She was educated in music and art, and in her twenties went to America to work as a fashion artist for the *New York Pictorial Review*. At the outbreak of the First World War she returned to Europe, and went to France as an army nurse. After the war, she worked as fashion editor of the *Gentlewoman,* and in 1930 became editor of the *Needlewoman.* She took up freelance writing in 1935.

*Mary Thomas's Dictionary of Embroidery Stitches,* published in 1934, was the first of her highly successful books, and it was followed in 1936 by *Mary Thomas's Embroidery Book.* Although embroidery was, of course, her first subject, she also developed an interest in knitting. In 1936, she began work on an exhaustive compendium of knitting history and technique, which was published in 1938 and 1943 in two volumes.

Both her embroidery and her knitting books have remained in print for nearly half a century, and are regarded as standard reference works for the techniques of these crafts.

First paperback edition published in the United States of America 1998 by
Trafalgar Square Books, North Pomfret, Vermont 05053

Reprinted 2001, 2002, 2007

**Printed at: Oriental Press Dubai  U.A.E**

All rights reserved. No part of this publication may be reproduced or transmitted in any form or by any means, electronic or mechanical including photocopying, recording, or any information storage and retrieval system, without either prior permission in writing from the publisher or  a license are permitting  restricted copying.

ISBN 978-1-57076-118-8
Library of Congress Catalog Card Number: 97 - 81406

CREDITS

This edition created and directed by Salamander Book Ltd.
EDITOR: Krystyna Mayer
Design : Bridgewater Design Ltd/
Peter Bridgewater and Nicki Simmonds
PHOTOGRAPHY : Steve Tanner
COLOUR  ARTWORK : Malcom Porter
INDEX : Myra Clark
COLOUR REPRODUCTION : Scantrans Pty, Ltd.

# CONTENTS

# INTRODUCTION

One of the delights of embroidery lies in the simplicity of the materials and the lack of complicated equipment and techniques. Fabric, threads, needles and a simple frame, together with time, practice and patience, are all that is needed to create beautiful embroideries.

## FABRIC

Fabric for embroidery falls into three groups: plain- or common-weave, even-weave and canvas. To ensure that an embroidery will last and give pleasure for many years, always buy the best quality of fabric available.

### Plain-weave Fabric (Common-weave fabric)

This first group of fabrics comprises all woven materials that do not have a regular weave. They are available in cotton, wool, linen, synthetics and blends of these, and in weights ranging from fine, semi-transparent voile and organdie right through to heavy-weight tweeds and velvet. When working embroidery on a plain-weave fabric, always match the weight of the thread and needle to the fabric.

### Even-weave Fabric

Fabrics in this group are also plain-weave, however in this case the same number of identical warp and weft threads is included in every 1 inch (2.5cm) square of fabric. This number, called the gauge or count, is usually stated on the fabric label. Stitches are worked accurately on even-weave fabrics by counting the threads. These fabrics are usually quite loosely woven, and made of linen, cotton or wool, often blended with a small percentage of a synthetic fibre. In the case of Hardanger, Aida and Binca cotton fabrics, either two or four warp and weft threads are woven together, providing regular blocks over which the stitches are worked.

### Canvas

Canvas, the third group, consists of warp and weft threads woven together to produce a precise mesh or grid which is usually completely covered by the stitching. The weight of the embroidery thread should always be carefully matched to the canvas gauge to ensure good coverage of the canvas. Canvas is available in a wide range of sizes or gauges ranging from delicate silk gauze with 72 threads to 1 inch (2.5cm) to coarse, 3- or 5-gauge cotton rug canvas. Canvas is usually made of stiffened cotton, but is also available in silk or linen.

The mesh of single or mono canvas is formed by the intersection of a single warp and weft thread. Double or Penelope canvas is similar in construction to single canvas, but the mesh is made up of pairs of warp and weft threads.

## EMBROIDERY FRAMES

Most embroidery benefits from being worked on fabric or canvas held taut in a frame. This makes the work easy to handle, keeps the stitching even and reduces puckering to a minimum. The choice of frame depends on the type of fabric used, the size of the embroidery and your own preference.

### Embroidery Hoops

Hoops or ring frames are available in various sizes and are made of plastic, wood or metal. They consist of two circular sections, one of which fits neatly inside the other, holding the fabric firmly in between.

To mount a piece of fabric in a hoop, first bind the small inner ring with thin cotton bias binding or bias-cut fabric and secure it with a few small stitches. Next, position the fabric over the inner ring with the right side facing upwards, slacken the screw on the outer ring and place it over the top. Adjust the screw so that the outer ring fits over the inner ring. Work around the ring with your fingers, gently pulling the fabric taut and, at the same time, keeping the fabric grain straight. When the fabric is taut, tighten the screw to secure the outer ring.

### Rectangular Frames

Specialist embroidery suppliers sell adjustable rotating and slate frames with or without integral stands. Both types of frame consist of top and bottom rollers with strips of webbing attached and two side sections which are secured and tensioned with wooden or metal nuts, screws or pegs.

The method of mounting a piece of fabric in a frame is as follows. First, bind the edges of your fabric or canvas with bias binding or masking tape. Stitch the top and bottom to the webbing with a strong thread, working from the centre point outwards. Next, slot in the side sections, turn the rollers to tighten the fabric and secure the tensioning devices. Lace the sides of the fabric to the frame with fine string or a strong linen thread, securing each end of the string by knotting it around the frame.

PLAIN-WEAVE (COMMON-WEAVE) FABRIC

EVEN-WEAVE FABRIC

LOOSELY WOVEN EVEN-WEAVE FABRIC

SINGLE (MONO) CANVAS

DOUBLE (PENELOPE) CANVAS

# INTRODUCTION

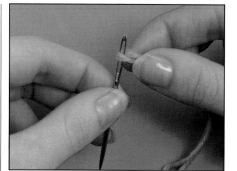

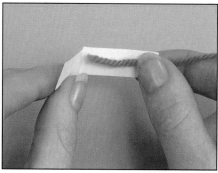

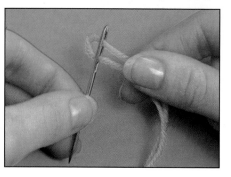

## ■ THREADING A NEEDLE

There are three basic ways of threading an embroidery needle.

A needle threader has a loop of fine wire at one end. Pass the loop through the eye of the needle, push the end of the thread through the loop, then carefully withdraw the needle threader. The wire loop will pull the thread through the eye.

Use the fold method (above) for soft threads. Fold the end of the thread over the needle and pull it tight. Slip the folded thread off the needle and push it through the eye.

A paper strip (above, right) will often succeed where the other two methods fail. Cut a strip of thin paper 2 inches (5cm) long and narrower than the needle eye. Fold the strip in half and place the end of the thread inside the paper. Push the folded paper with the thread inside through the eye of the needle.

## ■ STARTING TO STITCH

When you start to stitch, do not make a knot at the end of the thread. A knot can cause an unsightly bulge on the right side of the fabric or canvas. Instead, leave about 2 inches (5cm) of the thread hanging loose. Darn this loose thread

in on the wrong side when you have finished your embroidery.

Alternatively, work one or two tiny back stitches (page 13) to anchor the thread in an area that will be covered by the embroidery. If you are continuing to work an area which has been partly stitched, secure the end of the thread neatly on the wrong side under a group of stitches. To finish, secure the thread under a group of stitches and cut off the loose end.

## ■ NEEDLES FOR EMBROIDERY

The three types of needles used for embroidery have longer eyes than those used for plain sewing. They are graded in size from fine (high numbers) to coarse (low numbers). The choice of needle depends largely on the embroidery technique being worked.

Crewel needles are medium-length, sharp-pointed needles (sizes 1 to 10) used for fine and medium-weight embroidery on plain-weave fabric. Chenille needles (sizes 14 to 26) are similar, but they are longer and thicker, with larger eyes to accommodate heavier threads. Tapestry needles (sizes 14 to 26) have blunt points and are used for canvaswork and embroidery on even-weave fabric.

## ■ THREADS FOR EMBROIDERY

Embroidery threads are available in a wide range of weights and colours. The most commonly used threads are made of cotton and wool, but linen, pure silk, synthetic and metallic threads can also be bought. Wool threads are hardwearing, colourfast and proofed against moths. Some threads are twisted and cannot be divided, while others are made up of several strands which can be separated to provide a thread suitable for fine work. The strands can also be mixed together to create different weights and colour combinations.

### Stranded Cotton (Stranded Floss)

A slightly shiny thread made up of six strands twisted together which can be divided.

### Pearl Cotton

A tightly twisted thread with a lustrous finish available in three weights, 3, 5 and 8 and in a wide range of colours. Pearl cotton cannot be divided into separate strands.

### Soft Cotton

A heavy, twisted thread with a matt finish which cannot be divided.

### Coton à Broder

A tightly twisted thread, similar to a fine weight of pearl cotton but without the lustre.

### Pure Silk

A shiny thread with an extensive colour range, including some brilliant shades not available in cotton threads. Available as a stranded or twisted thread, silk is expensive, difficult to work with and needs to be dry cleaned.

### Crewel Wool

A fine thread used for free embroidery and canvaswork. Available in a good range of subtle colours. Several strands can be used together in the needle to make a thicker thread.

### Persian Wool

A loosely twisted, stranded thread which can be divided. Available in brighter colours than crewel wool.

### Tapestry Wool

A twisted, 4-ply thread available in an extensive range of colours. Used on coarse canvas.

STRANDED COTTON (STRANDED FLOSS)

PEARL COTTON

SOFT COTTON

COTON A BRODER

PURE SILK

CREWEL WOOL

PERSIAN WOOL

TAPESTRY WOOL

# CHAPTER ONE

# OUTLINE STITCHES

**T**his chapter contains many of the basic stitches used for embroidery on fabric, beginning with easy-to-work running stitch. With the exception of Holbein stitch, these stitches can all be worked on either plain- or even-weave fabric. Select from this chapter when you wish to outline an intricate or curved design, decorate the edge of an applied shape or work a linear detail. Different effects can be created by the stitch chosen, as well as by the weight and texture of the fabric and embroidery thread used.

When making your choice, take into account the varying weights of line produced by different stitches. For example, back stitch, stem stitch and couching will make plain, narrow lines, while twisted chain stitch, Pekinese stitch and knotted cable stitch will produce wider and much more decorative lines. Choose pearl stitch, satin couching or overcast stitch when you need a raised line. A number of the stitches included in this chapter can be worked in two or more colours or weights of thread to add interest to your design.

# OUTLINE STITCHES

## ■ RUNNING STITCH

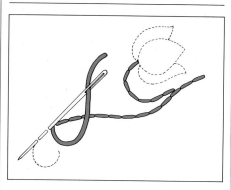

## ■ WHIPPED RUNNING STITCH

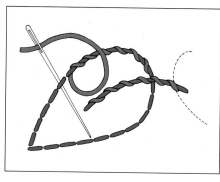

## ■ HOLBEIN STITCH

the stitches. Using a second thread, whip over this foundation, working from right to left, without picking up any of the ground fabric. Work the whipping stitches in either the same thread or one of a contrasting colour. Use a blunt-ended tapestry needle to avoid splitting the stitches in the foundation row.

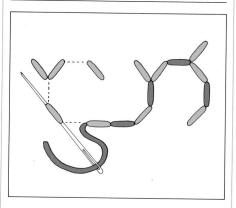

Running stitch is the most basic of all stitches and can be used on either plain- or even-weave fabric. The stitch is a versatile one with many uses, both in embroidery and in plain sewing, and it is quick and easy to work. Use it to stitch delicate outlines, which are ideal for intricate designs, or work it in multiple rows for a light filling and as a component of more complex stitches, such as whipped running stitch and Holbein stitch (right). Running stitch can also be used as a strengthening stitch in cutwork and for outlining designs in hand quilting. Any type of embroidery thread can be used to work the stitch, depending on the weight of the ground fabric and the size of the stitch. An embroidery hoop or frame need not be used.

Work running stitch along the line to be filled by passing the needle through the fabric at regular intervals with an in-and-out movement. For a closely worked effect (above) pick up just one or two fabric threads in between each stitch. Leave wider spaces in between the stitches for a different result.

(Also known as cordonnet stitch.)

Whipped running stitch makes a heavier line than ordinary running stitch (left), producing a raised, almost corded effect. This stitch is used for outlines and linear details because it follows intricate curves smoothly and delineates complex designs.

Any type of embroidery thread can be used to work the stitch, but two contrasting or toning thread colours provide a more decorative effect than one colour used alone. Use a twisted thread such as coton à broder or a heavy weight of pearl cotton to enhance the raised quality of the stitch. Whip the row twice in opposite directions to make a heavier line, or use a really thick thread for the whipping stitches. Metallic threads can also be used, providing they are supple and will not fray. Whipped running stitch benefits from being worked on fabric held taut in an embroidery hoop or frame.

To work this stitch, first make a foundation of running stitches on the line to be covered, leaving smaller spaces than usual in between

(Also known as double running stitch, line stitch, two-sided line stitch, two-sided stroke stitch, square stitch, Roumanian stitch and Chiara stitch.)

Holbein stitch is a simple stitch to work and is used on even-weave fabric, where the threads can be counted to ensure perfect regularity. The stitch is identical on both sides of the fabric and it can either be worked in a straight line or stepped to make a zigzag line. It is used extensively in two forms of traditional European counted-thread embroidery, Assissi embroidery from Italy and blackwork from Spain. Holbein stitch works well both as a delicate outline

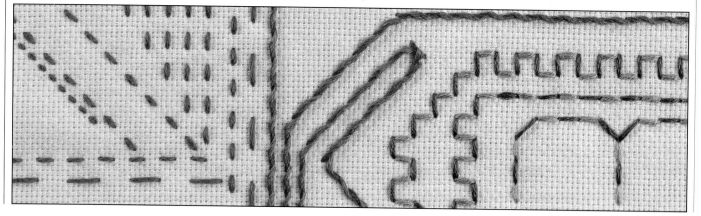

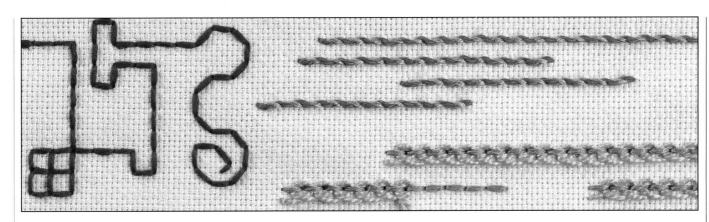

stitch and as a filling stitch used to create intricate geometric patterns.

First, work a row of evenly spaced running stitches (left) along the line to be covered. Fill in the spaces left on the first journey with running stitches worked in the opposite direction, as shown in the diagram. A contrasting thread colour can be used for the second journey.

## ▌BACK STITCH

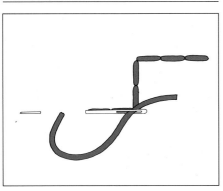

(Also known as point de sable and stitching.)

Back stitch can be worked as a delicate line stitch on both plain- and even-weave fabric. It is also used to make firm foundation rows for composite stitches such as herringbone ladder filling stitch (page 62). It follows complicated designs well when worked on a small scale. On the surface, a row of these stitches looks almost identical to a row of Holbein stitches (left), but here the line is slightly raised. Back stitch is occasionally worked on canvas when a well-defined outline or centre line is required.

Work back stitch from right to left, making small, neat and regular stitches across the

fabric. Work the stitches forwards and backwards along the line to be filled, as shown in the diagram. Keep all the stitches small and even, and position them close to each other so that the line looks as near as possible like machine stitching.

## ▌WHIPPED BACK STITCH

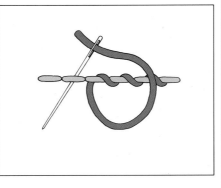

Whipped back stitch makes a heavier line than the previous stitch. The effect created by it varies depending on the choice of whipping thread. Use a heavy, shiny thread in the same colour as the foundation row to make the line of stitches look like fine cord. This technique is useful when a raised line is required on a fabric which is too delicate for a heavy thread to be embroidered directly through the weave. Whipped back stitch benefits from being worked on fabric stretched taut in an embroidery hoop or frame.

First, work a foundation row of back stitches (left), making the stitches slightly longer than usual. Using a second thread, whip over this line from right to left, as shown, without picking

up any ground fabric. Use a blunt-ended tapestry needle for the whipping thread to avoid splitting the foundation stitches.

## ▌PEKINESE STITCH

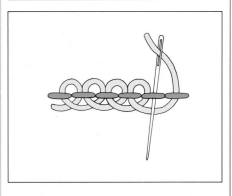

(Also known as Chinese stitch, blind stitch and forbidden stitch.)

In China, Pekinese stitch was traditionally worked as a solid filling stitch in carefully blended shades of silk thread. The stitch makes a braided line and can be used singly or in multiple rows to fill shapes in the Chinese manner. For an attractive effect, the lacing can be worked in a supple metallic thread.

First, work a foundation row of back stitches (left) along the line to be filled, leaving the stitches fairly loose on the surface of the fabric. Lace a thread in a contrasting colour through the back stitch foundation from left to right, as shown, without picking up any of the ground fabric, and tighten each loop after it has been formed. Use a blunt-ended tapestry needle for the lacing to avoid splitting the back stitches in the foundation row.

# OUTLINE STITCHES

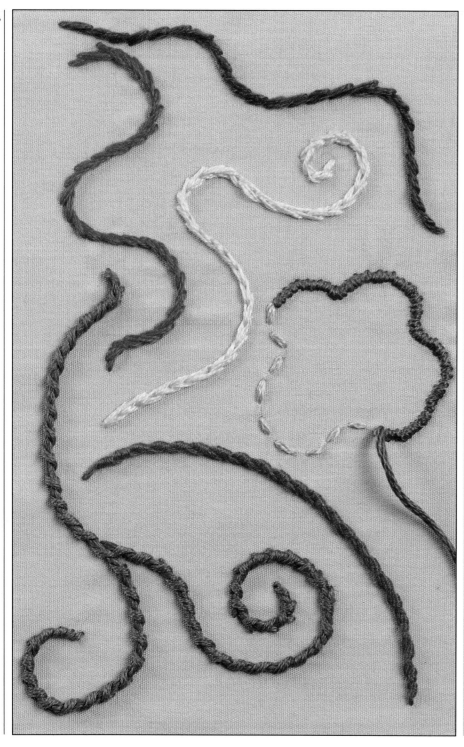

## STEM STITCH

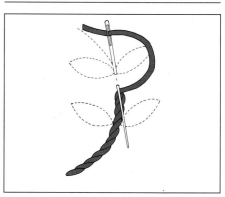

(Also known as crewel stitch, stalk stitch and South Kensington stitch.)

Stem stitch is one of the most frequently used outline stitches. It is quick and easy to work and follows intricate curves and linear designs well. Each stitch should be kept quite small and of an even size. A somewhat wider line can be made by inserting the needle into the fabric at a slight angle, instead of directly into the line to be covered by the stitches.

Work stem stitch upwards, with a simple forwards and backwards motion along the row, as shown, always keeping the working thread to the right of the needle. When the thread is kept to the left of the needle, the effect of the stitch is slightly different and it is then known as outline stitch (right).

## WHIPPED STEM STITCH

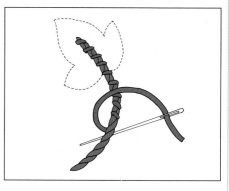

Whipped stem stitch makes a stronger line than ordinary stem stitch (above). Use it when you need a heavy outline which will follow a complex design well. The stitch can be made more decorative if a contrasting colour and texture of thread is used for the whipping stitches. The effect created by whipped stem stitch depends on the choice of whipping thread. When a heavy, twisted thread in the same colour as the foundation row is used, the stitching looks like fine cord. A flat, stranded cotton in a contrasting colour produces an entirely different effect.

First work a foundation row of ordinary stem stitches, then whip this row with a second thread, without picking up any ground fabric. Use a blunt-ended tapestry needle for the whipping stitches to avoid splitting the stitches in the foundation row.

## PORTUGUESE KNOTTED STEM STITCH

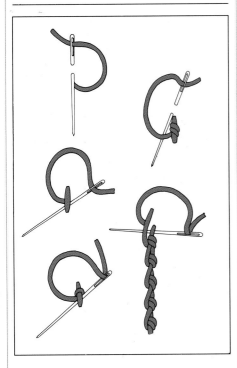

Portuguese knotted stem stitch makes a knotted, rope-like line which is accentuated when it is stitched in a thick, twisted thread such as pearl cotton. This stitch is ideal for outlining shapes and can also be used for working intricate linear designs where a heavy effect is required.

Work this stitch upwards in a similar way to ordinary stem stitch (left). Carry two whipping

stitches under and over the line to be filled, as shown, to form the small knots. Work the whipping stitches over two consecutive stem stitches without picking up any of the ground fabric with the needle.

## OUTLINE STITCH

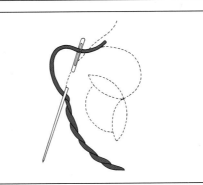

Outline stitch is a versatile stitch which is perfect for outlines and for working complicated linear designs as it follows curves well. Use it in single or multiple rows, depending on the effect required. It makes a neat, twisted line and can be worked in any type of embroidery thread, depending on the weight of the fabric. The stitches should be kept quite small and of an even size, and should be neatly worked.

Work this stitch in the same way as stem stitch (left), but always keep the working thread to the left of the needle. The stitches will twist in the opposite direction to that of stem stitch.

## SPLIT STITCH

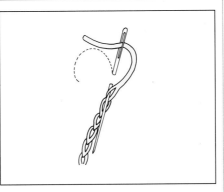

(Also known as Kensington outline stitch.)
Split stitch is used as both a line stitch and a solid filling stitch. Worked in multiple rows, this

stitch lends itself to subtle shading and it is particularly popular for working figurative designs because of the 'painted' effect it can create. Split stitch was extensively used during the Middle Ages for embroidering the faces, hands and feet of human figures on ecclesiastical vestments.

It is essential to use a soft, loosely twisted embroidery thread such as tapestry or crewel wool to work the stitch, since the thread at the base of each stitch is split by the needle as it emerges from the fabric.

Work split stitch upwards, in a similar way to stem stitch (left), using a forwards and backwards motion along the line to be covered. Split the thread with the point of the needle each time it emerges from the fabric, as shown in the diagram. Keep the stitches quite small and of an even size. The resulting stitching is similar in appearance to chain stitch (page 18).

## OVERCAST STITCH

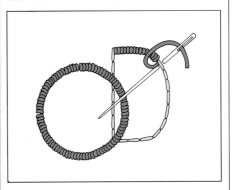

Overcast stitch forms a smooth, raised line which is particularly useful for working initials and monograms, although it can also be used for outlining floral shapes. A flat overcasting thread such as stranded cotton or silk gives good results; a round, twisted thread like pearl cotton should be used for the padding row. This stitch should always be worked with the fabric stretched taut in an embroidery hoop or frame to prevent puckering.

First, work a padding row of Holbein stitches or running stitches (page 12) along the line to be filled. Cover this row with small straight stitches worked at right angles to the padding, as shown in the diagram. Pick up a tiny amount of fabric when making each straight stitch and work the stitches closely together so that no ground fabric is visible.

## BLANKET STITCH

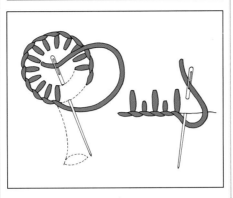

(Also known as open buttonhole stitch.)

Blanket stitch is worked in the same way as buttonhole stitch (below). The only difference between them lies in the spacing of the stitches. Blanket stitch is used as an edging stitch for appliqué and as a surface stitch. The name probably derives from its traditional use as a finish for the edges of blankets. To vary the effect of the stitch, make the uprights alternately long and short, either singly or in groups of two or three, or graduate their lengths to form pyramid shapes.

Work blanket stitch from left to right along straight lines and curves, pulling the needle through the fabric over the top of the working thread. Space the stitches at intervals along the row, as shown in the diagram.

## BUTTONHOLE STITCH

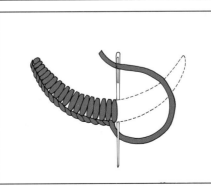

(Also known as button stitch and close stitch.)

Buttonhole stitch is a looped line stitch which is worked along straight lines and curves and has both practical and decorative applications.

You can use it for finishing raw edges and for working buttonholes, although a knotted variation, tailor's buttonhole stitch (page 27), is more durable for these purposes. Variations of this stitch are used for many types of fancy embroidery, including cutwork and Richelieu work. In these embroidery styles, the stitch is used as an edging for raw areas of fabric that have been cut away.

Work buttonhole stitch from left to right along straight lines and curves, pulling the needle through the fabric over the top of the working thread. Work the stitches closely together so that no ground fabric is visible.

## SINGLE FEATHER STITCH

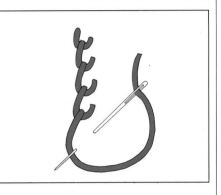

(Also known as slanted buttonhole stitch.)

Single feather stitch is a simple variation of ordinary feather stitch (page 28) which produces a plainer line. This stitch can either be worked in a straight line or it can be made to follow a gradual curve, with the looped edge facing the outside or inside of the curve. Work it in multiple rows with the lines of stitches touching along their lengths to make a delicate, lacy filling.

Work single feather stitch downwards in a similar way to feather stitch, but position the looped stitches only at the right-hand side of the row, as shown in the diagram. Set the looped stitches at an angle to the line being followed, spacing them evenly and keeping them all of the same length.

*The picture on the left shows part of a 1930s satin bedcover. The design of poppies and delphiniums has been cut from a contrasting fabric and outlined with buttonhole stitches.*

# OUTLINE STITCHES

## ▌CHAIN STITCH

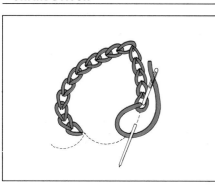

(Also known as tambour stitch and point de chainette.)

Chain stitch is one of the oldest and most widely used embroidery stitches, and examples of it can be found on both antique and contemporary textiles from many countries. It is a simple stitch to work, and can be used either as an outline or filling stitch on all types of fabric and canvas. Work it in multiple rows to fill a shape, or in a single row spiralling outwards from the centre. Any type of embroidery thread can be used, depending on the size of the stitch and the weight of the fabric.

Work chain stitch downwards, as shown in the diagram, by making a series of loops of identical size. Anchor the last loop with a tiny straight stitch.

## ▌WHIPPED CHAIN STITCH

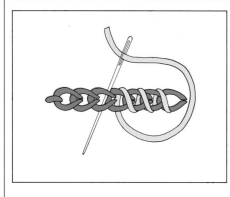

Whipped chain stitch makes a neat, raised line and is often used where a strong outline or border is required. Any type of embroidery thread can be used, but a round, twisted thread such as coton à broder or a medium weight of

pearl cotton enhances the raised quality of the stitch more than a flat, stranded thread. This stitch benefits from being worked on fabric held taut in an embroidery hoop or frame. Although this is not essential, it helps prevent puckering of the fabric and enables the stitches to be worked evenly.

Two variations of whipped chain stitch are equally attractive: whip the row twice in opposite directions to make a heavier line. Alternatively, work the whipping stitches over the left- or right-hand loops instead of over the whole stitch.

First, work a foundation row of ordinary chain stitches (left) along the line to be covered, then whip over the row from right to left with a contrasting or matching thread, without picking up the ground fabric. The whipping stitches should fall neatly over the junction of each chain stitch. Use a blunt-ended tapestry needle for the second thread to avoid splitting the stitches in the foundation row.

## ▌BACK STITCHED CHAIN STITCH

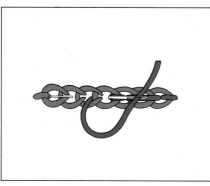

Back stitched chain stitch is a simple variation of ordinary chain stitch (left) which can be used on both fabric and canvas. It makes a heavy line that may be worked in two contrasting or toning colours and is effective for creating strong outlines and borders. On fabric, the stitch works well with intricate linear designs as it follows both tight and gradual curves smoothly. Work it in multiple rows to produce an unusual, solidly stitched filling or stitch a single row spiralling outwards from the centre of a shape. Back stitched chain stitch is often used on canvas in preference to chain stitch as it covers the canvas threads extremely effectively.

First, work a row of ordinary chain stitches along the line to be covered. Then work a row of

back stitches (page 13) from right to left along the centre of the loops, as shown in the diagram. Use either the same thread or one of a contrasting colour and weight for the row of back stitches.

## ▌TWISTED CHAIN STITCH

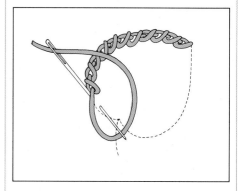

Twisted chain stitch has a neat, textured appearance. It is always worked downwards and is a simple variation of ordinary chain stitch (left) which produces a more decorative line that is ideal for outlining shapes and working linear details. Any type of embroidery thread can be used, but a round thread such as pearl cotton makes the line slightly more raised than a flat thread like stranded silk or cotton. The most attractive effect is achieved when the stitches are kept small and positioned close to each other.

Hold the working thread on the surface of the fabric with your left thumb, then make a slanting chain stitch over the thread, as shown in the diagram. Work the stitches downwards along the line to be covered.

## ▌KNOTTED CHAIN STITCH

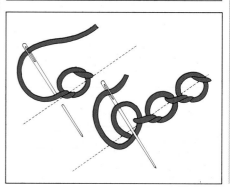

(Also known as link stitch.)

Knotted chain stitch is a fancy line stitch worked on both plain- and even-weave fabric in any type of embroidery thread. It makes a raised, knotted line which follows intricate curves well. Although this stitch is easy to work if the sequence shown in the diagram is followed, some practice is needed to work the loops neatly and evenly.

Working from right to left, bring the needle out at the end of the line to be covered and make a short slanting stitch under the line to the left. Hold the working thread down on the surface of the fabric with the left thumb, then slip the needle under the slanting stitch. Pull the thread through, adjusting the loop until it is of the required size. Hold the loop in place, then pass the needle through it, as shown, pulling the working thread through to complete the knot. Repeat along the line.

## ▌HEAVY CHAIN STITCH

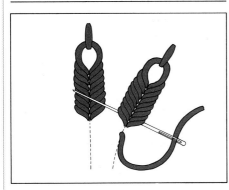

(Also known as heavy braid chain stitch.)

Heavy chain stitch produces a cord-like line which is useful when a heavy outline is required in a design. It is similar in construction to broad chain stitch (page 20), but in this case the needle travels back under two chain loops, rather than one.

First, work a short straight stitch at the top of the row, bringing the needle back through the fabric a little further down the row. Next, work a chain loop by taking the needle under the straight stitch and then back through the fabric. Work a second chain loop under the straight stitch in the same way. Position the subsequent chains as shown, threading the needle back underneath the two previous loops without picking up any fabric. Always work the stitches downwards along the line to be covered.

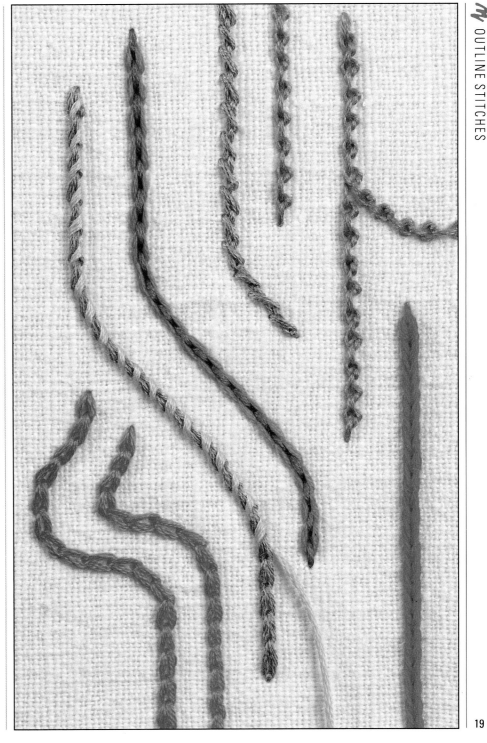

# OUTLINE STITCHES

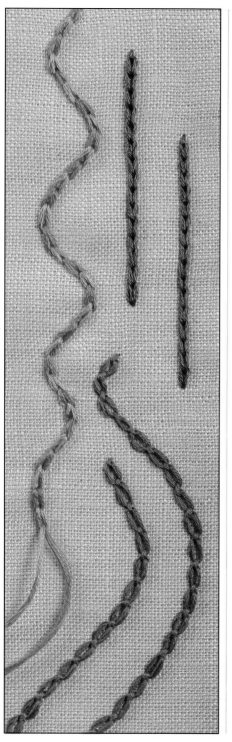

## CHEQUERED CHAIN STITCH

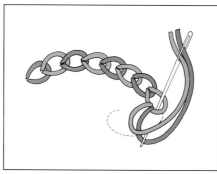

(Also known as magic chain stitch and magic stitch.)

Chequered chain stitch is a variation of ordinary chain stitch (page 18) which is used as a decorative line stitch or in multiple rows as a filling on both plain- and even-weave fabric. The stitch is worked in two threads of contrasting colours threaded into one needle. Change the colour after every stitch, or work two or three stitches in one colour before reversing the position of the threads.

First, thread two contrasting threads through the same needle, then work a row of chain stitches using the threads alternately. Keep the thread not in use above the point of the needle while one stitch is made, as shown in the diagram, then pull both threads through. If a loop of the contrasting colour remains on the surface, a slight pull on the thread will make it disappear. Reverse the position of the threads before working the next stitch along the line to be covered. Work the stitches downwards along this line.

## BROAD CHAIN STITCH

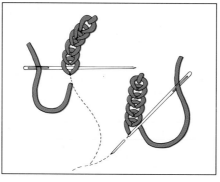

(Also known as reverse chain stitch.)

Broad chain stitch makes a bold, broad line which is worked downwards on both plain- and even-weave fabric. It is useful where a wide, strongly defined outline is required. Choose a firm, rather stiff thread to ensure that the individual stitches keep their shape well. The chain loops should not be pulled tight but should lie quite loosely on the surface of the fabric in order for the row of stitching to stay perfectly flat.

Work with the fabric stretched taut in an embroidery hoop or frame to prevent puckering and to enable the stitches to be worked evenly. Position the stitches closely together so that no ground fabric is visible.

To work broad chain stitch, make a short straight stitch at the top of the line to be covered to anchor the top chain. Then bring the needle through the fabric a little further down, ready to work the first chain stitch. Next, work a chain loop by taking the needle under the straight stitch and then back through the fabric, bringing it out further along the row. Work the subsequent chains as shown in the diagram, passing the needle underneath the previous stitch and taking care not to pick up any of the ground fabric.

## CABLE STITCH

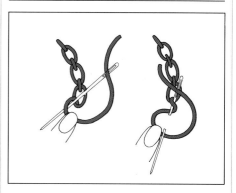

(Also known as cable chain stitch.)

Cable stitch is a variation of chain stitch (page 18). The stitch follows curves well and is used for working lines and borders. It also makes an attractive filling when worked in multiple rows. Alternatively, fill a shape by working evenly spaced, parallel rows of cable stitch across it, then lace the adjacent loops together using a thread in a contrasting colour and a blunt-ended tapestry needle.

Work this stitch downwards, twisting the thread around the needle after making a chain loop and before entering the fabric. Hold the thread down on the fabric when making the twist, as shown.

## KNOTTED CABLE STITCH

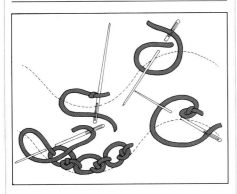

(Also known as knotted cable chain stitch.)

Knotted cable stitch can be used on both plain- and even-weave fabric. It is more ornate than ordinary cable stitch (left), producing a broader line with a knotted finish. It consists of chain stitches (page 18) set alternately with coral stitches (right).

Although this stitch looks more complicated to work than ordinary cable stitch, it is in fact quite simple to execute, as the knots hold the chain loops in place while the next stitch along the line is being worked.

Work from right to left of the line to be filled and begin by making a coral stitch. Pass the needle under this stitch and work a chain stitch, as shown. Alternate these two stitches along the row.

## DOUBLE KNOT STITCH

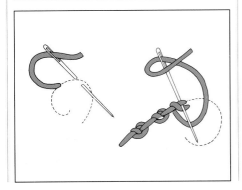

(Also known as tied coral stitch, old English knot stitch, Palestrina stitch and Smyrna stitch.)

Double knot stitch makes an attractive knotted line with a beaded texture and is used on both plain- and even-weave fabric. It is a characteristic Italian stitch used widely for outlines and borders, although it can also be worked in multiple rows to fill a shape with texture. The stitch is similar in appearance to coral stitch (below) but with a more raised effect. Use a round, twisted thread such as pearl cotton or coton à broder to show the knotted texture to best advantage.

Work double knot stitch from left to right. Make a straight stitch, then loop the thread over and under it, as shown in the diagram. Next, pull the needle through over the top of the working thread. Continue along the line to be filled. For a heavy, more textured effect, position the knots closer to each other by making the straight stitches shorter.

## CORAL STITCH

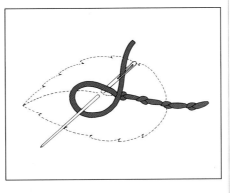

(Also known as coral knot, beaded stitch, German knot stitch, knotted stitch, scroll stitch and snail trail.)

Coral stitch is used for working outlines and as a filling; in the latter case it is worked in multiple rows, with the knots positioned so that they form lines across the shape or alternately on every row. The effect can be varied by altering the angle of the needle as it enters the fabric and by changing the spacing of the knots along the row.

Work from right to left of the line to be filled, holding the thread loosely in place on the surface of the fabric with your left thumb. Take short stitches through the fabric and pull the needle over the working thread to form a knot, as shown in the diagram.

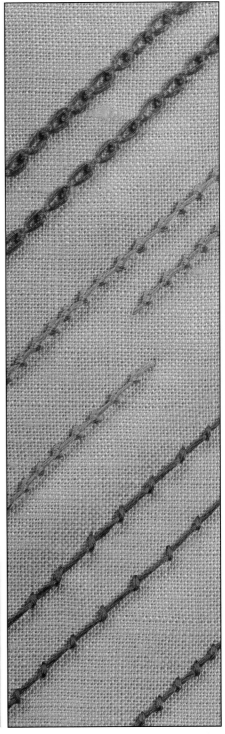

# OUTLINE STITCHES

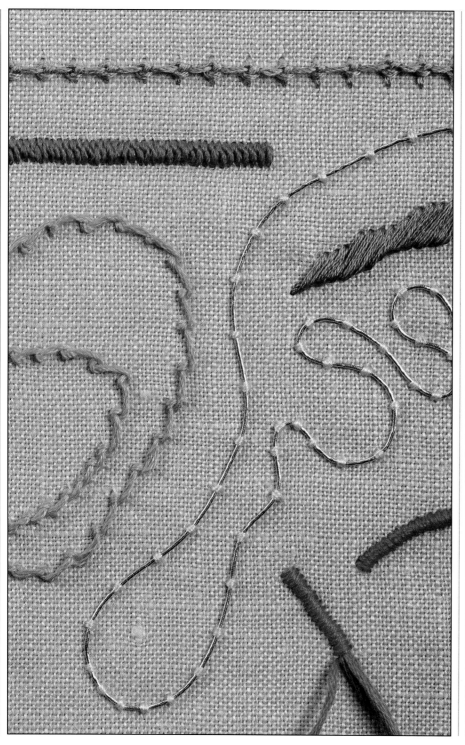

## ▊ BASQUE KNOT

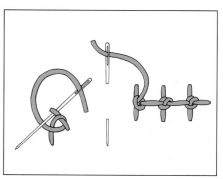

(Also known as knotted loop stitch.)

Basque knot can be used singly as a powdering or joined together in a row to make a pretty line stitch. Alternatively, use Basque knot as a heavy, textured filling by working it in multiple rows to fill a shape. The Basque knot is similar in construction to double knot stitch (page 21), but here the stitch is worked from right to left.

Begin by working a loose diagonal stitch, bringing the needle vertically through the fabric at the base of the row. Next, work the sequence of loops shown in the diagram, passing the needle over and under the diagonal stitch to form a knot. Hold the knot down on the fabric with your left thumb and gently pull the loops before proceeding to work the next stitch along the row.

## ▊ PEARL STITCH

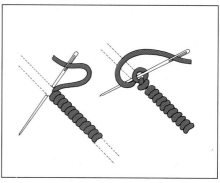

Pearl stitch makes a raised, corded line and is ideal for embroidering complicated linear designs. It looks most effective when worked in a thick thread such as soft cotton or the heaviest available weight of pearl cotton. Pearl stitch benefits from being worked on fabric stretched in an embroidery hoop or frame. Although this is not essential, it helps prevent puckering of the fabric and enables the stitches to be worked evenly. To stop the stitching from becoming ragged and untidy, work the stitches evenly. Arrange the stitches close to each other to ensure that none of the ground fabric shows through.

Work pearl stitch from right to left. First, take a small stitch at right angles to the line being followed, leaving a small loop on the surface of the fabric. Insert the needle through the loop and then downwards through the fabric, as shown. Tighten the working thread firmly before pulling the needle through to work the next stitch.

## ▌SCROLL STITCH

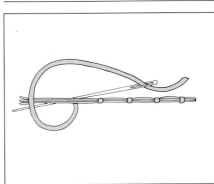

(Also known as single knotted line stitch.)

Scroll stitch makes an attractive knotted line and is used on both plain- and even-weave fabric. It is useful for all types of embroidery as it is quick and easy to work. This stitch is effective for working both tight and gradual curves and follows an intricate design with ease. Any type of embroidery thread can be used for working the stitch, depending on the weight of the ground fabric used and the effect required. A flat thread like stranded cotton or silk produces a wider, flatter line than a round, twisted thread such as pearl cotton or coton à broder. Scroll stitch should be worked with the fabric stretched taut in an embroidery hoop or frame, if possible, as this helps to prevent the ground fabric from pulling out of shape and enables the stitches to be worked evenly.

Work the stitch from left to right of the line being followed, making the knots by pulling the

needle through the fabric and over the working thread, as shown in the diagram. Pull the thread tightly when it is under the point of the needle and space the stitches evenly along the row to provide a regular effect.

## ▌ROPE STITCH

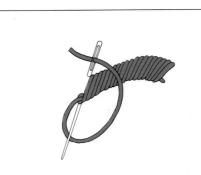

Rope stitch makes a solidly stitched line which is raised along its lower edge. It is effective for working curves and spirals when a lustrous thread such as stranded cotton or pure silk is used. It is easy to work, but the stitches must be kept even to give the correct effect. Work with the fabric stretched taut in an embroidery hoop or frame to prevent puckering and distortion.

Work rope stitch from right to left by making diagonal stitches which slant backwards at a sharp angle. Pull the needle through the fabric and over the working thread so that a small knot is formed at the base of each diagonal stitch. The knots at the lower edges of the stitches do not show on the surface, but act as a padding for the base of the line.

## ▌COUCHING

(Also known as Kloster stitch and convent stitch.)

Couching is used to attach a thread or group of threads to fabric when they are too thick, too highly textured or too fragile to be stitched directly into the fabric. The name comes from the French word *coucher*, meaning to lay down. Couching is used extensively in metal thread embroidery as a line stitch and also as a filling. It should be worked on a closely woven fabric stretched taut in an embroidery hoop or frame to prevent puckering.

Work couching from right to left. First, lay the thick thread on the fabric, following the line to be couched. Hold this thread in place with your left hand. Then, using a fine thread, work tiny stitches to tie down the first thread, as shown in the diagram. At the end of the row, pull the ends of all the threads through to the back and secure them. Arrange the tying-down stitches close to each other around curves, and work one or two extra stitches when turning a corner to prevent the angle from pulling out of shape.

## ▌SATIN COUCHING

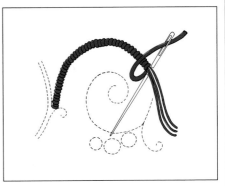

(Also known as trailing stitch.)

Satin couching produces a highly raised line which is useful when a well-defined, heavy outline is required. It is a variation of the previous stitch, but in this case the laid threads act as a padding and are hidden by the tying-down stitches.

To work satin couching, first lay the padding thread on the surface, guiding it with your left hand. Then work small satin stitches (page 102) over the padding, either at a slant or at right angles. Position the stitches close to each other so that the padding is completely covered. Secure the ends of all the threads on the back of the fabric.

# BORDER STITCHES

The majority of the stitches described in this chapter are worked in straight lines which can either be used individually, or in multiple rows to create deep borders and fillings. A few of the stitches can also be used along curves. Further decoration can be provided for many of the stitches by the addition of one of the isolated knot stitches described in Chapter 4. Most border stitches benefit from being worked on fabric stretched taut in an embroidery hoop or frame. Although this is not essential in every case, it helps prevent puckering of the fabric and enables the stitches to be worked evenly.

The effect created by these stitches varies widely from the broad, complex lines with a textured finish produced by plaited braid stitch, Russian cross stitch and crested chain stitch, to the much plainer, less dramatic lines made by Paris stitch and the buttonhole stitch variations.

# BORDER STITCHES

## ■ CLOSED BUTTONHOLE STITCH

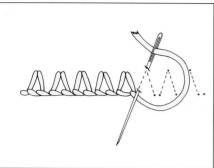

Closed buttonhole stitch is a variation of ordinary buttonhole stitch (page 17). It can be used instead of blanket stitch (page 17) to make an attractive edging for hems, or worked in multiple rows to make a pretty wide border or filling on either plain- or even-weave fabric.

Any type of embroidery thread can be used, depending on the weight of the fabric, stitch size and effect required. Stranded cotton gives a flatter appearance to the stitch than a round thread such as pearl cotton. When using the stitch as a filling, work with the fabric stretched taut in an embroidery hoop or frame to help prevent puckering and distortion, and to enable the stitches to be worked evenly.

Arrange closed buttonhole stitch from left to right in the same way as ordinary buttonhole stitch, but make the spaces in between the stitches wider. Work each pair of adjacent vertical stitches into the same hole in the fabric so that they form a triangular shape, as shown. A more complex variation of this stitch can be made by working three or four vertical stitches

into the same hole in the fabric.

When working this stitch as a wide border or filling, try positioning the rows with the base loops facing, or with the vertical stitches touching or interlocking. By varying the spaces in between the stitches, the filling can be made either light and lacy, or almost solid.

## ■ CROSSED BUTTONHOLE STITCH

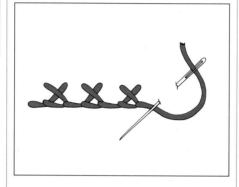

Crossed buttonhole stitch is another simple but effective variation of ordinary buttonhole stitch (page 17). It can be used as an edging, border or filling on either plain- or even-weave fabric.

Any type of embroidery thread can be used, depending on the weight of the fabric, stitch size and effect required. Stranded cotton gives a flatter appearance to the stitch than a round thread such as coton à broder or soft cotton. When using the stitch as an filling, work with the fabric stretched taut in a hoop or frame to help prevent puckering and to enable the stitches to be worked evenly. This is not necessary when only one or two rows are being worked,

or when the stitch is used as an edging.

Work the stitch from left to right, keeping the spaces in between the stitches quite wide. Work each pair of adjacent stitches at an angle so that they cross each other. When this stitch is worked as a wide border or filling, the spacing between the stitches can be varied to create different effects.

## ■ DOUBLE BUTTONHOLE STITCH

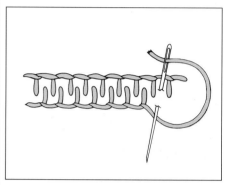

Double buttonhole stitch is an attractive edging or wide border stitch which can be used on either plain- or even-weave fabric. It is quick and easy to work and consists of two parallel rows of blanket stitches (page 17) arranged so that the vertical stitches face each other. Work the stitch in a straight line or along a very gentle curve for an equally effective result.

Any type of embroidery thread can be used, depending on the weight of the fabric, stitch size and effect required. Stranded cotton gives a flatter appearance to the stitch than a round thread such as pearl cotton. Two different threads of a contrasting colour, weight and

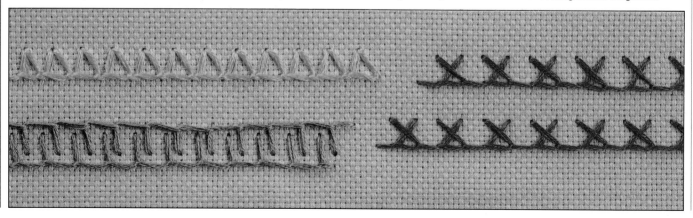

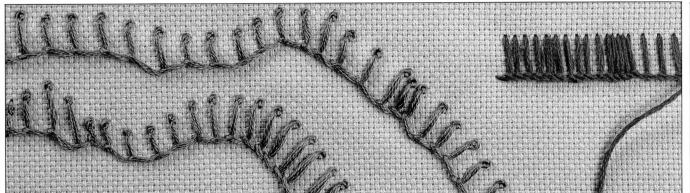

texture can be used for the two rows of stitching to add interest to a design. When working the stitch in multiple rows, first stretch the fabric in an embroidery hoop or frame to prevent puckering.

Work one row of blanket stitches from left to right along the line to be covered. Invert the fabric and work a second row underneath the first one so that the vertical stitches fit into the spaces left in the first row, as shown. The spacing and size of the stitches can be varied depending on the weight of the fabric and thread and the effect required.

When this stitch is worked as an edging on a length of hemmed fabric, the top row of stitching should follow the fold of the turned-under edge. Position the second row close to the base of the hem. To create a more decorative edging, work the two rows of blanket stitches closely together, elongating the vertical stitches, then slot a contrasting narrow ribbon through the centre of the line of stitches.

## ▌KNOTTED BUTTONHOLE STITCH

Knotted buttonhole stitch is a useful and decorative variation of ordinary buttonhole stitch (page 17) which is used for outlines and borders on both plain- and even-weave fabric. Each vertical stitch has a knot at the tip and the stitch is a little tricky to work at first, because some practice is needed to keep the knots even and of an identical size.

This stitch makes an attractive outline for a circle or curved shape. The vertical stitches can be worked either inside the shape pointing towards the centre, or outside the shape so that they fan out around the edge. To make a decorative, feathery border, work two rows

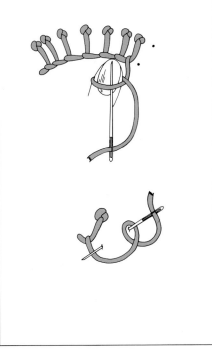

back to back and very close together, graduating the lengths of the vertical stitches. Knotted buttonhole stitch looks best when worked in a heavy, round thread such as pearl or soft cotton.

Work the stitch from left to right in the same way as ordinary buttonhole stitch. Make the knots by winding the thread once around the thumb of the left hand to make a loop. Pass the needle through the loop and proceed to work a buttonhole stitch, as shown.

## ▌TAILOR'S BUTTONHOLE STITCH

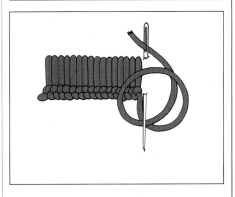

Tailor's buttonhole stitch is similar to ordinary buttonhole stitch (page 17), but it makes a strong, hardwearing edge which is particularly suitable for use on heavyweight fabric. Use it to finish raw edges and as a border stitch on either plain- or even-weave fabric. It is equally effective if worked in a straight line or along a gentle curve.

Any type of embroidery thread can be used, but choose a durable thread when finishing a raw edge. When working the stitch in multiple rows, stretch the fabric in an embroidery hoop or frame to prevent distortion. This is not necessary when the stitch is used as an edging.

Work the stitch from left to right in the same way as buttonhole stitch. Insert the needle into the fabric, then wind a loop of thread around the needle point before it is pulled through the fabric, as shown. The loop makes the firm, knotted edge. Work the stitches closely together so that no fabric shows between them: this will ensure that the knots lie neatly next to each other along the edge of the row.

# BORDER STITCHES

## ■ FEATHER STITCH

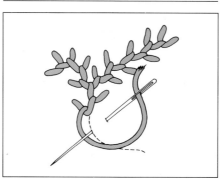

(Also known as single coral stitch and briar stitch.)

Feather stitch is an extremely attractive stitch which has a long history in English embroidery. It was used extensively to decorate traditional linen smocks, both as a smocking stitch and for the surface embroidery, and also as a joining stitch on crazy patchwork. The stitch makes a pretty, almost feathery line and can be worked either along a gentle curve or in a straight line. Any type of embroidery thread can be used, depending on the effect required. This stitch benefits from being worked on fabric stretched taut in an embroidery hoop or frame.

Bring the thread through the fabric at the top of the line to be covered and make alternate slanting stitches, first to the left and then to the right of the line, as shown, pulling the needle through over the working thread.

## ■ CLOSED FEATHER STITCH

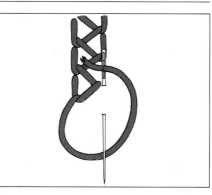

Closed feather stitch is a simple variation of feather stitch (above) used on both plain- and even-weave fabric. It makes a decorative, lacy line and is worked downwards between two parallel lines. Worked in multiple rows, this stitch makes an attractive wide border or light filling. It does not follow curves well, unless they are very gradual, and is therefore usually worked in a straight line. As a fancy couching stitch (page 55), it is used to attach groups of threads or narrow ribbon to fabric.

To work this stitch neatly, either choose an even-weave fabric and count the threads, or mark two parallel guidelines on plain-weave fabric with tailor's chalk or a special water-soluble marker. Any type of embroidery thread can be used, depending on the weight of the fabric, stitch size and effect required. When using the stitch in multiple rows as a wide border or filling, work with the fabric stretched taut in an embroidery hoop or frame.

Bring the thread through the fabric at the top of the line to be covered and make alternate looped stitches, first to the left and then to the right of the line, as shown, inserting the needle vertically through the fabric and pulling it through over the working thread.

## ■ DOUBLE FEATHER STITCH

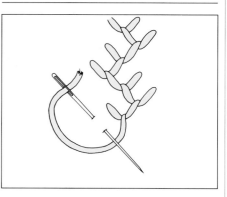

(Also known as double coral stitch.)

Double feather stitch is a great favourite with many embroiderers and is frequently used to decorate babies' and children's clothes. The stitch makes a branched, feathery line which is wider and more ornate than a row of ordinary feather stitches (left). It is used as a border stitch on both plain- and even-weave fabric, and can be worked along straight lines and curves, as well as in multiple rows to cover a shape with bands of delicate, lacy filling.

Any type of embroidery thread can be used, depending on the weight of the fabric, stitch size and effect required, but a stranded cotton or silk thread gives a flatter appearance to the stitching than a round thread such as coton à broder. When the stitch is worked as a filling, different threads of a contrasting colour, weight and texture can be used for alternate rows to add interest to the stitched surface. When used in this way, double feather stitch should be worked on fabric stretched taut in an embroidery hoop or frame to prevent puckering and distortion, and to enable the stitches to be worked evenly. This is not necessary when only single rows of the stitch are being worked.

Work this stitch downwards in the same way as ordinary feather stitch, but make two or more extra stitches alternately at the right and left of the line to be covered, as shown. The stitch can be worked irregularly, with two stitches to one side, four to the next, three to the next, and so on. This method produces a light, feathery line of a varying width.

## ▌ SPANISH KNOTTED FEATHER STITCH

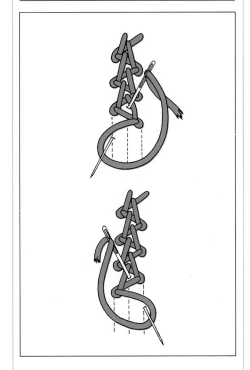

(Also known as twisted zigzag chain stitch.)

Spanish knotted feather stitch is an ornamental stitch used on both plain- and even-weave fabric. It makes a wide, decorative line with a braided appearance and is used for bands

and borders. The stitch is worked downwards along three parallel lines and is rather difficult to work evenly without practice.

To enable this stitch to be worked evenly, either choose an even-weave fabric and count the threads, or mark three parallel guidelines on plain-weave fabric with tailor's chalk or a special water-soluble marker. A round, twisted thread such as pearl cotton produces a bolder effect than a flat, stranded cotton.

Bring the needle through at the top of the line to be covered. Hold the thread down to the left of the centre line with your left thumb, then make a slanting stitch, as shown in the first diagram, pulling the needle through over the working thread. Work a similar stitch at the right of the line, inserting the needle into the fabric just above the last stitch, as shown in the second diagram. Repeat along the line.

## ▌ MAIDENHAIR STITCH

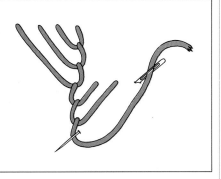

Maidenhair stitch is worked in straight rows on both plain- and even-weave fabric. Its unusual name derives from the delicate, branched line it produces, which has an almost fern-like quality. It is a variation of single feather stitch (page 17) and looks equally effective worked on a small or large scale.

To work the stitch evenly, either choose an even-weave fabric and count the threads, or mark a central guideline on plain-weave fabric with tailor's chalk or a special water-soluble marker. Use a round, lightweight thread such as coton à broder for the best results.

Bring the thread through at the top of the line, then work three single feather stitches at the left of the line. Graduate the lengths of these stitches, making sure that they line up vertically. Work a similar group of stitches at the right of the line. Repeat along the line.

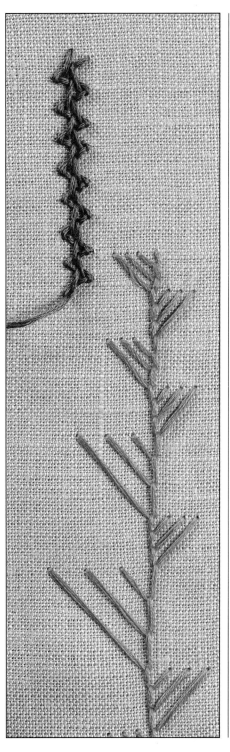

# BORDER STITCHES

## CRETAN STITCH

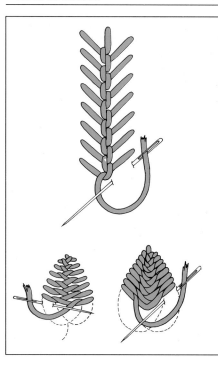

(Also known as Persian stitch and long-armed feather stitch, or quill stitch when worked in a straight, vertical line.)

Cretan stitch is worked downwards on both plain- and even-weave fabric as a line stitch and as a filling for narrow shapes. It originated on the island of Crete, where it is used to decorate clothing and household linen. Any type of embroidery thread can be used, although stranded silk or cotton threads give the best fabric coverage when the stitch is used to fill a shape. This stitch benefits from being worked on fabric stretched taut in an embroidery hoop or frame, although this is not essential.

To work Cretan stitch in a line, bring the needle through the fabric and make alternate loop stitches, first to the left and then to the right of a central line, as shown in the first diagram. Space the stitches out to make a pretty, spiked line which will curve.

To use Cretan stitch as a filling, work it from alternate sides of the shape to be filled until it is covered. The second diagram shows the stitches widely spaced, allowing the ground fabric to show through, and the third diagram shows the stitches worked closely together.

## OPEN CRETAN STITCH

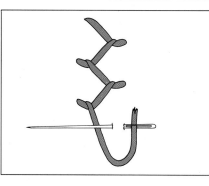

Open Cretan stitch is used to work lines and fill shapes in a similar way to Cretan stitch (left). It produces a light, zigzag line that can be worked along either a straight row or a gentle curve. Any type of embroidery thread can be used, depending on the weight of the fabric, stitch size and effect required. This stitch benefits from being worked on fabric stretched taut in an embroidery hoop or frame.

To work open Cretan stitch, first bring the needle through the fabric at the top of the line to be covered, then insert the needle horizontally into the fabric and pull it through over the working thread, as shown. Continue in this way, making alternate stitches to the left and then to the right of the line, spacing them well apart.

Various isolated stitches can be used to decorate this stitch. Work them in the spaces left in between the stitches, using a contrasting colour and weight of thread. French and Chinese knots (page 68), as well as daisy stitches (page 76), are suitable for this purpose.

## SCOTTISH CRETAN STITCH

Scottish Cretan stitch is a variation of open Cretan stitch (above) which is used to work rich, ornamental straight lines on both plain- and even-weave fabric. It consists of blocks of open Cretan stitches which are linked together without picking up the ground fabric. This stitch should always be worked on fabric stretched taut in an embroidery hoop or frame.

Begin stitching at the top of the line to be covered and first work a block of open Cretan stitches. This can be of any size, but five stitches are normally used to make up one block. Pass the working thread upwards

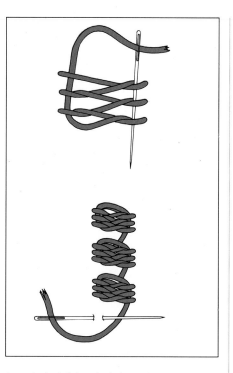

through the left-hand stitches without picking up any of the ground fabric, then pull it over the top of the block and downwards through the right-hand stitches. Tension the thread carefully before proceeding to work the next block: if the thread is pulled too tightly the stitches will become distorted.

Experiment by working Scottish Cretan stitch as an isolated stitch to make a pretty, powdered filling. After each block has been threaded, secure the thread on the back of the fabric, then proceed to work the next block.

## ZIGZAG CORAL STITCH

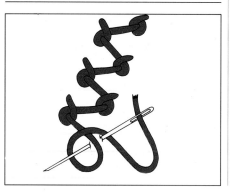

Zigzag coral stitch is a wide, decorative stitch used on both plain- and even-weave fabric. It follows gradual curves well, and produces an attractive, strongly defined outline when the stitches are kept small and even. It is a variation of ordinary coral stitch (page 21) and is always worked downwards.

Any type of embroidery thread can be used to work zigzag coral stitch, depending on the weight of the fabric, stitch size and effect required, but a twisted thread such as coton à broder gives the best results. To work this stitch neatly, choose an even-weave fabric and count the threads, or mark parallel guidelines on plain-weave fabric with tailor's chalk or a special water-soluble marker.

Work the left-hand stitches in exactly the same way as coral stitches. Loop the thread as shown to make the right-hand stitches.

## ▌BASKET STITCH

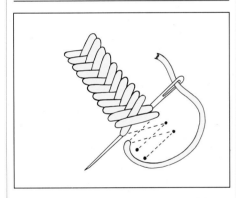

Basket stitch is used on plain-weave fabric to produce an attractive, braided line which can be worked alone as a border or in multiple rows to fill a shape. It can be given an open or closed finish, depending on the effect required, and looks best when the edges are kept parallel. To achieve this, mark two parallel guidelines on the fabric with a dressmaker's pencil or special water-soluble marker. Basket stitch looks most effective when it is worked in a lustrous thread like stranded cotton.

Bring the needle through the fabric at the top of the left-hand guideline. Insert the needle a little further down on the opposite line and bring it out exactly opposite on the left. Work the next stitch by inserting the needle at the right just above the first stitch, letting it emerge very slightly below the first stitch at the left. Repeat along the row.

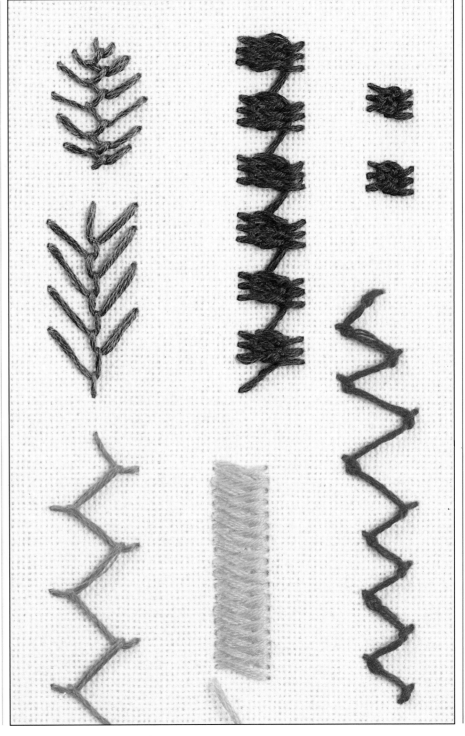

# BORDER STITCHES

## ▌BRAID STITCH

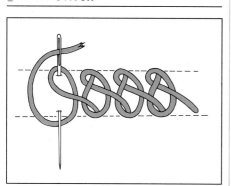

(Also known as Gordian knot stitch.)

Braid stitch is a wide line stitch used on plain-weave fabric to make a textured border with a braided appearance. It can be worked either in straight lines or along curves. Stranded cotton is too flat to be used successfully with this stitch and a firm, twisted thread such as pearl cotton should be used. To work braid stitch neatly, mark parallel guidelines spaced fairly closely together on the fabric with tailor's chalk or a special water-soluble marker. Keep the stitches small to prevent the loops from slipping. Braid stitch should not be used on articles which will be laundered unless the stitches are kept less than ¼ inch (5mm) high because the loops tend to pull out of shape.

Work braid stitch from right to left, bringing the needle through the fabric on the lower guideline. Loop the thread as shown, then hold it down with your left thumb and insert the needle. Tighten the loop, then pull the needle through over the working thread to complete the first stitch. Repeat along the row.

## ▌ROSETTE CHAIN STITCH

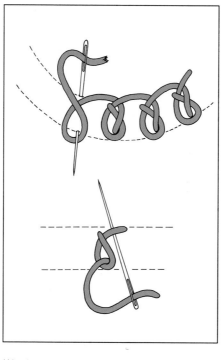

(Also known as bead edging stitch.)

Rosette chain stitch is a decorative line stitch used on both plain- and even-weave fabric. It is a variation of twisted chain stitch (page 18) which is worked from right to left between two parallel lines and produces a pretty, braided line. This stitch is a useful outline stitch which is equally effective when worked in a straight line or along a curved shape. It can also be used to make floral motifs by working small circles with the chain stitches pointing outwards.

A heavy thread such as pearl or soft cotton works best with this stitch, as stranded threads are too flat, and it benefits from being worked on fabric stretched taut in an embroidery hoop or frame, although this is not essential.

To work rosette chain stitch, bring the needle through on the top line, then make a loop of thread, as shown in the large diagram. Hold the loop in place on the fabric with the left thumb until the needle has been pulled through and the twisted chain stitch is completed. Pass the needle under the top right-hand thread of this stitch, as shown in the smaller diagram, and gently pull it through, without picking up the ground fabric. Proceed in this way along the row to be covered.

## ▌ZIGZAG CHAIN STITCH

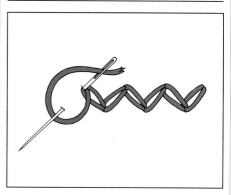

(Also known as Vandyke chain stitch.)

Zigzag chain stitch is used as a line stitch and filling on both plain- and even-weave fabric. As its name suggests, it produces a decorative, zigzag line. The stitch is normally worked in

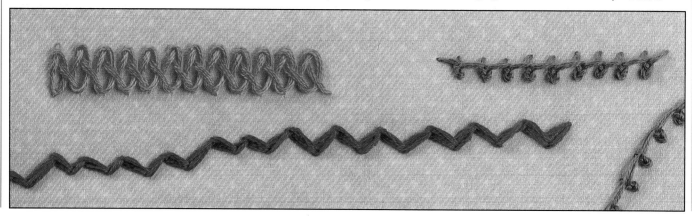

straight rows, but it can also be used along a very gentle curve. It makes an attractive filling when worked solidly over an area and lends itself to being striped in contrasting bands of colour or gradually shaded in close tones of the same colour of thread. Examples of this very old variation of ordinary chain stitch (page 18) worked on a very small scale in silk have been found on many ancient Chinese embroideries.

Any type of embroidery thread can be used, depending on the weight of the fabric, stitch size and effect required. A lustrous thread such as stranded cotton or silk works well when the stitch is used as a filling. This stitch benefits from being worked on fabric stretched taut in an embroidery hoop or frame.

Work zigzag chain stitch in the same way as ordinary chain stitch, but set each chain loop at right angles to the previous loop in order to create a zigzag line. To make sure that the chain loops lie perfectly flat on the surface of the fabric, pierce the end of each preceding chain loop with the point of the needle.

## PETAL STITCH

(Also known as pendant chain stitch.)

Petal stitch is an attractive stitch which can be used on both plain- and even-weave fabric. It is a combination of stem stitches (page 14) and daisy stitches (page 76) with the latter arranged so that they hang down to form pendants. This stitch is particularly suitable for working curves, circles and spirals, with the pendant daisy stitches arranged on the outside of the curves. It can also be used in a straight line, either singly or in multiple rows, to make a wide border or pretty, textured filling.

Any type of embroidery thread can be used, depending on the weight of the ground fabric,

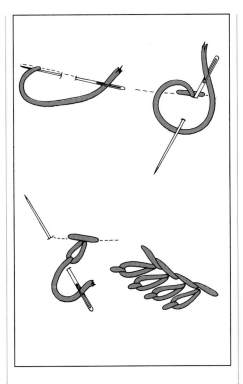

but the stitch looks most attractive when worked in stranded cotton or silk. Petal stitch benefits from being worked on fabric stretched taut in an embroidery hoop or frame.

Work from right to left, beginning by making a short straight stitch. Bring the needle through halfway along this stitch and proceed to work a daisy stitch at an acute angle to the line. Bring the needle out further along the line and work a stem stitch, inserting the needle at the top of the daisy stitch. Repeat along the row.

## SWORD-EDGING STITCH

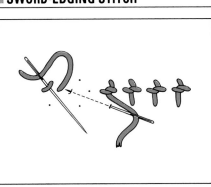

Sword-edging stitch makes a soft, pretty line on both plain- and even-weave fabric. Each stitch looks like an elongated cross and is quick and simple to work. Because this stitch can also be used individually to make a powdered filling worked at random over a shape, it is sometimes classified as an isolated stitch.

Choice of thread depends on the weight of the fabric, stitch size and effect required. A round thread such as pearl cotton makes the stitch stand out from the background rather more than a stranded silk or cotton.

Make a loose slanting stitch from left to right of the line being worked. Bring the needle through the fabric at the right, as shown, then slip it down under the slanting stitch and take it back through the fabric a little lower down to form a slightly elongated 'tail'. Do not pick up any of the ground fabric when working the second stitch, which should pull the first stitch into a V-shape. Repeat along the line to be covered, arranging the stitches close to each other to form a broken line.

# BORDER STITCHES

## ■ CROSS STITCH

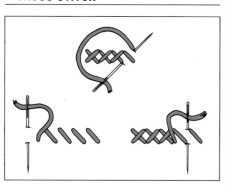

(Also known as sampler stitch, Berlin stitch and point de marque.)

Cross stitch is probably the oldest and best known of all embroidery stitches. It is quick to work and is used mainly on even-weave fabric and canvas where the threads can be counted to keep the crosses of an even shape and size.

There are different methods of working cross stitch, but one basic rule applies: the top diagonal stitches should always slant in the same direction unless a variation of light and shade is required. In this case, the direction of the stitches can be varied to catch the light.

The first diagram shows cross stitch worked individually. This method should be used when working cross stitch on canvas. Complete each cross before proceeding to make the next one. The other diagrams show a row of cross stitches worked on a plain- or even-weave fabric. Work a row of diagonal stitches from right to left, then cross them with a second row of diagonal stitches worked in the opposite direction.

## ■ ALTERNATE CROSS STITCH

A row of alternate cross stitches looks the same on the right side of the fabric as a row of ordinary cross stitches which has been worked in two journeys. However, this method of working cross stitch requires four journeys to complete one row of crosses. This stitch should only be used on even-weave fabric to ensure a perfectly even tension and neat appearance, which is particularly important when covering a large area on a design.

Alternate cross stitch is particularly suitable for working large areas of embroidery. When working tiny details on the same piece of work, use individual cross stitches (above), taking care

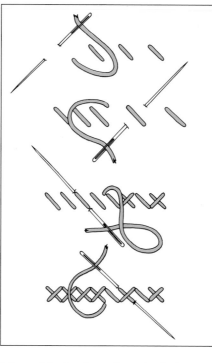

to keep all the top diagonals running in the correct direction. This stitch benefits from being worked on fabric stretched in an embroidery hoop or frame, although this is not essential.

On the first journey, which is stitched from right to left, work every alternate diagonal stitch along the row. Complete these diagonals on the second journey, working from left to right. Finish the stitches by working the top row of diagonals in the same way on two more journeys, as shown.

## ■ MARKING CROSS STITCH

Marking cross stitch is a variation of ordinary cross stitch (left) used on both plain- and even-weave fabric. It is reversible, with each stitch forming a cross on the front of the fabric and a square of straight stitches on the back. As its name suggests, this stitch is useful for working lettering and monograms on clothing and household linen. It can also be used in a very decorative way on a semi-transparent fabric such as voile or organdie. On this type of fabric, the stitches on the reverse show through to the front, creating a shadow pattern. Some of the stitches are re-crossed in order to form the squares on the reverse.

Follow the diagram carefully. The stitches formed on the back of the fabric are shown next to each stitch. You may need to make further re-crosses in order to complete every square. This should be done as neatly as possible, with the beginning and end of each length of thread secured neatly under an existing stitch.

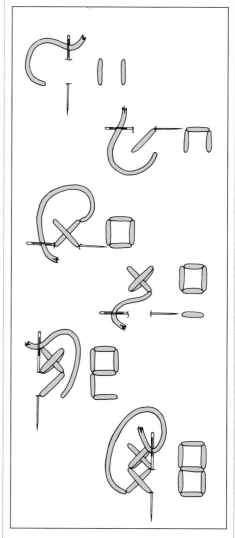

*Cross stitch is a great favourite for decorating household linen. The 1920s table runner shown on the right features various floral motifs embroidered in a variety of bright thread colours.*

# BORDER STITCHES

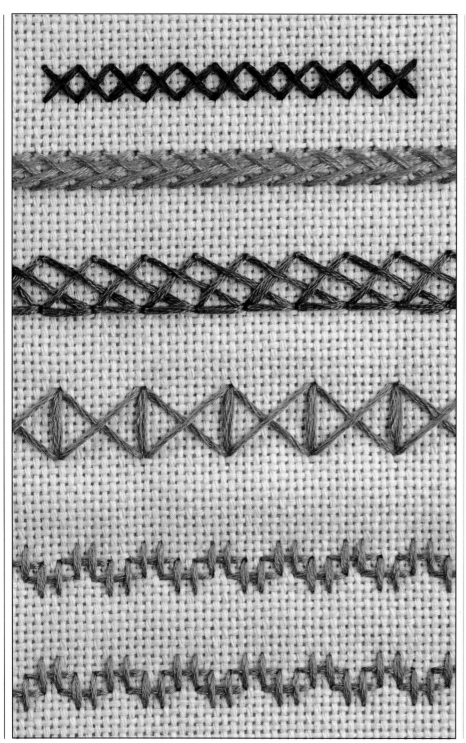

## ▍TWO-SIDED CROSS STITCH

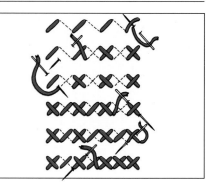

(Also known as marking stitch and brave bred stitch.)

Two-sided cross stitch is a reversible variation of ordinary cross stitch (page 34) which is used on both plain- and even-weave fabric. As its name suggests, it makes an identical stitch on both sides of the fabric. It is the ideal cross stitch to use on a small scale on fine, semi-transparent fabrics such as organdie, voile and silk Habotai. Each row is worked in four journeys and the secret of working the stitch neatly lies in making two half stitches at the beginning of the second and fourth rows.

Begin at the left of the line to be covered, working every alternate diagonal stitch along the row. Make an extra half stitch on the right-hand side before returning along the line to complete the alternate crosses. On the third journey, work the missing diagonals from left to right. Turn, then work another half stitch, as shown, and complete the cross stitches on the fourth journey from right to left.

## ▍RUSSIAN CROSS STITCH

Russian cross stitch is used on canvas and on plain- and even-weave fabric to produce a rich, plaited line which can be used singly or in multiple rows to fill a shape. It is worked in a similar way to long-armed cross stitch (page 134), but in this case the stitches are longer and more complicated to work.

To work this stitch neatly, choose an appropriate even-weave fabric or canvas which will enable you to count the threads and keep the stitches regular and even. Plain-weave fabric can also be used, providing guidelines are marked on it with a dressmaker's pencil, tailor's chalk or special water-soluble marker. On fabric,

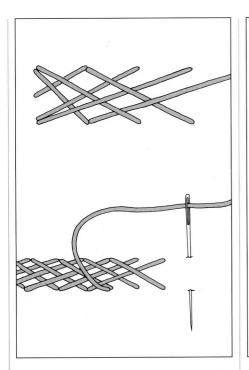

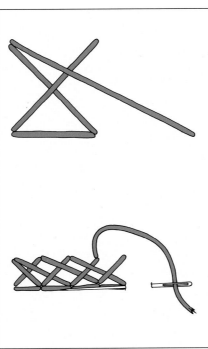

any type of embroidery thread can be used, depending on the weight of the fabric and the stitch size, but coton à broder or the finest available weight of pearl cotton provide the best results. When using this stitch on canvas, choose a weight of thread which is compatible with the gauge of canvas selected.

Begin by working one Russian cross stitch, carefully following the sequence of overlapping stitches shown in the first diagram. Repeat along the row, working from left to right.

## BELGIAN CROSS STITCH

Belgian cross stitch is a variation of ordinary cross stitch (page 34) used on canvas and on plain- and even-weave fabric. It produces an attractive line which can be worked either singly or in multiple rows to fill a shape.

To work this stitch neatly, choose an even-weave fabric and count the threads, or mark guidelines on plain-weave fabric with tailor's chalk or a special water-soluble marker. On fabric, any type of embroidery thread can be used, depending on the weight of the fabric and the stitch size, but a stranded cotton or silk thread provides a flatter appearance than pearl or soft cotton. When working the stitch on

canvas, choose a weight of thread which is compatible with the gauge of canvas.

Begin by working one Belgian cross stitch, carefully following the sequence of overlapping stitches shown in the first diagram. Repeat along the row, working from left to right.

## ZIGZAG STITCH

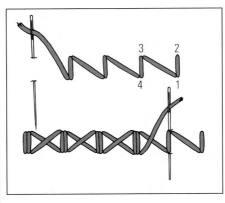

Zigzag stitch can be used as a line stitch or filling on both plain- and even-weave fabric. It makes a decorative outline or border with a pretty geometric pattern and can be worked in

multiple rows to fill a shape. Each horizontal row of stitches is worked in two journeys.

For preference, choose an even-weave fabric and count the threads to keep the stitches even. If using plain-weave fabric, mark parallel guidelines on it with tailor's chalk or a special water-soluble marker. A fine embroidery thread such as coton à broder or fine pearl cotton accentuates the delicate geometric pattern of the stitch. When using it as a filling, arrange the rows close to each other so that the vertical stitches touch.

Begin at the right of the line to be covered and work a row of alternate vertical and diagonal stitches, as shown. On the return journey, stitching from left to right, work an identical set of vertical and diagonal stitches to share the same holes as those in the previous row. This row of stitches completes the crosses.

## CHINESE STITCH

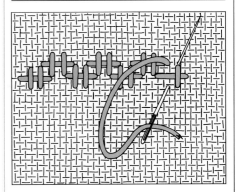

(Also known as Chinese cross stitch.)

Chinese stitch is used as a border stitch or filling on even-weave fabric. It is simple to work and looks most effective when a loosely woven linen or cotton fabric is chosen for the background. The loose threads of the fabric can be drawn together by the stitching if the thread is tightened after each stitch has been made. Chinese stitch can also be used as a decorative surface stitch on other types of even-weave fabric, either worked in rows as a border or scattered in random blocks over a shape to make a powdered filling.

First, make a central horizontal stitch over six threads of fabric, then cross this stitch with two vertical stitches worked over four threads. Set the next block with a half drop, as shown, and continue along the row in this way.

# BORDER STITCHES

## FERN STITCH

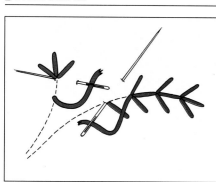

Fern stitch is a line stitch used on both plain- and even-weave fabric. It is extremely simple to work and any type of embroidery thread can be used, depending on the weight of the ground fabric. The stitch makes a pretty, branched line and is often used for decorating leaf and flower shapes and for working small sprays of leaves in floral designs.

To make a light filling, work the stitch in multiple rows. The effect can be varied by altering the spacing between the rows: to produce a delicate trellis over a shape, arrange the rows close to each other with the stitches touching; to obtain a textured, solidly stitched shape, overlap the rows. Experiment by filling the shape with either horizontal, vertical or diagonal rows and by varying the thread.

Begin at the top of the line to be covered and make a group of three straight stitches of equal length worked at angles to each other. All three of these stitches should share the same base hole. Work further groups of stitches downwards to form a line, as shown.

## WHEATEAR STITCH

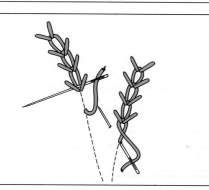

Wheatear stitch is a decorative line stitch used on both plain- and even-weave fabric. It is worked downwards and makes a wide, branched line with a heavy central band which looks rather like an ear of corn. The stitch can be worked along a gentle curve, but it is normally used to work straight lines, often in short lengths, depicting wheat, barley or wild grasses. Wheatear stitch was frequently used to embroider monochrome surface decorations on traditional English smocks made from hand-woven linen.

Any type of embroidery thread can be used to work this stitch, depending on the weight of the fabric, stitch size and effect required. Pearl cotton or a thick wool thread make the stitch stand out from the background more effectively than a flat, stranded cotton or silk. Wheatear stitch benefits from being worked on fabric stretched taut in an embroidery hoop or frame, although this is not essential.

Begin at the top of the line to be covered. First, make two straight stitches set at an angle to each other, then bring the needle through the fabric lower down the line and slip it from right to left under the first two stitches, as shown, without picking up any of the fabric. Take the needle back through the fabric at the spot where it last emerged, and gently pull it to make a chain loop. Work the next two straight stitches into the base of the chain loop. If desired, the length of the diagonal stitches can be varied to make a pretty, irregular line.

## SPINE CHAIN STITCH

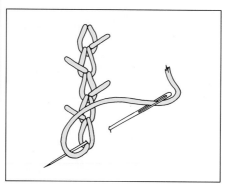

Spine chain stitch is a decorative variation of ordinary chain stitch (page 18) which is quick and easy to work. It is a line and filling stitch used on both plain- and even-weave fabric. The stitch is most attractive when worked on a small scale, and can be used for outlining shapes and working linear details as it follows all types of curves well. Work it in multiple rows to make an unusual filling for any size of shape.

Any type of embroidery thread can be used, depending on the weight of the fabric, stitch size and effect required. This stitch benefits from being worked on fabric stretched taut in an embroidery hoop or frame. Although this is not essential, it helps prevent distortion and puckering of the ground fabric.

Work spine chain stitch in the same way as ordinary chain stitch, but add a diagonal straight stitch at the base of each chain, as shown. Work these diagonal stitches or 'spines' alternately to the right and left of the chain, or arrange them in groups of two or three at either side. Make the diagonal stitches either of an identical length or vary them along the row.

As an additional decoration, rows of spine chain stitches can be embellished with isolated stitches such as French or Chinese knots (page 68), bullion knots (page 69) or daisy stitches (page 76) worked at the tips of the spines in a contrasting colour. A variation of the stitch can be created by whipping the central chain line with a contrasting colour, weight or texture of thread, or by working a French or Chinese knot at the centre of each chain.

## ROMAN STITCH

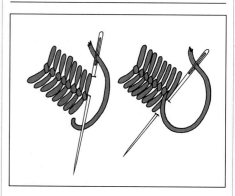

(Also known as branch stitch.)

Roman stitch is a wide line stitch used on both plain- and even-weave fabric to make a pretty, solidly stitched line. It can be used either as a border or in multiple rows to fill a shape and is worked from left to right between two widely spaced parallel lines. To work the stitch neatly, choose an even-weave fabric and count the threads, or mark parallel guidelines on plain-weave fabric with tailor's chalk or a dressmaker's pencil. This stitch should always be worked on fabric stretched taut in an embroidery hoop or frame to prevent distortion.

First, make a long, loose stitch from left to right across the line to be covered. Bring the needle out at the centre of this stitch, then pull it through over the working thread. Make a short crossing stitch over the long stitch to tie it down, and bring the needle out on the left to commence the next long stitch. Repeat along the line. The long stitches can be pulled by the crossing stitches to give them a gentle curve. If you want the long stitches to lie flat and straight across the fabric, work the crossing stitches quite loosely. The stitches can be spaced out along the row or, as is more usual, worked closely together to make a solid line.

## ▮ ROUMANIAN STITCH

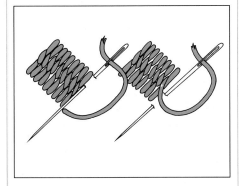

(Also known as Oriental stitch, antique stitch, Indian filling stitch and Janina stitch.)

Roumanian stitch is a wide line stitch used on both plain- and even-weave fabric. It makes an attractive border when worked between two parallel lines, and it can also be used to fill long, narrow shapes by graduating the width of the stitches. The stitch is similar to Roman stitch (left), but in this case the crossing stitches are long and slanted. It looks very effective when worked in stranded cotton or silk.

Make a long, loose stitch from left to right across the line to be covered. Bring the needle out a short distance in towards the centre of this stitch, then pull it through over the working thread. Make a slanting stitch to tie down the long stitch, and bring the needle out on the left to commence the next stitch. Repeat the sequence along the line, working the stitches closely together to cover the ground fabric.

# BORDER STITCHES

## ▌ CHEVRON STITCH

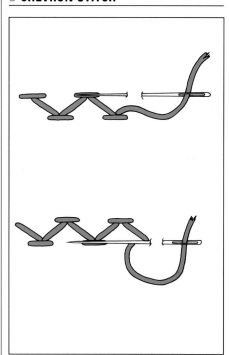

Chevron stitch is used as a border stitch and filling on both plain- and even-weave fabric. It is worked from left to right between two parallel lines, in a similar way to herringbone stitch (page 47), and produces a pretty zigzag line. Chevron stitch is also used in smocking to make both diamond and surface honeycomb patterns across tiny folds of gathered fabric. It does not follow curves well, unless they are very gradual, and is therefore normally used in straight rows.

To work chevron stitch neatly and keep the line of an even width, choose an even-weave fabric and count the threads, or mark two parallel guidelines on plain-weave fabric with a dressmaker's pencil, tailor's chalk or special water-soluble marker. Any type of embroidery thread can be used to work chevron stitch, depending on the weight of the fabric, stitch size and effect required. Rows of this stitch can be threaded in a contrasting colour and weight of thread in the same way as threaded herringbone stitch (page 61).

To work this stitch, bring the needle through the fabric on the lower guideline and make a straight stitch, as shown in the second diagram, bringing the needle out at the centre of this stitch. Take a diagonal stitch across to the upper line, as shown in the first diagram, then make a second straight stitch along this line. Repeat along the row. When using the stitch as a filling, arrange the rows closely together to produce a diamond-shaped lattice, which should be worked neatly and regularly.

## ▌ FLY STITCH

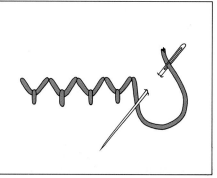

(Also known as Y-stitch and open loop stitch.)

Fly stitch makes an attractive line on both plain- and even-weave fabric. Each separate stitch looks like a capital Y and the stitches are repeated along the row from left to right. This stitch is extremely quick and easy to work successfully, even for a novice embroiderer. Fly stitch is also used individually to create a powdered filling worked at random to decorate a shape, and because of this is often classified in embroidery books as an isolated stitch.

Choice of embroidery thread depends on the weight of the fabric, stitch size and effect required. A round, twisted thread such as soft cotton or coton à broder makes a row of fly stitches stand out from the background rather more than a stranded cotton or silk. This stitch benefits from being worked on fabric stretched taut in an embroidery hoop or frame, although this is not essential.

Each stitch is very easy to work. Bring the needle through at the top left of the line to be covered and insert it diagonally back into the fabric, making a V-shaped loop, as shown. Pull the needle through over the working thread and work a vertical straight stitch or 'tail' to hold the loop in place. Arrange the fly stitches side by side to make a horizontal row, or work them underneath each other to make a vertical row. The stitches can touch or be spaced regularly apart and the length of the tail may be varied to produce different effects.

When using the stitches as a filling, either space them evenly or scatter them randomly over a shape. To make the stitches more decorative, work an isolated stitch such as daisy stitch (page 76), dot stitch (page 69) or Chinese knot (page 68) in the centre of the V or at the tips of the stitches in a contrasting thread colour.

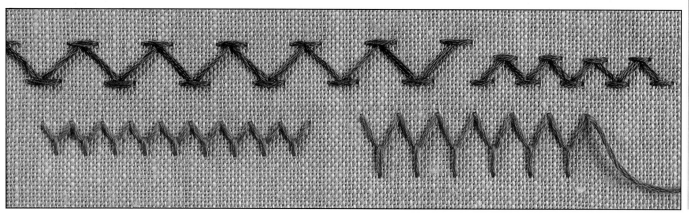

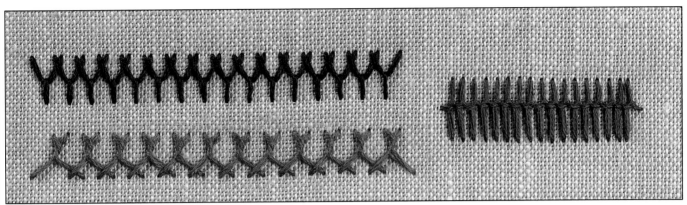

## ▍PLAITED FLY STITCH

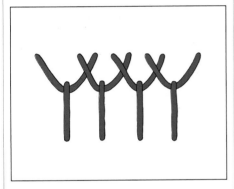

Plaited fly stitch is used as a border stitch or filling on both plain- and even-weave fabric. It is worked in the same way as ordinary fly stitch (left), but in this case the stitches are elongated and overlap along the row to produce an attractive plaited line. Work multiple rows of the stitch to make a light filling, varying the effect by altering the length of the tails. Any type of embroidery thread can be used to work this stitch, depending on the weight of the fabric, stitch size and effect required.

Bring the needle through the fabric at the top left of the line to be covered, then work a row of ordinary fly stitches with elongated tails. Arrange the stitches so that each new stitch overlaps the preceding stitch by a small amount, as shown. To make a wide border, work a double row of plaited fly stitches with the V-shapes touching. The tail stitches will create a row of spines along each side. A border with either an unusual zigzag or gently undulating edge can be produced by graduating the length of the tails along the row.

## ▍BRETON STITCH

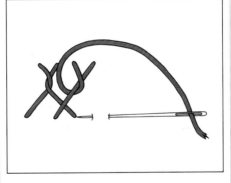

This unusual stitch is characteristic of the embroidery of Brittany and echoes the shape of the carved spindles found on traditional Breton furniture. It is used on both plain- and even-weave fabric and was originally worked in just two colour combinations: dark blue thread on white fabric, and white on blue. When rows of Breton stitch are worked together to fill a shape, an attractive grillwork pattern is created over the fabric which allows the colour of the background to show through.

Breton stitch is worked in the same way as herringbone stitch (page 47), but with a twist. Position it between two parallel lines and choose an even-weave fabric and count the threads, or mark guidelines on plain-weave fabric with a special water-soluble marker. For the best results, use a thread with a definite twist and work on fabric stretched taut in an embroidery hoop or frame.

Work a row of herringbone stitches from left to right, taking the needle under each preceding stitch from right to left to create a twist.

## ▍LOOP STITCH

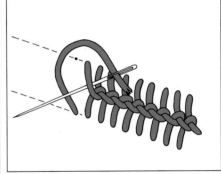

(Also known as centipede stitch and knotted loop stitch.)

Loop stitch is a line stitch with a raised, plaited centre which is used on both plain- and even-weave fabric. It is normally worked in straight rows but can also be used along very gentle curves. Loop stitch can be worked as a filling for narrow shapes if the length of the outside stitches is varied to fit the contours. An outline can be created around shapes filled in this way with a row of back stitches (page 13), outline stitches (page 15) or stem stitches (page 14). Work this stitch from right to left between two parallel lines. Use an even-weave fabric and count the threads, or mark guidelines on plain-weave fabric with tailor's chalk or a special water-soluble marker.

Bring the needle through at the centre of the row, then insert it on the top guideline to make a diagonal stitch and bring it out along the lower line. Work a buttonhole stitch (page 17) over the first stitch, then insert the needle on the top line to work the next stitch.

41

# BORDER STITCHES

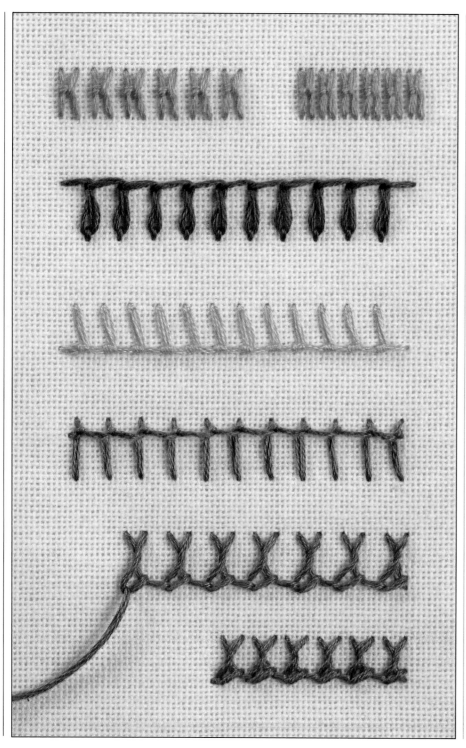

## ▌SIENNESE STITCH

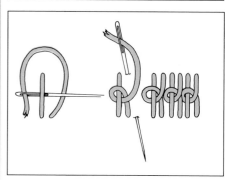

Siennese stitch is a wide line stitch used on both plain- and even-weave fabric to make a delicate, rather spiky line. The stitch should always be worked in a straight line as it does not follow curves successfully. It is very simple to work and is stitched from left to right along two parallel lines. To work Siennese stitch neatly, choose an even-weave fabric and count the threads, or mark parallel guidelines on plain-weave fabric with tailor's chalk or a special water-soluble marker.

Bring the needle through the fabric along the lower guideline and work a vertical straight stitch, bringing the needle out a short distance away on the lower line. Loop the needle over the first stitch, as shown, then pull the needle through and tighten the loop. Insert the needle into the fabric as shown and commence working the next stitch. Proceed in this way along the row, either working the stitches closely together to cover the ground fabric, or spacing them out at regular intervals, depending on the effect required.

## ▌BASQUE STITCH

(Also known as twisted daisy border stitch.)

Basque stitch, as its name suggests, originated in the Basque provinces of northern Spain. Traditionally, it was worked in one of two colour combinations: red thread on green fabric or white on blue-green. Basque stitch is a looped line stitch with a twist and it is worked from left to right on plain-weave fabric. It lends itself well to working curved lines, spirals and scrolls and is most effective when stitched in a white thread on a dark fabric. At first sight, the stitch looks quite complicated, but with practice it can be worked quickly and easily.

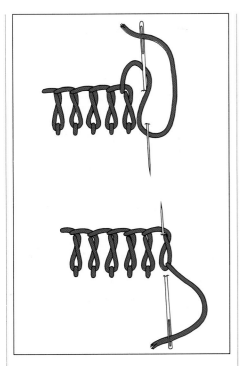

Bring the needle through the fabric and work a vertical stitch, looping the thread around the needle, as shown. Tighten the loops, and hold them down on the fabric with your left thumb while pulling the needle through. Insert the needle vertically into the fabric, as shown, pulling it through before starting to work the next stitch.

## BERWICK STITCH

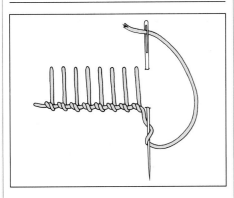

Berwick stitch is a line stitch worked only on plain-weave fabric. The stitch has a knotted lower edge with upright stitches protruding like spines along the top. It is quick and easy to work successfully and is similar to buttonhole stitch (page 17). Use it to outline circular shapes, arranging the knotted edge either to the inside or outside of the curve, or make a wide border or unusual filling by working it in multiple rows. This stitch benefits from being worked on fabric stretched taut in an embroidery hoop or frame.

Work the stitch in the same way as buttonhole stitch, but loop the thread around the needle, as shown, to make the knot. Each knot should be tightened carefully before the needle is pulled through the fabric again. When using Berwick stitch to make a border, work two rows with the knotted edges touching and vary the length of the spines to give a zigzag or wavy edge. French or Chinese knots (page 68), or tiny bullion knots (page 69) can be used to decorate the tips of the spines.

## KNOTTED PEARL STITCH

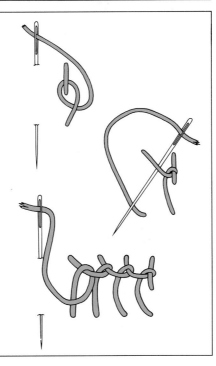

Knotted pearl stitch is used on both plain- and even-weave fabric. It is a variation of pearl stitch (page 22), but this stitch produces a more open line with a knotted surface. Use it to work outlines and linear details or stitch it in multiple rows to make wide borders and fillings. Any type of embroidery thread can be used, depending on the weight of the fabric, stitch size and effect required. A round, twisted thread such as pearl cotton accentuates the knots more than a flat, stranded thread.

Begin at the right of the line to be covered. Make a short vertical stitch, then loop the thread through it, as shown in the first diagram. Insert the needle vertically into the fabric, pull it through and tighten the thread. Take the needle over and under the second stitch, as shown, then insert it vertically into the fabric and commence working the next stitch. Space the stitches evenly apart along the line.

## BONNET STITCH

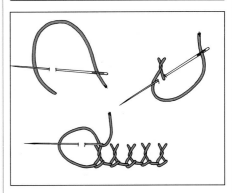

Bonnet stitch gets its unusual name from the discovery of a previously unknown stitch used on a bonnet featured in a 1923 issue of *Embroidery* magazine. It is a looped line stitch which is worked from right to left on plain-weave fabric and can also be arranged in multiple rows with the twisted uprights touching to produce a light, lacy filling. The effect of the stitch can be varied by altering the length and spacing of the upright stitches.

Most types of embroidery thread can be used to work bonnet stitch, depending on the effect required and the weight of the ground fabric chosen. Coton à broder, for example, produces a delicate, spidery line, while a thick wool thread creates a solid line.

Bring the needle through and make a short horizontal stitch along the upper edge of the line to be covered, as shown, pulling the needle through over the working thread. Make the loop stitch shown in the second diagram, then insert the needle a short distance away on the upper edge and commence working the next stitch.

# BORDER STITCHES

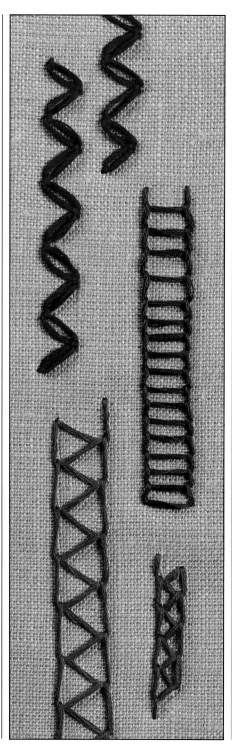

## ▋ ZIGZAG CABLE STITCH

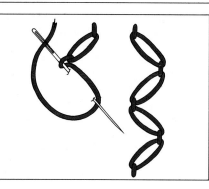

(Also known as double cable stitch.)

Zigzag cable stitch is a simple but effective variation of ordinary cable stitch (page 20) which produces a decorative, zigzag line. It is used as a line stitch and filling on both plain- and even-weave fabric. When used as a line stitch, zigzag cable stitch is normally worked in a straight line as it does not follow curves successfully. It makes an attractive light filling when several spaced parallel rows are worked to fill a shape.

Any type of embroidery thread can be used, depending on the weight of the fabric, stitch size and effect required. This stitch benefits from being worked on fabric stretched taut in an embroidery hoop or frame.

Work the stitch downwards in the same way as ordinary cable stitch, but in this case position each stitch at right angles to the preceding stitch to make a zigzag line.

## ▋ OPEN CHAIN STITCH

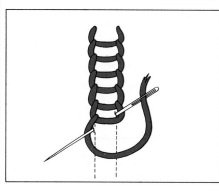

(Also known as square chain stitch, Roman chain stitch, small writing (when the stitches are narrow), big writing (when the stitches are wide) and ladder stitch.)

Open chain stitch is always worked downwards and can be used on both plain- and even-weave fabric. It is a wide variation of ordinary chain stitch (page 18) which is quick and easy to work. In East European countries – particularly Hungary and Yugoslavia – and in India, rows of solidly worked open chain stitches are extensively used in embroidery.

Work this stitch between two parallel lines to make a heavy border, or use it to couch down cord, narrow ribbon or flat, metallic braid. The stitch is also suitable for filling narrow shapes and looks attractive when worked solidly in multiple rows. To work it neatly and keep the line of an even width, choose an even-weave fabric and count the threads, or mark guidelines on plain-weave fabric with tailor's chalk or a special water-soluble marker.

Work the stitch in the same way as chain stitch, but in this case insert the needle diagonally from the right-hand side of the row to the left. Anchor the last chain in the row by working a tiny straight stitch across each of the base corners. The spacing of the stitches can be varied to create an open or closed effect.

## ▋ DOUBLE CHAIN STITCH

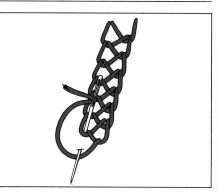

(Also known as Turkmen stitch.)

Double chain stitch is a simple variation of ordinary chain stitch (page 18) used on both plain- and even-weave fabric. It makes an attractive wide border when worked between two parallel lines, or it can be used to fill narrow shapes if the size of the stitches is varied. If worked in multiple, parallel rows, the stitch can be used to fill large shapes. Double chain stitch works best when used in a straight line, but can also be worked along a very gradual curve. Any type of embroidery thread can be used, depending on the weight of the fabric, stitch size and effect required. To work double chain stitch neatly in a straight line, either choose an even-weave fabric and count the threads, or mark guidelines on plain-weave fabric with tailor's chalk or a special embroidery marker.

Bring the needle through at the top left of the line to be covered and work a row of wide chain stitches, arranging them alternately at the right and then the left of the line, as shown in the diagram. To make the row more decorative, work an isolated knot stitch such as a French knot (page 68) in the centre of each chain.

## ▌CRESTED CHAIN STITCH

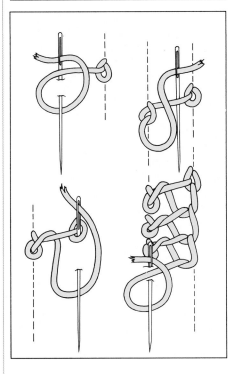

(Also known as Spanish coral stitch.)

Crested chain stitch is a wide line stitch used on both plain- and even-weave fabric. It is a combination of ordinary chain stitch (page 18) and coral stitch (page 21), and is easy to work if these stitches have been practised previously. A decorative, braided line is produced when the stitches are worked closely together; for a lacy effect, the stitches can be spaced widely apart. The stitch is also effective when worked along a gradual curve with the coral stitch edge arranged on the outside.

To keep the stitches evenly spaced, choose an even-weave fabric and count the threads, or mark parallel guidelines on plain-weave fabric with tailor's chalk or a special water-soluble marker. Any type of embroidery thread can be used, depending on the weight of the fabric, stitch size and effect required.

To work crested chain stitch, make a small chain stitch at the right-hand side of the row to be covered. Take the needle to the left of the row and work a coral stitch. Loop the thread as shown in the second diagram, then work a chain stitch on the right-hand side, inserting the needle into the previous chain loop. Continue in this way, making coral and chain stitches alternately along the row.

## ▌FEATHERED CHAIN STITCH

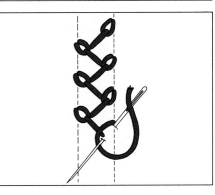

(Also known as chained feather stitch.)

Feathered chain stitch is a wide border stitch which is worked downwards on both plain- and even-weave fabric and makes a pretty, zigzag line. Short, isolated rows of feathered chain stitch look effective when scattered across a shape to make a powdered filling. If worked in multiple rows, the stitch can be used to fill a shape with an interesting texture.

To keep the stitches evenly spaced, either choose an even-weave fabric and count the threads, or mark parallel guidelines on plain-weave fabric with tailor's chalk or a special water-soluble marker.

Begin at the top right of the row to be covered. Work an ordinary chain stitch (page 18) which slants towards the centre of the row, then insert the needle close to the left-hand side to make a diagonal stitch, as shown. Bring the needle out on the dotted line slightly above this stitch, then work another slanting chain stitch. Repeat along the row.

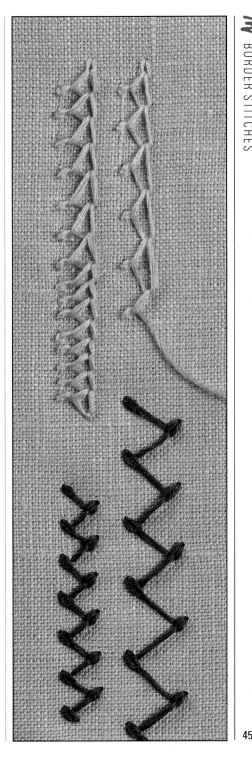

## ❚ HERRINGBONE STITCH

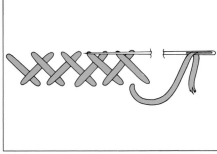

(Also known as plaited stitch, catch stitch, fishnet stitch, witch stitch, Mossoul stitch, Persian stitch, Russian stitch and Russian cross stitch.)

Herringbone stitch is a border stitch which is used to make a crossed zigzag line on both plain- and even-weave fabric. It is worked in straight rows from left to right. To work the stitch neatly and keep the stitches even, choose an even-weave fabric and count the threads, or mark parallel guidelines on plain-weave fabric with tailor's chalk.

Bring the needle through the fabric on the lower guideline, then make a short stitch from right to left a little further along the top line. Make a second short stitch along the lower line, spacing the stitches evenly, as shown. Repeat along the row.

## ❚ CLOSE HERRINGBONE STITCH

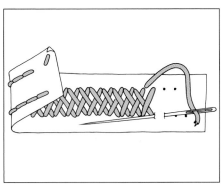

(Also known as shadow stitch.)

Close herringbone stitch is used to make a heavy, braided line on both plain- and even-weave fabric. It is usually worked as a border,

but can also be utilized for shadow-work on fine, semi-transparent fabrics such as voile and organdie. In addition, it is an attractive stitch to use for couching down a narrow ribbon, metallic braid or group of laid threads. To work this stitch neatly and in a straight row on an opaque fabric, choose one with an even-weave and count the threads, or mark parallel guidelines on plain-weave fabric with tailor's chalk or a special water-soluble marker.

Work this stitch from left to right in the same way as herringbone stitch (left), but position the stitches close to each other so that the diagonal stitches touch at the top and bottom of the row, as shown in the diagram.

## ❚ DOUBLE BACK STITCH

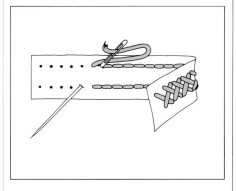

(Also known as crossed back stitch.)

Double back stitch is used mainly for shadow-work embroidery. On the right side of the fabric, it produces two rows of ordinary back stitches (page 13) at the same time, while on the reverse, a row of close herringbone stitches (left) is formed. The back stitches outline the design while the herringbone stitches show through the fabric in shadow form.

Work the stitch from right to left in the same way as back stitch, but after completing the first stitch on the upper line, take the needle under the fabric, and bring it through to work the second stitch on the lower line. Take the needle under the fabric again, and work the third stitch on the upper line. Repeat along the row.

*The colourful appliquéd design on the left dates from the 1930s. A variety of stitches, including herringbone stitch, has been used to define and decorate the edges of the fabric shapes.*

# BORDER STITCHES

### ■ PARIS STITCH

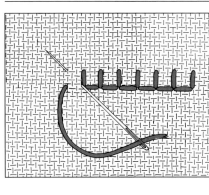

Paris stitch is a line stitch used only on even-weave fabric. It makes a neat line with branched stitches along the upper edge and should be worked in straight rows. It is a pretty variation of back stitch (page 13) which is quick and easy to work. When used on a loosely woven ground fabric, each stitch can be pulled tightly to create a pattern of holes along the row. Paris stitch also looks effective when worked in multiple rows to fill a shape. It can be worked over any number of threads, but a square of four fabric threads is the norm.

Any type of embroidery thread can be used to work Paris stitch, depending on the weight of the fabric, stitch size and effect required. Use a fine, strong thread when making a pattern of holes on a loosely woven ground fabric and do not stretch the fabric in an embroidery hoop or frame.

Work the stitch from right to left in the same way as back stitch, but make an upright stitch in between each pair of back stitches.

### ■ TWO-SIDED PLAITED SPANISH STITCH

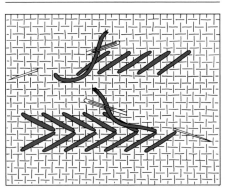

Two-sided plaited Spanish stitch is a border stitch used in straight rows on even-weave fabric. It makes a simple but stylish pattern of V-shapes which point towards the right, and is identical on both sides of the fabric. Any type of embroidery thread can be used, depending on the weight of the fabric and effect required, but a lightweight thread such as coton à broder or the finest available weight of pearl cotton accentuates the geometric pattern produced by the stitch.

Work this stitch in two journeys, beginning at the right of the line to be covered. On the first journey, work a row of stitches which slant from bottom left to top right. Use a backwards and forwards motion, as shown, making sure that each stitch spans five vertical and three horizontal fabric threads. Work another row of similar stitches on the second journey. These stitches are worked directly above the first row and slant in the opposite direction. If both sides of the piece of work are to be visible, break off the thread at the end of the first journey and secure it neatly out of sight. Rejoin the thread for the second journey, securing the beginning and end as neatly as possible.

### ■ ONE-SIDED INSERTION STITCH

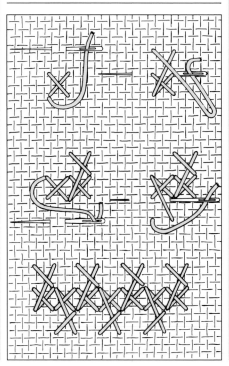

One-sided insertion stitch is, in spite of its name, an unusual border stitch, not a stitch used to join two pieces of fabric together. It can be worked on plain-weave fabric, but a much neater finish is possible if an even-weave fabric is used. The stitch is an ornate and decorative variation of ordinary cross stitch (page 34) which is always worked from right to left in a straight line.

Any type of embroidery thread can be used to work one-sided insertion stitch, depending on the weight of the fabric and effect required. A round, twisted thread such as pearl cotton makes the stitch stand out from the background more effectively than a flat, stranded cotton or silk. Choose a firm fabric and, for preference, stretch it in an embroidery hoop or frame. The sequence of stitches which makes up one-sided insertion stitch is rather complicated to grasp at first, so follow each stage carefully from the diagrams.

First, work a cross stitch over three horizontal and three vertical fabric threads, bringing the thread through at the lower left-hand corner of the cross. Next, insert the needle six threads up and three threads to the right, bringing it out again three threads to the left, as shown in the first diagram. Insert the needle at the top right-hand corner of the original cross, as shown in the second diagram, bringing it out six threads to the left. Following the third diagram, work another cross stitch next to the first one, bringing the thread through at the top left-hand corner. Next, insert the needle six threads down and three threads to the right. Insert the needle at the lower right-hand corner of the second cross, bringing it out six threads to the left, as shown in the fourth diagram. From this point, repeat the sequence along the row.

### ■ TWO-SIDED INSERTION STITCH

Two-sided insertion stitch is, like the previous stitch, an attractive border stitch. It should be worked on an even-weave fabric to ensure perfect regularity. As the name suggests, the stitch is reversible. On the front of the fabric, it builds up into a plaited border consisting of a broad zigzag line interlaced with a narrow, closely stitched zigzag line. On the reverse of the fabric a diamond lattice is produced.

First, bring the needle through the fabric and insert it nine threads up and three threads to the right. Bring it out three threads down and three threads to the right. Next, insert the needle three threads down and three threads to the

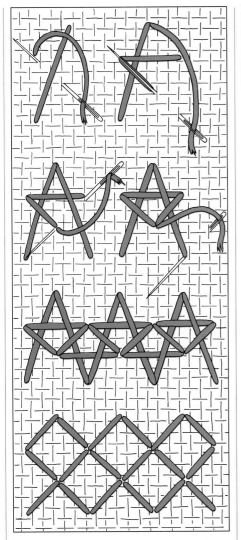

right. Bring it out at the beginning of the second stitch, as shown in the first diagram. Following the second diagram, insert the needle six threads to the right, bring it out at the top of the first stitch, and insert it nine threads down and three threads to the right. Bring the needle through at the base of the second stitch, insert it at the right-hand edge of the third stitch, and then at the base of the second stitch, as shown in the third diagram. Complete the sequence by following the fourth diagram, inserting the needle six threads to the right and bringing it through at the base of the fourth stitch. Repeat this sequence along the row.

# BORDER STITCHES

## VANDYKE STITCH

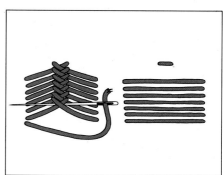

Vandyke stitch is used as a border stitch and filling on both plain- and even-weave fabric. It makes a wide line with a plaited, raised centre and looks effective when worked in multiple rows to make a deep, rather heavy border. Vandyke stitch can also be used to fill a narrow shape if the width of the stitches is varied to fit the contours. Work this stitch downwards and arrange the stitches close to each other. Choose an even-weave fabric and count the threads, or mark parallel guidelines on plain-weave fabric with tailor's chalk or a special water-soluble marker.

Bring the needle through at the left-hand edge of the row to be covered. Make a small stitch higher up at the centre of the line to anchor the row, then insert the needle at the right-hand edge. Take the thread under the fabric and let it emerge on the left-hand line just below the first stitch. The subsequent stitches should cross the row from left to right and pass behind the preceding stitches at the centre, as shown, without picking up the fabric.

## LADDER STITCH

Ladder stitch is a wide line stitch which is worked downwards on both plain- and even-weave fabric. It can be used to work straight borders and as a filling for long, narrow shapes. To work the stitch neatly, choose an even-weave fabric and count the threads, or mark two parallel guidelines on plain-weave fabric. Use any type of embroidery thread, and always work on fabric stretched taut in an embroidery hoop or frame.

Begin at the left of the row and follow the diagrams to work the sequence of crossing stitches and loops. In the first diagram, the

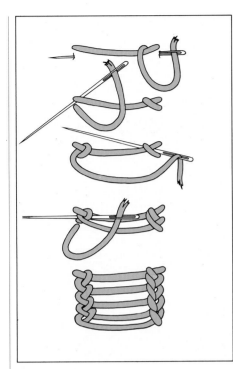

thread can be used to work thorn stitch, depending on the weight of the fabric, stitch size and effect required. For an attractive result, use a heavy thread such as the thickest available weight of pearl cotton for the laid thread, and a finer one for the diagonal stitches. This stitch should always be worked with the fabric stretched taut in an embroidery hoop or frame to prevent distortion.

To work thorn stitch, bring the first thread out at the top and lay it loosely along the line to be covered. Then, using the second thread, work pairs of diagonal stitches so that they cross over the laid thread, as shown, anchoring it to the fabric. The diagonal stitches create the 'thorns' at each side of the line.

the needle just below this knot and bring it out further down on the left-hand line. At the centre of the row, as shown, make a knot over the previous stitch without picking up the fabric. Work a tiny stitch on the right-hand line and repeat the sequence from the beginning.

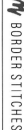

needle is brought back through the fabric to make a loop over the first stitch before being taken back to the left-hand side. In the second and third diagrams, the needle does not enter the fabric. Repeat the third and fourth steps from side to side of the row.

## THORN STITCH

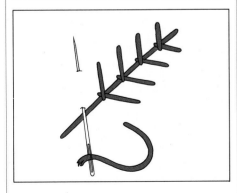

Thorn stitch is a decorative form of couching (page 23) used on both plain- and even-weave fabric. It makes a wide, branching line which is often used to depict ferns and grasses in naturalistic designs. Any type of embroidery

## DIAMOND STITCH

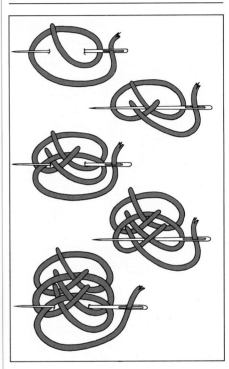

Diamond stitch is a wide line stitch used as a border on both plain- and even-weave fabric. It makes a broad, knotted line which is worked downwards between two parallel lines.

Work a horizontal stitch from left to right across the row, then bring the thread out just below this stitch and make a knot at the end, as shown in the first diagram. Carry the thread across and make a similar knot at the left. Insert

## PLAITED BRAID STITCH

Plaited braid stitch is a heavy line stitch which is worked downwards on plain-weave fabric. It has been used since the early sixteenth century, reaching the height of popularity during the early seventeenth century, when heavy metal threads were used to decorate clothes and furnishings. Work the stitch in a heavy, fairly stiff thread as the loops will tangle and pull out of shape if a soft thread is used, and stretch the fabric in an embroidery hoop or frame.

Follow the sequence of stitches carefully from the diagrams, passing the needle alternately through the fabric and under the loops. Begin by working all of the five stages shown in the diagrams, then continue along the row by repeating the movements shown in the fourth and fifth diagrams only. The reverse of the fabric should show a line of small, evenly sized horizontal stitches.

# CHAPTER THREE

# COMPOSITE BAND STITCHES

**T**he majority of the stitches described in this chapter are worked only in straight lines, and all are made up of a combination of two or more stitches. To ensure a neat result, the fabric on which these stitches are worked should preferably be stretched in an embroidery hoop or frame. Some of the stitches described, such as laced double running stitch and threaded chain stitch, are easy to work and ideal for a beginner. Others, like raised lattice band and sheaf stitch, are more complex and require some practice before they can be mastered.

Choice of thread is particularly important, as many of the stitches can be worked in more than one colour and weight of thread. When making your selection, consider the different effects created by using bright, contrasting colours, subtle shades of a single colour, or textured and metallic threads. A number of the stitches are laced or threaded: whenever possible, work this stage with a blunt-ended tapestry needle to avoid splitting the foundation stitches.

# COMPOSITE BAND STITCHES

## ■ THREADED BACK STITCH

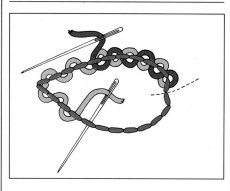

Threaded back stitch is quick to work and is used to make attractive outlines for shapes on either plain- or even-weave fabric. The stitch produces a wider, heavier line than ordinary back stitch (page 13).

This stitch can be worked in either one, two or three colours and any type of embroidery thread can be used, depending on the weight of the fabric, stitch size and effect required. If a fine thread interlaced with a soft woollen yarn is used, the stitching takes on an almost embossed appearance. A different effect is produced when extra long stitches are worked on the foundation row, and then threaded with a textured or supple metallic thread. This stitch benefits from being worked on fabric stretched taut in an embroidery hoop or frame, although this is not essential.

Begin by working a foundation row of ordinary back stitches along the line to be covered, making the stitches slightly longer than usual. Pass a second thread alternately up and down behind these stitches, as shown,

without picking up any of the ground fabric. Leave the stitch as it is with just a single row of threading, or fill in the spaces left on the first journey with a third thread to make a richer, heavier line.

## ■ LACED DOUBLE RUNNING STITCH

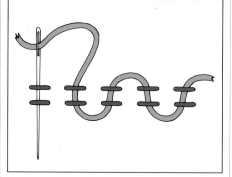

Laced double running stitch can be used as a border stitch or filling on both plain- and even-weave fabric. It is a wide, decorative variation of ordinary running stitch (page 12) which is usually worked in a single straight line, but can also be stitched in multiple rows to make an attractive filling. Any type of embroidery thread can be used, depending on the weight of the fabric, stitch size and effect required, but a metallic lacing thread looks very effective.

Work a double row of evenly spaced running stitches. Lace a second thread up and down behind the stitches, as shown, without picking up the fabric. Work the lacing from right to left. To make laced treble running stitch, add an extra row of running stitches and lace a thread through all three rows.

## ■ LACED BUTTONHOLE STITCH

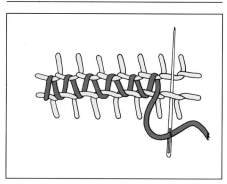

Laced buttonhole stitch is used on both plain- and even-weave fabric. It produces an attractive, wide line which is usually worked in more than one colour and weight of thread. Any type of embroidery thread can be used, depending on the weight of the fabric, stitch size and effect required. For a very decorative effect, the lacing can be worked in a supple metallic or textured thread.

This stitch should be worked with the fabric stretched taut in an embroidery hoop or frame to help prevent the lacing from tightening and distorting the ground fabric. Leave the lacing thread quite loose on the fabric to stop the foundation rows from pulling towards each other and creating an untidy effect.

To work laced buttonhole stitch, first make two parallel rows of ordinary buttonhole stitches (page 17), spacing the stitches evenly apart. Arrange the two rows so that the looped edges of the stitches face each other and leave a small gap in between the rows. Working from left to right, lace a second thread up and down

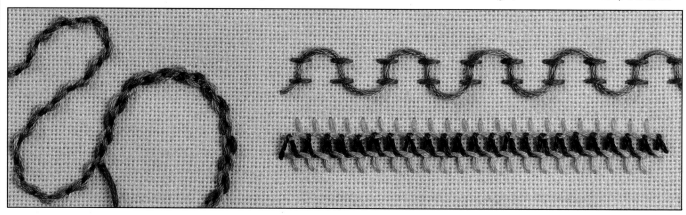

between the foundation rows, as shown, without picking up the ground fabric.

To vary the look of this stitch, use one of the buttonhole stitch variations described in Chapter 2 to make the foundation rows. Closed buttonhole stitch, crossed buttonhole stitch (page 26) and knotted buttonhole stitch (page 27) are all suitable for this purpose.

## FANCY COUCHING

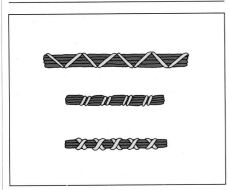

Fancy couching is a variation of ordinary couching (page 23) used on both plain- and even-weave fabric to hold down groups of laid threads. Narrow ribbon, braid or cord can be used instead: turn the ends neatly under on the right side of the fabric and secure them. This stitch should be worked on fabric stretched taut in an embroidery hoop or frame.

Work the stitch in the same way as ordinary couching, but use a decorative stitch to hold down the laid threads. Buttonhole stitches (page 17), open chain stitches (page 44), cross stitches (page 34) and blocks of satin stitches (page 102) work well as couching stitches.

## THREADED CHAIN STITCH

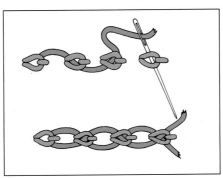

Threaded chain stitch is used on both plain- and even-weave fabric. It can be worked in more than one colour and any type of embroidery thread can be used, depending on the weight of the fabric, stitch size and effect required. This stitch benefits from being worked on fabric stretched taut in an embroidery hoop or frame.

Begin by working a foundation row of evenly spaced daisy stitches (page 76) facing in the same direction. Pass a second thread up and down behind these stitches, working along the row from left to right without picking up the ground fabric, as shown in the first diagram. To produce a heavier, more decorative line, thread the row again, as shown in the second diagram. Use a blunt-ended tapestry needle for the threading to avoid splitting the stitches in the foundation row.

For added decoration, work one of the isolated knot stitches described in Chapter 4 in between each pair of daisy stitches. Choose from French or Chinese knot (page 68), Danish knot or knot stitch (page 69).

## BUTTERFLY CHAIN STITCH

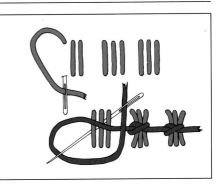

Butterfly chain stitch is a pretty, wide line stitch used on both plain- and even-weave fabric. Use the stitch as a light, decorative filling by working it in spaced multiple rows to fill a shape. To produce a more solid effect, arrange the rows so that the groups of straight stitches interlock.

Each row of stitches is worked in two journeys, using either the same thread for both journeys or two threads of contrasting colours, weights and textures. This stitch should be worked on fabric stretched taut in an embroidery hoop or frame.

Make a foundation row consisting of regular groups of three vertical straight stitches. Space the groups evenly apart, as shown. Work a row of twisted chain stitches (page 18) across the groups of foundation stitches. Tighten each twisted chain stitch after it has been worked to bunch the straight stitches together. On this journey, the needle should enter the ground fabric only at the beginning and end of the row. A blunt-ended tapestry needle makes this stage easier to work.

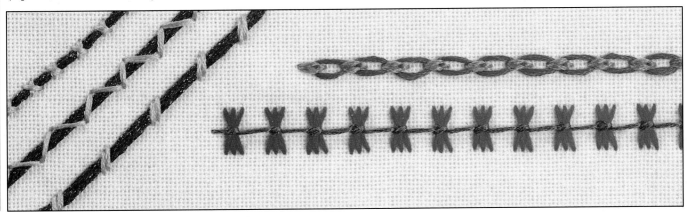

# COMPOSITE BAND STITCHES

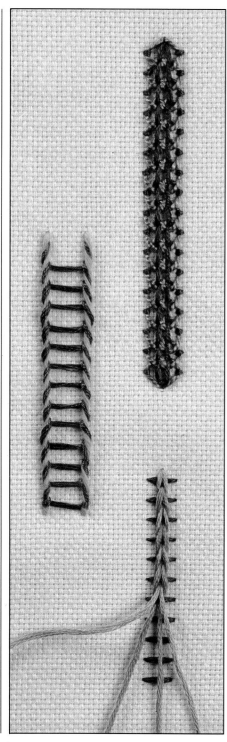

## ◼ SINGHALESE CHAIN STITCH

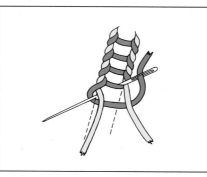

Singhalese chain stitch is used extensively on the traditional embroideries of Sri Lanka, and is normally worked in two contrasting thread colours. It is a variation of open chain stitch (page 44) which is worked downwards on both plain- and even-weave fabric. The stitch looks most attractive when it is used in a straight line to form a border, and it can be worked over a narrow ribbon, tape or flat braid. Work the stitch on an even-weave fabric and count the threads, or mark guidelines on plain-weave fabric with tailor's chalk.

First, bring a thread through at the top of each guideline. Lay the two threads loosely on the fabric along the lines. Work open chain stitches in a contrasting thread colour over these threads, as shown. Tighten the laid threads at the end of each row, then pull them through to the back of the fabric and secure them neatly.

## ◼ INTERLACED CHAIN STITCH

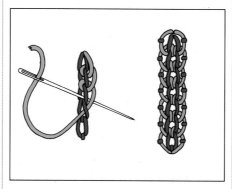

Interlaced chain stitch is an unusual variation of ordinary chain stitch (page 18) used on both plain- and even-weave fabric. It is an old stitch,

possibly of French origin, which produces a rich, wide line. It is simple to use once the working method has been mastered. Always work this stitch downwards.

Make a vertical row of large chain stitches. Working downwards, interlace a second thread through the side loops of the chain stitches, following the diagram carefully. Work the interlacing in two journeys, one on each side of the row, always beginning at the top. Do not pick up any of the ground fabric when working the interlaced stitches and, for preference, use a blunt-ended tapestry needle to avoid splitting the stitches in the foundation row. Leave the interlacing thread quite loose, and anchor the loops to the fabric with small horizontal stitches set at regular intervals along the row.

## ◼ CHEQUERED CHAIN BAND

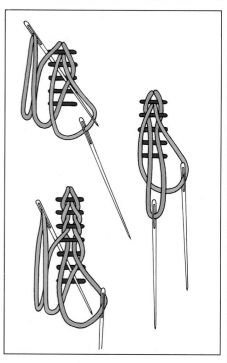

Chequered chain band is used on both plain- and even-weave fabric. It is used as a heavy line stitch and can only be worked in straight rows. This stitch should be worked on fabric stretched in an embroidery hoop or frame.

Make a foundation row of short, evenly spaced horizontal stitches. Thread two needles with threads of contrasting colours, doubling the thread in each needle. Bring the first doubled thread through just above the first horizontal stitch and the second thread just below it. Following the diagram, work a row of chain stitches (page 18) over the foundation stitches, without picking up the fabric. Use the two needles alternately, as shown.

## RAISED CHAIN BAND

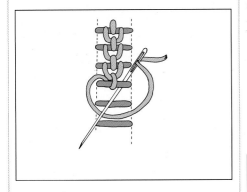

Raised chain band is worked downwards in straight rows on both plain- and even-weave fabric. It makes an attractive, raised line which can be worked in two colours. Work this stitch on fabric stretched taut in an embroidery hoop or frame.

Work a foundation row of small horizontal stitches, keeping them quite close together. Bring the thread through just above the top stitch. Pass it first over this stitch, then under it from below, so that the thread emerges at the top left of the line. Work a looped stitch over the foundation stitch. Repeat these two movements along the row, without picking up any of the ground fabric.

## RAISED STEM STITCH BAND

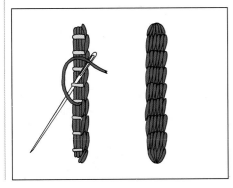

Raised stem stitch band makes a solidly stitched, raised band on both plain- and even-weave fabric. The stitch can only be worked in straight rows. Stretch the fabric in an embroidery hoop or frame.

Make a foundation row of long surface satin stitches (page 114) of the required width along the line to be covered. Work them closely together and add more stitches in the centre to produce a raised effect. Work single straight stitches across and at right angles to the foundation stitches. Then, beginning at the base of the row, work a row of stem stitches (page 14) over the short stitches, without picking up the long threads underneath. Repeat this row until the foundation threads are covered. The stem stitch rows should share the same base hole at each end of the band.

## RAISED FEATHER STITCH BAND

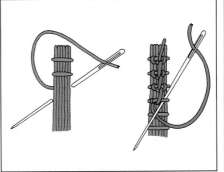

Raised feather stitch band is used on both plain- and even-weave fabric and produces a heavy, textured line which can only be worked in straight rows. It consists of a line of feather stitches (page 28) worked over a padded foundation. Any type of embroidery thread can be used, depending on the weight of the fabric, stitch size and effect required. This stitch should be worked on fabric stretched taut in an embroidery hoop or frame to enable the padding stitches to be kept parallel.

Work the stitch in three journeys. First, make a padding of five or six vertical surface satin stitches (page 114) spaced closely together. Then work a foundation of short, evenly spaced horizontal stitches across and at right angles to the foundation. Finally, work a row of feather stitches over the foundation stitches, without picking up the padding stitches, as shown in the second diagram.

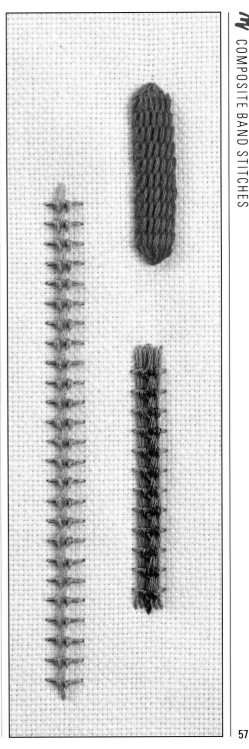

# COMPOSITE BAND STITCHES

## ▋ RAISED LATTICE BAND

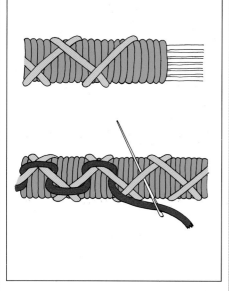

(Also known as raised lace band.)

Raised lattice band is a border stitch used on both plain- and even-weave fabric. It makes an ornate, padded line which is usually worked in more than one colour and weight of thread. The stitch can be worked either in a single row, or in multiple rows on a firm fabric to make a rich, heavy border.

Any type of embroidery thread can be used, depending on the weight of the fabric and effect required, although a flat thread such as stranded cotton or silk provides the most effective coverage for the foundation row. Use a shiny, light-reflecting synthetic or metallic thread for the final journey to make the stitch more decorative. Raised lattice band should be worked on fabric stretched taut in an embroidery hoop or frame to enable the padding stitches to be kept parallel.

Make a padding of long horizontal surface satin stitches (page 114) along the row to be covered. Work a few extra stitches over these in the centre to produce a rounded surface. Cover the padding with a foundation of vertical satin stitches (page 102) worked very closely together. Try to make all the vertical stitches of

an identical length. Finally, work a row of threaded herringbone stitches (page 61) over the satin stitches, as shown. Arrange the tips of the herringbone stitches so that they enter the fabric just above and below the line of satin stitches. Use a blunt-ended tapestry needle for threading the herringbone stitches.

## ▋ TWISTED LATTICE BAND

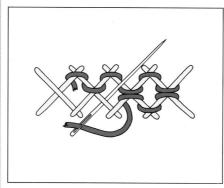

Twisted lattice band is used on both plain- and even-weave fabric to produce a delicate band with an attractive lattice appearance. The stitch can either be used alone as a lightweight border worked in two contrasting or toning colours of thread, or arranged in multiple rows to make a decorative filling.

To work this stitch neatly, either choose an even-weave fabric and count the threads, or mark parallel guidelines on plain-weave fabric with tailor's chalk. Any type of embroidery thread can be used, depending on the weight of the fabric, stitch size and effect required. This stitch should be worked on fabric stretched taut in an embroidery hoop or frame.

Begin by working a row of rather loose double herringbone stitches, following the method shown in the second diagram on page 60. Work the lacing in two journeys, as shown, without picking up the ground fabric. Proceed from left to right and work the upper row, then return in the opposite direction, using a blunt-ended tapestry needle to avoid splitting the herringbone stitches.

*Both raised and twisted lattice band have been worked on the embroidery shown opposite. A range of thread weights has been used to provide a varied appearance to the stitching.*

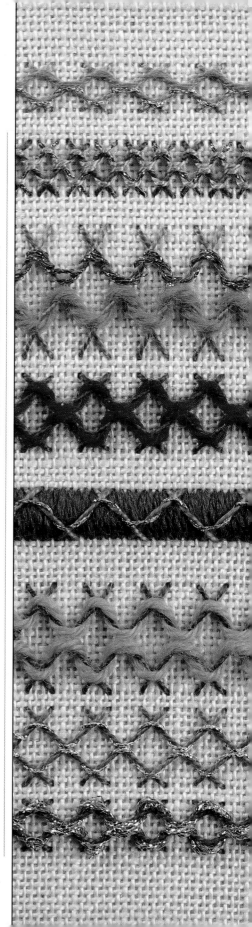

# COMPOSITE BAND STITCHES

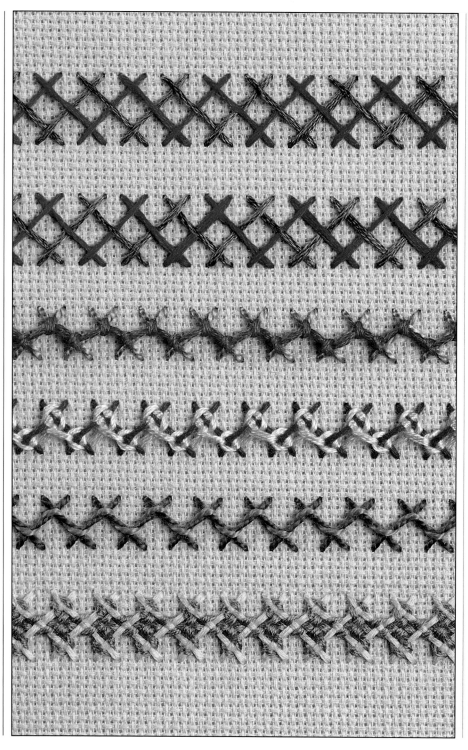

## ▌DOUBLE HERRINGBONE STITCH

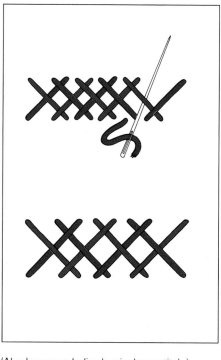

(Also known as Indian herringbone stitch.)

Double herringbone stitch is used on both plain- and even-weave fabric as a decorative border or as a foundation for more complicated stitches. The method of working the stitch differs depending on its use. For both methods, choose an even-weave fabric and count the threads, or mark parallel guidelines on plain-weave fabric with tailor's chalk or a special water-soluble marker.

To work double herringbone stitch as a decorative border, follow the first diagram. Begin by working a row of ordinary herringbone stitches (page 47). Work a second row over the top of the first row, spacing the stitches evenly apart and interlacing them where they cross each other, as shown.

To work this stitch as a foundation for stitches such as twisted lattice band (page 58), follow the second diagram. When working the stitches along the top line of both rows, slip the needle under each preceding stitch, instead of over it in the usual way. On the second row, after working a stitch along the lower line, slip the needle under the next stitch of the preceding row as it moves upwards.

## ▌TIED HERRINGBONE STITCH

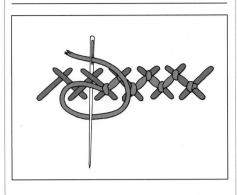

(Also known as coral knotted herringbone stitch.)

Tied herringbone stitch makes a knotted, zigzag line and is usually worked in two contrasting colours of thread. The stitch is used on both plain- and even-weave fabric and can be worked either as a border, or in multiple rows to make a knotted filling.

Work a row of ordinary herringbone stitches (page 47) along the line to be covered. Use a second thread to work a row of coral stitches (page 21) over the foundation, without picking up the ground fabric. Position the coral knots over the intersections of the herringbone stitches, tying them together. When using tied herringbone stitch as a filling, arrange the foundation rows so that the stitches touch at the tips of the crosses.

## ▌LACED HERRINGBONE STITCH

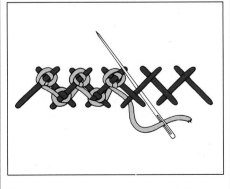

(Also known as woven herringbone stitch and German interlacing stitch.)

Laced herringbone stitch is an extremely decorative stitch used on both plain- and even-

weave fabric. It makes a wide border with a circular lacing. To work the stitch neatly, choose an even-weave fabric and count the threads, or mark parallel guidelines on plain-weave fabric with tailor's chalk or a special water-soluble marker. Laced herringbone stitch should be worked with the fabric stretched taut in an embroidery hoop or frame to prevent the lacing from tightening around the herringbone stitches and pulling them out of shape.

Begin by working a foundation row of ordinary herringbone stitches (page 47). The row should be at least ¾ inch (2cm) wide for the lacing to be worked successfully. Turn the work upside-down before starting the lacing. This ensures that the lacing is worked around the herringbone stitches in the correct order. Work the lacing around the crossed part of the stitches from left to right. Make two complete circles around each upper cross and one and a half circles around each lower cross, as shown, interlacing the thread under and over both the foundation stitches and itself.

## ▌THREADED HERRINGBONE STITCH

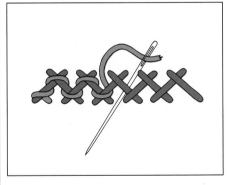

(Also known as barred witch stitch.)

Threaded herringbone stitch is used in straight rows on both plain- and even-weave fabric. It produces a narrow, decorative border which is usually worked in two contrasting or toning colours of thread. Work the stitch in a single row, or in multiple rows to create a pretty filling or deep band. To enable the foundation row to be worked neatly and evenly, choose an even-weave fabric and count the threads, or mark parallel guidelines on plain-weave fabric with tailor's chalk.

Make a row of ordinary herringbone stitches (page 47). Work the lacing from left to right, taking the second thread over and under the

foundation stitches, as shown. Take this thread through the fabric only at the beginning and end of each row, and always use a blunt-ended tapestry needle for this stage to avoid splitting the foundation stitches. When working the stitch as a filling, arrange the rows so that the herringbone stitches touch at the tips.

## ▌INTERLACED HERRINGBONE STITCH

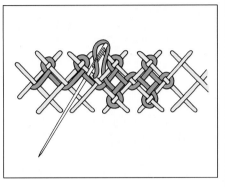

(Also known as interlacing stitch and Armenian cross stitch.)

Interlaced herringbone stitch is a wide, complex stitch used on both plain- and even-weave fabric. It produces an interlaced line which is always worked in straight rows. To enable the foundation row to be worked neatly, choose an even-weave fabric and count the threads, or mark guidelines on plain-weave fabric with tailor's chalk or a special water-soluble marker. Any type of thread can be used, depending on the weight of the fabric, stitch size and effect required, although the lacing thread should be thick enough to fill and cover the foundation stitches. Work on fabric stretched taut in an embroidery hoop or frame to enable the stitches to be worked evenly.

Work a foundation row of rather loose double herringbone stitches (left), using the second method shown. Check that the sequence of crossing stitches is correct before proceeding. Two journeys are needed to work the interlacing. Bring the interlacing thread through at the centre left of the line and work the lacing along the top of the foundation row, as shown. Lace the thread around the centre of the cross at the end of the row, then return in the opposite direction, as shown, to complete the row. Follow the sequence of 'unders' and 'overs' carefully from the diagram, and do not pick up any of the ground fabric.

# COMPOSITE BAND STITCHES

## ▌FANCY HERRINGBONE STITCH

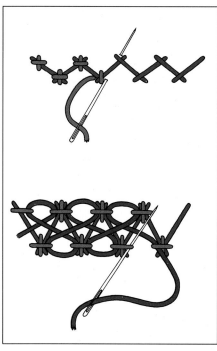

Fancy herringbone stitch is an ornamental stitch which is worked in more than one colour on both plain- and even-weave fabric. It makes a rich border which can easily be adapted to fill a shape if it is worked in spaced multiple rows, using a carefully selected range of colours. At first sight, fancy herringbone stitch looks rather complicated, but it is actually very easy to work. To work this stitch neatly and keep the row straight, choose an even-weave fabric and count the threads, or mark parallel guidelines on plain-weave fabric with tailor's chalk or a special water-soluble marker.

Work each row in three journeys. Begin by making a foundation row of ordinary herringbone stitches (page 47). Space the stitches quite widely apart, as shown. Next, work St George cross stitches (page 86) over the top and bottom crosses of the herringbone row. Make sure that the vertical bar of each St George cross stitch is worked first, then cross it with the horizontal bar. On the third journey, lace a thread from left to right through the horizontal bars of the St George cross stitches, as shown in the diagram, without picking up the ground fabric.

## ▌HERRINGBONE LADDER FILLING STITCH

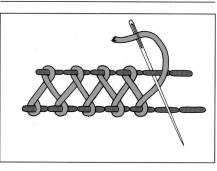

(Also known as interlaced band stitch, laced Cretan stitch and double Pekinese stitch.)

Herringbone ladder filling stitch is used on both plain- and even-weave fabric as a border and filling stitch. It has a pretty, laced appearance and can be worked in more than one colour of thread for an attractive effect. To work it neatly and keep the row of an even width, choose an even-weave fabric and count the threads, or mark parallel guidelines on plain-weave fabric with tailor's chalk or a special water-soluble marker.

Work a foundation of two parallel rows of Holbein stitches (page 12), arranging the rows so that the stitches are placed alternately, as shown. Lace a second thread from left to right between the rows, as shown, without picking up the ground fabric. To use this stitch as a filling, work further parallel rows of Holbein stitches and arrange the lacing in between adjacent rows. Holbein stitch is identical on both sides of the fabric, and if required, the interlacing can be worked on both sides.

## ▌GUILLOCHE STITCH

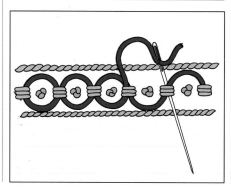

Guilloche stitch is used to produce a pretty, composite border on both plain- and even-weave fabric. The stitch produces an extremely decorative effect when it is used in straight, single rows worked in several contrasting or toning colours of thread. To work guilloche stitch neatly, choose an even-weave fabric and count the threads, or mark widely spaced guidelines on plain-weave fabric.

First, work the outer lines in stem stitches (page 14), then work groups of three satin stitches (page 102) at regular intervals in between the lines. Lace a thread up and down under the groups of satin stitches from left to right. Fill in the gaps on the second journey, as shown, again working from left to right. Use a blunt-ended tapestry needle and do not pick up any of the ground fabric. Stitch a French knot (page 68) in the centre of each circle.

## ▌SHAM HEM STITCH

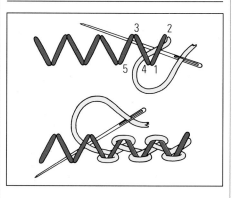

(Also known as zigzag sham hem stitch.)

Sham hem stitch is used on all types of lightweight fabric. The stitch makes an effective covering for a seam line, particularly on semi-transparent fabric, imitating the effect of a hem-stitched seam (page 183) on fabric which is too delicate for the threads to be removed. It is also used on plain- and even-weave fabric as a decorative line stitch worked in two colours.

Work a row of diagonal straight stitches from right to left to make a zigzag pattern. To do this, bring the thread through at the bottom of the first stitch. Take a diagonal stitch to the top of the line. Bring the thread out at the top left, making a horizontal stitch through the fabric, and insert the needle just next to the first stitch on the lower line. Repeat along the row. Lace a second thread over and under the foundation stitches, without picking up the ground fabric.

## RAISED CHEVRON STITCH

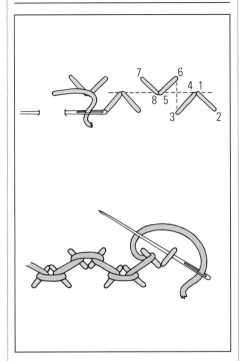

Raised chevron stitch is a heavy stitch used in straight rows on both plain- and even-weave fabric. This variation of ordinary chevron stitch (page 40) makes a bold, raised line, and is used for borders and in multiple rows to make deep bands. To work the stitch neatly and keep the V-shapes of an identical size, choose an even-weave fabric and count the threads, or mark guidelines on plain-weave fabric with tailor's chalk or a special water-soluble marker. Any type of embroidery thread can be used, depending on the weight of the fabric, stitch size and effect required. This stitch should be worked on fabric stretched taut in an embroidery hoop or frame.

Work a foundation of diagonal stitches arranged in V-shapes, as shown in the diagram. Work from right to left, bringing the needle through at the top of the first V. Make a horizontal stitch, then insert the needle at the top of the first stitch to complete the V. Continue in this way, taking horizontal stitches through the fabric and travelling from the lower to the upper V-shapes alternately. Work a row of chevron stitches over this foundation from left to right, without picking up the fabric.

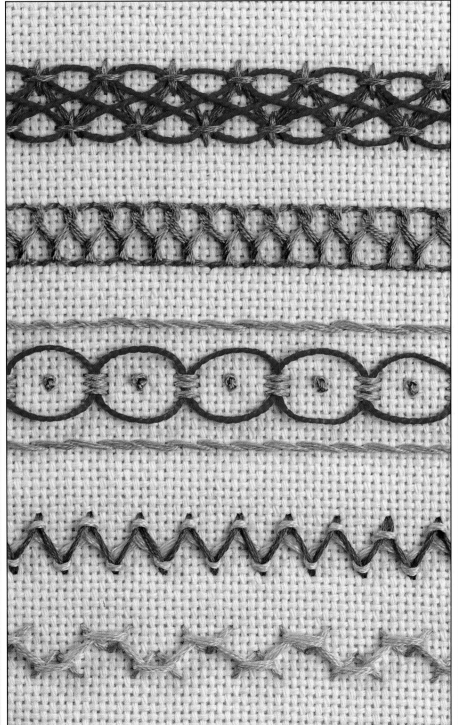

# COMPOSITE BAND STITCHES

## ■ SHEAF STITCH

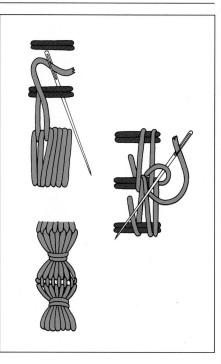

Sheaf stitch is a handsome and unusual border stitch used in straight lines on both plain- and even-weave fabric. Any type of embroidery thread can be used, but a stiff, firm thread gives the best results. Sheaf stitch is always worked vertically upwards, and the fabric should be stretched taut in an embroidery hoop or frame to help prevent puckering.

Work a foundation of pairs of horizontal straight stitches, spacing each pair evenly apart according to the length of sheaf required. Bring the thread through at the bottom right of the line. Work six or seven satin stitches (page 102) over the first and second pairs of straight stitches, without picking up the ground fabric. Working upwards, link the pairs of foundation stitches in this way, taking each stitch between two of the previous group of stitches.

After this journey has been completed, bring the thread through at the right of the bottom pair of foundation stitches. Take the needle over the first two satin stitches, one above the row and one below it, then slip it down behind the foundation stitches, without picking up the fabric. Before pulling the thread through, slip the needle through it, as shown in the second diagram, then tighten the thread to make a knot. Work a knot between each pair of satin stitches until you reach the left-hand side of the row. Work a similar row of knots along each pair of foundation stitches. As the needle passes from sheaf to sheaf to work the knots, tie each sheaf around the centre with two satin stitches.

## ■ STEP STITCH

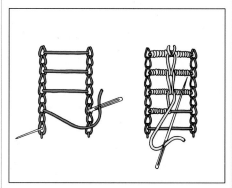

(Also known as ladder stitch.)

Step stitch is used on both plain- and even-weave fabric. It makes a wide border which looks rather like a ladder and is usually worked in more than one colour. The stitch is worked vertically between two parallel lines. To work it neatly and keep the stitches even, choose an even-weave fabric and count the threads, or mark guidelines on plain-weave fabric with tailor's chalk or a special water-soluble marker. A fine thread provides the best results and the stitch should always be worked with the fabric stretched taut in an embroidery hoop or frame.

Work two vertical rows of ordinary chain stitches (page 18) of an identical size. Work a row of horizontal straight stitches from left to right of the row, inserting the needle into the centre of the chains and through the fabric. Work the straight stitches through every alternate chain loop down the border to make the rungs of the ladder. Bring a second thread through at the top left of the line. Slip the needle under the first rung, then whip over it six times, without picking up the ground fabric. At the centre of the rung, take a stitch through the fabric, then proceed to whip the remainder of the rung. At the end of the rung, take the thread through the fabric and bring it out at the left. At the centre of the second and subsequent rows, loop the thread around the stitch in the row above, as shown, to join the rungs together.

## PORTUGUESE BORDER STITCH

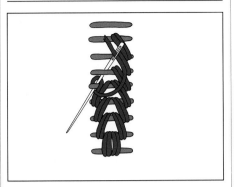

Portuguese border stitch makes a wide, raised border on both plain- and even-weave fabric. It can be used alone as a border, or worked solidly to make a rich, heavy filling. A firm thread should be used to work this stitch.

Work a row of horizontal straight stitches. Thread the left-hand side of the row, working upwards. First, work four satin stitches (page 102) over the bottom two straight stitches, without picking up the ground fabric. Take a small stitch through the fabric and bring the thread out near the centre, just below the second stitch. Join the remaining pairs of stitches together with groups of two satin stitches, always keeping the thread to the right of the needle. Work the right-hand side of the line in the same way from the bottom, keeping the thread to the left of the needle.

## DIAGONAL WOVEN BAND

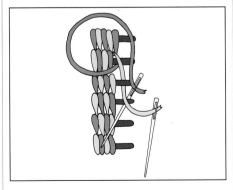

Diagonal woven band is worked in two colours to make a solid, diagonally striped band on both plain- and even-weave fabric. It should be worked on fabric stretched taut in an embroidery hoop or frame and any type of embroidery thread can be used.

Work a foundation of evenly spaced horizontal straight stitches, as shown, beginning at the top left of the row to be covered. Thread two needles with threads of contrasting colours. Bring both threads through the fabric at the top left-hand corner of the foundation row. Working downwards, weave alternate threads over and under the foundation stitches, as shown in the diagram. Begin each row of weaving with alternate colours to form the diagonal stripes. Arrange the rows of weaving closely together. Work a preliminary padding of long vertical surface satin stitches (page 114) under the foundation stitches when a raised effect is required.

## STRIPED WOVEN BAND

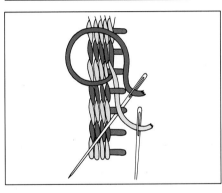

Striped woven band is worked in two colours to make a solidly stitched, striped band on both plain- and even-weave fabric. It is a simply worked variation of diagonal woven band (above), but in this case the arrangement of colours is slightly different.

Work a foundation of evenly spaced horizontal straight stitches, beginning at the top left of the row to be covered. Thread two needles with threads of contrasting colours. Bring both threads through the fabric at the top left-hand corner of the foundation row. Working downwards, weave alternate threads over and under the foundation stitches, as shown. Begin each row of weaving with the same thread colour to form the stripes, and arrange the rows of weaving close to each other so that they cover the foundation stitches completely. Work a preliminary padding of long vertical surface satin stitches (page 114) under the foundation stitches when a raised effect is required.

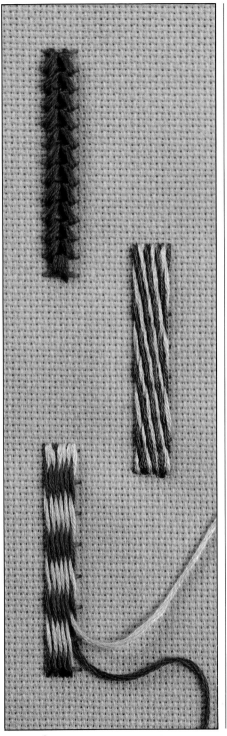

# CHAPTER FOUR

# ISOLATED STITCHES

The stitches described in this chapter can all be used alone to provide splashes of a contrasting colour or texture against a smoothly stitched surface or flat area of embroidered canvas. These stitches range in size from tiny, flat stitches like dot stitch, through knotted, ribbed and wrapped stitches, to large motif stitches such as Catherine wheel and Maltese cross.

Choose from these stitches when you want to create powdered fillings with the stitches scattered randomly across the fabric, or use them to decorate many of the border and band stitches in Chapters 2 and 3. When making your selection, take into account the different sizes of the stitches and the weight of the ground fabric. Where indicated, the stitches can be worked in two or more colours or weights of thread to add interest to a design. Included in this chapter are three unusual stitches used to attach shisha mirrors to fabric.

# ISOLATED STITCHES

## FRENCH KNOT

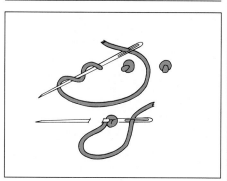

(Also known as twisted knot stitch, wound stitch, French dot and knotted stitch.)

French knots are used on both plain- and even-weave fabric. They can be worked as accent stitches or as a powdering over a shape. If arranged closely together, they can be used to cover an area with texture or in rows as an outline. French knots can also be worked over canvas stitching to add texture or splashes of colour. Any type of embroidery thread can be used, but bear in mind that the weight of the thread determines the size of the knot.

Bring the thread through the fabric and hold it taut with the left hand. Twist the needle around the thread two or three times and then tighten the twists. Still holding the thread in the left hand, turn the needle and insert it into the fabric at the point where it originally emerged. Pull the needle and thread through the twists.

## CHINESE KNOT

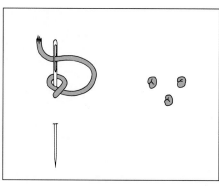

(Also known as blind knot, forbidden knot and Pekin knot.)

Chinese knots are used on both plain- and

even-weave fabric in the same way as the previous stitch. They look rather like French knots (left) but in this case the knots are flatter and have a slightly different shape. This stitch is a characteristic of old Chinese silk embroideries: Chinese knots were worked on these *en masse*, on a minute scale, to produce subtly shaded fillings. Chinese knots are easy to work, particularly when the fabric is stretched taut in an embroidery hoop or frame. This enables the knots to be worked neatly.

Begin by making a loose loop on the fabric, then insert the needle point through the centre of the loop and into the fabric, as shown. Tighten the loop, then pull the needle through the fabric and commence working the next stitch. To make the stitch easier to work, hold the loop down on the fabric while the needle is being pulled through.

## ▌ BULLION KNOT

(Also known as bullion stitch, caterpillar stitch, worm stitch, coil stitch, knot stitch, post stitch, roll stitch, grub knot and Porto Rico rose.)

Bullion knot is a long, coiled knot stitch used on both plain- and even-weave fabric. It can be worked as an accent, as a powdering over a shape, or *en masse* to make a textured filling. If worked in a coil, the stitch can be used to form a small flower. Use a thick needle with a small eye which will pass easily through the coil.

Bring the needle through the fabric, then insert it a short distance away, letting the point emerge at the same place as the thread. Coil the thread around the needle six or seven times, then pull the needle through the coil. Hold the coil down on the fabric with the left thumb. Pull the working thread in the opposite direction to make the coil lie flat, then insert the needle in the same place as before.

## ▌ DANISH KNOT

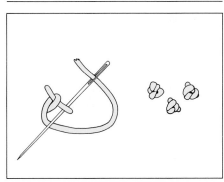

Danish knots are easy to work and can be used on both plain- and even-weave fabric. This stitch makes a slightly raised knot which looks most attractive when a round, twisted thread such as pearl cotton is used. It can be worked as an accent stitch, as a powdering, or to provide a dense texture if the knots are arranged closely together. When working the stitch solidly, use different weights and colours of thread to create an interesting surface.

Begin by making a short diagonal stitch slanting from bottom right to top left. This creates the foundation over which the knot will be made. Bring the needle through the fabric close to the centre of the diagonal stitch, then make two looped stitches over the foundation, as shown in the diagram, without picking up any of the ground fabric. Take the needle back through the fabric close to the looped stitches.

## ▌ KNOT STITCH

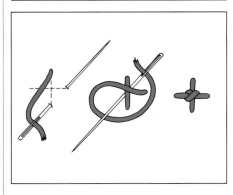

(Also known as four-legged knot stitch.)

Knot stitch is an attractive little stitch used on both plain- and even-weave fabric. It looks like

an upright cross stitch with a knot added in the centre. Use this stitch as an accent stitch where you require extra colour or texture, or work it closely together in a row to make a narrow border. To make an attractive light powdering, arrange the stitches to make a regular pattern over a shape, or scatter them at random for a more informal look. Any type of embroidery thread can be used to work knot stitch, depending on the weight of the fabric, stitch size and effect required.

Work over an imaginary cross. Make a vertical stitch, then bring the needle through at the right of the cross. Work a horizontal stitch across the first stitch, looping it to make a knot at the centre without picking up the fabric.

## ▌ DOT STITCH

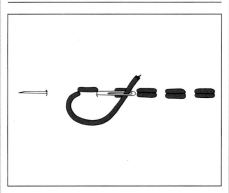

(Also known as simple knot stitch, rice grain and seed stitch.)

Dot stitch is used on both plain- and even-weave fabric. As its name suggests, the stitch makes a small, raised dot. Use it individually as an accent stitch or work it in rows to produce a dotted outline. Dot stitch also makes an effective light powdering when the stitches are scattered across a shape. When used in this way, the stitch is often known as seeding.

Dot stitch is very simple to work and any type of embroidery thread can be used, depending on the weight of the fabric and size of dot required. Use a lightweight thread such as coton à broder when working dot stitch on a small scale. For a heavier effect, choose tapestry wool, or thread several strands of crewel wool through the needle.

Work two back stitches (page 13) into the same holes to make one dot stitch. When using this stitch as an outline, leave a small amount of fabric unworked between each pair of stitches.

# ISOLATED STITCHES

## ▌ STRAIGHT STITCH

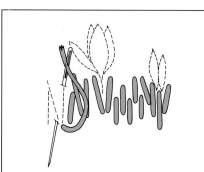

(Also known as stroke stitch.)

Straight stitch is used on both plain- and even-weave fabric to create areas of texture and blended colour. The stitch is particularly useful for working leaves, grasses and other landscape details. Any type of embroidery thread can be used, depending on the weight of the fabric, stitch size and effect required. The stitch can be shaded and blended if it is worked in threads in close tones of a single colour, or if more than one fine thread is used in the needle at the same time. Keep the stitches quite small to prevent them from looking loose and untidy.

Work individual satin stitches (page 102) over the shape to be covered, making them of varying lengths and changing direction at will, as shown in the diagram. To create areas of dense texture, overlap the stitches.

## ▌ SWEDISH SPLIT STITCH

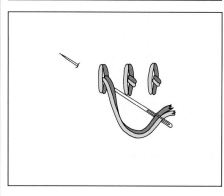

(Also known as detached split stitch.)

Swedish split stitch is used on both plain- and even-weave fabric. It can be worked as an accent stitch, or arranged in a circle to form a flower shape. To make a powdering, scatter it over the fabric, or use it as a solid filling with the stitches arranged in the same way as long and short stitches (page 104). Swedish split stitch is worked rather like split stitch (page 15), but in this case two threads are used in the needle together. Any type of embroidery thread can be used, depending on the weight of the fabric, stitch size and effect required.

Thread a needle with two threads and work a long straight stitch. Bring the needle through the fabric so that it splits the long stitch at the centre, between the two threads. Work a downwards slanting stitch to anchor the long stitch to the fabric, as shown.

## ▌ POINT RUSSE STITCH

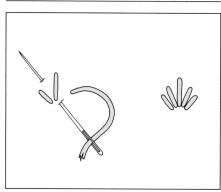

Point Russe stitch is quick and simple to work and can be used on both plain- and even-weave fabric. It makes a pretty, fan-shaped motif which can be used individually as an accent of colour. The motifs can also be used as an unusual powdering, or arranged in vertical or horizontal rows to make an attractive filling for any size of shape.

Any type of embroidery thread can be used, depending on the weight of the fabric, stitch size and effect required, but the stitch looks most attractive worked in a thread colour which contrasts strongly with that of the ground fabric. Try working the stitch in black or in shades of dark grey on a white background. Point Russe stitch benefits from being worked on fabric stretched taut in an embroidery hoop or frame, although this is not essential.

Begin by working a vertical straight stitch to form the centre of the fan, then work the outside straight stitches, starting with the short outside pair, as shown. Complete the stitch by working the remaining pair of straight stitches.

## ▌ CROWN STITCH

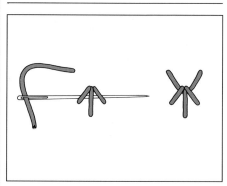

Crown stitch is used on both plain- and even-weave fabric to make a powdering with a slight texture. It can also be arranged in horizontal rows to make a pretty border. Any type of embroidery thread can be used, depending on the weight of the fabric, stitch size and effect required. A very effective result is achieved when the stitch is worked on a small scale in a fine thread such as coton à broder.

Work the three bottom straight stitches first, arranging them so that they all radiate from the same hole. Bring the thread through the fabric above these stitches at the left, then work the top stitch to pass underneath the straight stitches, without picking up the fabric.

## ▌ STAR DARN

(Also known as woven star.)

Star darn is a simple stitch used on both plain- and even-weave fabric. Work this pretty motif in any type of embroidery thread, scattering it over a shape to form a rather attractive powdering. To work the stitch neatly and evenly, choose an even-weave fabric and count the threads, or mark the points of the star on plain-weave fabric with tailor's chalk.

Bring the thread through at the top of the star. Work the star using five straight stitches, as shown in the diagram, interlacing the stitches where they cross each other. Decorate star darn by working a small isolated stitch such as a Danish knot (page 69), square boss (page 77) or daisy stitch (page 76) at the centre.

## ■EYE STITCH

Eye stitch is used on fabric and on single canvas. Each stitch makes a pretty square block which can be used alone or as a filling worked in more than one thread colour.

On even-weave fabric or canvas, arrange each block over eight vertical and eight horizontal threads. Work sixteen satin stitches (page 102) of graduated length around the block, as shown, arranging them so that they all radiate from the same hole. Around the outside of the block, leave two fabric or canvas threads unworked between the stitches, as shown in the diagram. The blocks can then be framed with a row of back stitches (page 13) worked around the edges in either the same or a contrasting thread colour.

## SHISHA STITCH 1

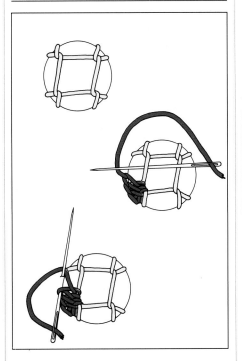

Shisha embroidery is a traditional Indian technique used to attach round pieces of mirror or tin to a fabric background by means of an embroidered border. Originally developed during the early seventeenth century, shisha embroidery is still worked today in parts of India, Pakistan and Afghanistan. The tiny mirrors are available from specialist craft suppliers. Alternatively, use large sequins or paillettes with a hole near the edge.

The stitches on this page are alternative ways of making the framework to hold the mirror securely on the fabric. The framework made when working the first two stitches is covered with a decorative stitched edge, but in the third method, the framing stitches are left uncovered.

Shisha stitch 1 is the traditional method of attaching mirrors. Any type of thread can be used, but one or two thicknesses of stranded cotton (depending on the size of mirror) produce a good, firm edge. Use the same thread for both the framework and the border. In the diagrams, two contrasting threads have been used for clarity.

First work the framework. Hold the mirror securely on the fabric with your left thumb and

work two horizontal stitches across the mirror. Link these stitches with two vertical stitches, threading them over and under the horizontal stitches where they cross. When the mirror is firmly attached, work the decorative twisted edging, taking the needle alternately through the fabric and under the framework, as shown.

## SHISHA STITCH 2

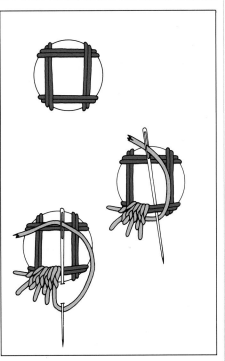

In shisha stitch 2, eight straight stitches arranged in pairs are used to anchor the mirror to the fabric. A snugly fitting framework is essential in this type of embroidery to prevent the mirror from dislodging. When stitching the framework, insert the needle vertically as close to the mirror as possible, and tighten the stitches as they are worked. Any type of embroidery thread can be used, but make sure that the thread will not break when the stitches are tightened as you work the framework. These stitches benefit from being worked on fabric stretched taut in an embroidery hoop or frame, although this is not essential.

To work this version of shisha stitch, first make the framework. Hold the mirror on the fabric with the left thumb, then work four pairs of straight stitches across the mirror, as shown,

taking the last pair of stitches under the first pair where they cross. If attaching a very large mirror or paillette, use twelve stitches split into groups of three to make a heavier framework.

To continue, work the decorative band around the edge. Inserting the needle vertically at all times, take the thread alternately under the framework and into the fabric, as shown in the diagram. Make all the stitches of an identical length or alternately long and short, as shown, to create a more decorative outside edge. Buttonhole stitches (page 17) can be used for the border with this framework to make a plainer edge.

## SHISHA STITCH 3

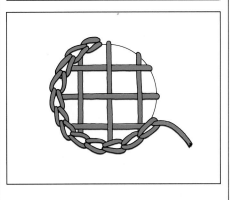

Shisha stitch 3 is a modern American variation of the traditional Indian technique and it is much easier to work than the previous shisha stitches. It differs from the other stitches in that the framework stitches are left uncovered to form part of the decoration. Regularly shaped mirrors with smooth edges, or large sequins or paillettes, should be used because the edges are not covered by the border.

Hold the mirror on the fabric and make three vertical straight stitches across it. Cross these stitches with three horizontal stitches, weaving them through the vertical stitches. Work the stitches quite tightly. To finish the stitch, work an outline of ordinary chain stitches (page 18) through the fabric, as close to the edge of the mirror as possible.

*Indian embroidery is always rich in both colour and pattern. The shisha embroidery shown on the left is actually a tiny pouch, complete with beaded drawstrings and bobble fringe.*

# ISOLATED STITCHES

## ■ MALTESE CROSS

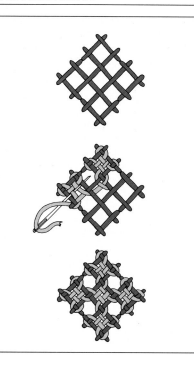

Maltese cross is used on both plain- and even-weave fabric. It makes an intricate, interlaced, diamond-shaped cross and can be used alone as a large accent stitch, or joined together to make a rich, heavy border. The stitch can also be used to form a square if the foundation stitches are worked vertically and horizontally rather than diagonally. When using the stitch as a border, arrange the diamond-shaped crosses so that they join together at adjacent corners; join square crosses along adjacent edges. The interlacing will tighten up the foundation grid as it is worked, so keep the grid stitches quite loose, and work the stitch on fabric stretched in an embroidery hoop or frame.

Make a foundation grid of long, crossed straight stitches. Begin at the left of the top point and make sure that the stitches pass over and under each other in the manner shown in the diagram. Check that the grid is correctly worked before proceeding to the interlacing. Beginning at the top of the centre diamond of the grid, work the interlacing in a similar way to interlaced herringbone stitch (page 61) using either the same or a contrasting thread. Use a blunt-ended tapestry needle for the interlacing.

## ■ INTERLACED CROSS STITCH

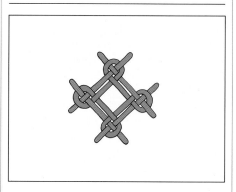

Interlaced cross stitch is used on both plain- and even-weave fabric. It looks quite decorative when combined with a plainer stitch like ordinary cross stitch (page 34) to make a border. Any type of embroidery thread can be used, depending on the weight of the fabric, but a supple, metallic interlacing thread provides the most decorative effect.

Work a foundation of four interlocking straight stitches to form a diamond shape, taking the last stitch under the first stitch. Use a second thread to work the interlacing through the foundation, as shown, without picking up any of the ground fabric. Begin and end this thread under one of the foundation stitches.

## ■ SPIDER'S WEB

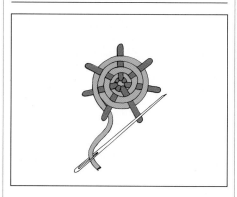

(Also known as woven wheel, woven spot and woven spoke stitch.)

Spider's web makes a raised, circular shape on both plain- and even-weave fabric. It can be used alone as an accent of colour, or worked in different sizes as a powdering for a shape. Any type of thread can be used.

First, work a foundation of spokes. These should be of an odd number, seven or nine being the usual number. Work evenly spaced straight stitches radiating from the centre of a circle to make the foundation, then weave a second thread over and under the spokes. Start at the centre point and work outwards in a spiral, without picking up the fabric.

## ■ RIBBED SPIDER'S WEB

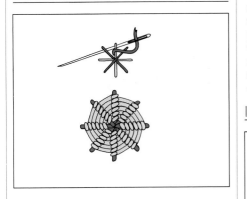

(Also known as ribbed wheel and back-stitched spider's web.)

Ribbed spider's web is a variation of the previous stitch and makes a circular shape with pronounced ribs radiating from the centre.

First, make a foundation consisting of an even number of spokes, eight or twelve being the usual number. For an eight-spoke foundation work an ordinary cross stitch (page 34) over a St George cross stitch (page 86). Other numbers of spokes can be worked in straight stitches. Work a spiral of back stitches (page 13) over the spokes from the centre, without picking up the fabric.

## ■ CATHERINE WHEEL

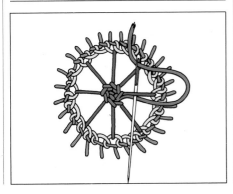

Catherine wheel has been adapted from a nineteenth-century open needlepoint filling to make a large, decorative surface stitch used on plain-weave fabric. This stitch should be worked in a firm, round thread such as pearl cotton, which makes the wheel stand out from the background most effectively.

First, work a large circle of blanket stitches (page 17), arranging the loops towards the inside. Next, work a second row of the same stitches inside the circle, working the stitches through the loops of the first circle without picking up the fabric. Work four straight stitches through the fabric, spanning the centre space to make eight spokes. Work two rings of back stitches (page 13) over the spokes at the centre, without picking up the fabric.

## ■ BUTTONHOLE WHEEL

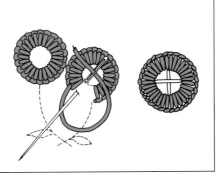

(Also known as wheel stitch.)

Buttonhole wheel is the circular form of buttonhole stitch (page 17) used on both plain- and even-weave fabric. The most successful effect is achieved when the stitch is worked on fabric with a fairly loose weave. Use any type of thread and do not stretch the fabric in an embroidery hoop or frame.

Work buttonhole stitches closely together around a circle, arranging them so that each vertical stitch goes into the same hole in the centre. The fabric threads are pulled back during the stitching so that a neat, circular hole is formed at the centre. When the fabric weave is too dense for this to be achieved easily, start the hole with the help of a stiletto. A variation of this stitch can be worked in the same way on an open-weave fabric, but in this case leave a pair of crossed fabric threads unworked at the centre of the hole. The stitch is then known as barred buttonhole wheel.

# ISOLATED STITCHES

## ◼ DOUBLE FLY STITCH

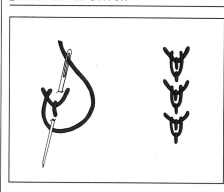

Double fly stitch is a variation of ordinary fly stitch (page 40) used on both plain- and even-weave fabric. It can be used alone to provide an accent of colour, or scattered across a shape as a powdered filling. To make a pretty, light border, work the stitch in a neat row. Any type of thread can be used, depending on the effect required, but the stitch looks best when worked in two colours and weights of thread.

First, work an ordinary fly stitch with a short tail, then work an elongated fly stitch over the top, as shown in the diagram. To work the stitches in a line, arrange them closely together, either vertically, as shown, or horizontally, with the arms of the stitches touching. Work the stitches in two journeys when using two colours of thread: use one thread to work all the underneath stitches, then return along the row with a second thread to complete the stitches.

## ◼ REVERSED FLY STITCH

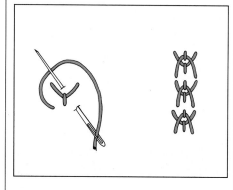

Reversed fly stitch is a variation of ordinary fly stitch (page 40) used on both plain- and even-weave fabric. It can be used alone as an accent stitch, or scattered across a shape as a powdered filling. To make a deep border, work the stitch in evenly spaced multiple rows. Any type of embroidery thread can be used, depending on the weight of the fabric, stitch size and effect required, and the stitch can be worked in two colours and weights of thread. This stitch benefits from being worked on fabric stretched taut in an embroidery hoop or frame. Although this is not essential, it helps prevent puckering and distortion of the fabric and enables the stitches to be worked evenly.

First, work an ordinary fly stitch with a short tail. Then work a second, slightly narrower fly stitch upside down over the top of the first one, as shown in the diagram. To work the stitches in a line, arrange them closely together, either vertically, as shown, or horizontally, with the arms of the underneath stitches touching. Work the stitches in two journeys when using two different colours of thread: use one thread to work all the underneath stitches, then return along the row with a second thread to complete the stitches.

## ◼ DAISY STITCH

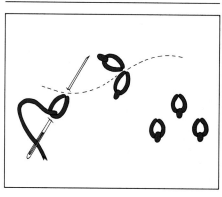

(Also known as detached chain stitch, lazy daisy stitch, tail chain stitch, loop stitch, tied loop stitch, knotted knot stitch and picot stitch.)

Daisy stitch is actually a single chain stitch (page 18) and is well known under its alternative name of detached chain stitch. It is commonly worked in groups on plain-weave fabric to make leaf and flower shapes, but it can also be used as a pretty powdering over a shape. In addition, it provides the foundation row for threaded chain stitch (page 55) and it can be worked on top of a flat area of canvaswork when an accent in a contrasting colour is needed. Any type of embroidery thread can be used to work daisy stitch, depending on the weight of the fabric, but bear in mind that the size of the stitch is determined by the weight of the thread.

Work daisy stitch in the same way as chain stitch, but anchor each loop with a small vertical stitch before commencing the next loop.

## ◼ LONG-TAILED DAISY STITCH

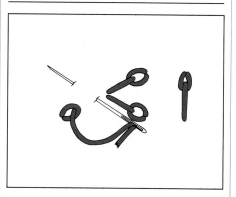

Long-tailed daisy stitch is a variation of the previous stitch which is used on both plain- and even-weave fabric. The stitch is often worked in circular groups with either the tails or the loops positioned at the centre of the circle. It makes an attractive powdering, and can also be worked closely together in a row with the loops arranged alternately at the top and bottom of the row. As with daisy stitch, any type of embroidery thread can be used.

Work long-tailed daisy stitch in the same way as the previous stitch, but in this case make the loop small and elongate the tying-down stitch to form an exaggerated tail. Use one of the knot stitches on page 68 or 69 to add a dash of contrasting colour to the centre of each loop.

## ◼ CROSS AND TWIST STITCH

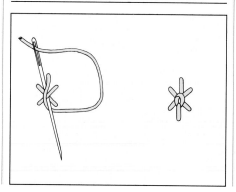

Cross and twist stitch is used on both plain- and even-weave fabric. Its delicate quality is enhanced when it is worked on a small scale in a fine, round thread such as coton à broder. Use it to provide an accent of colour, or work it as a powdering to decorate a shape. Cross and twist stitches can also be placed side by side to form a border, with the top stitches worked in a thread of a contrasting colour and weight.

Begin by working an ordinary cross stitch (page 34) as a foundation, then cross this stitch with a long vertical stitch. The vertical stitch should enter the fabric only at the top and bottom, and should loop around the centre of the cross stitch, making a twisted chain stitch (page 18) with a long tail. The vertical stitch can be made shorter to give a different effect.

## ■ SQUARE BOSS

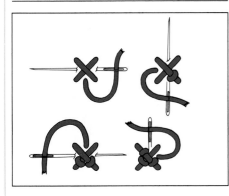

(Also known as raised knot.)

Square boss is easy to work and can be used on both plain- and even-weave fabric. The stitch makes neat, square knots and can be worked individually when splashes of extra colour are required, or scattered randomly over a shape to make a knotted powdering. Any type of embroidery thread can be used, depending on the weight of the fabric, stitch size and effect required, but a round thread such as coton à broder or pearl cotton makes the stitch stand out well from the background.

First, work an ordinary cross stitch (page 34). Then, beginning at the bottom right of the cross, cover each arm with a back stitch (page 13) worked through the fabric, as shown in the diagram. When the stitch is used as a powdered filling, two threads in contrasting colours can be used. Work all the cross stitches in one journey. On the second journey, change the thread colour to work the back stitches.

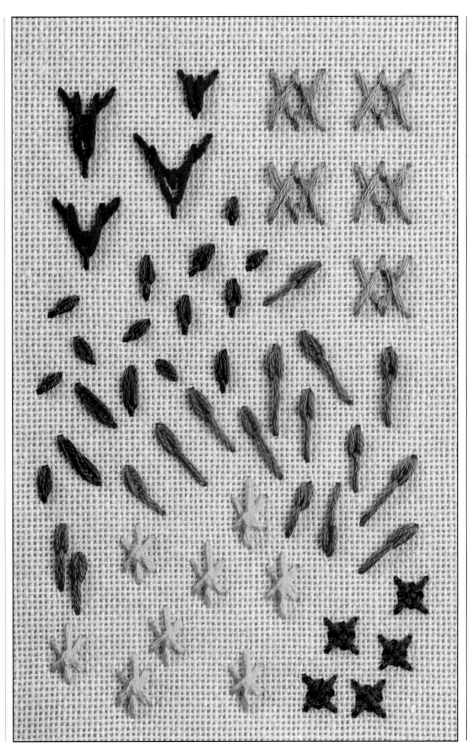

# ISOLATED STITCHES

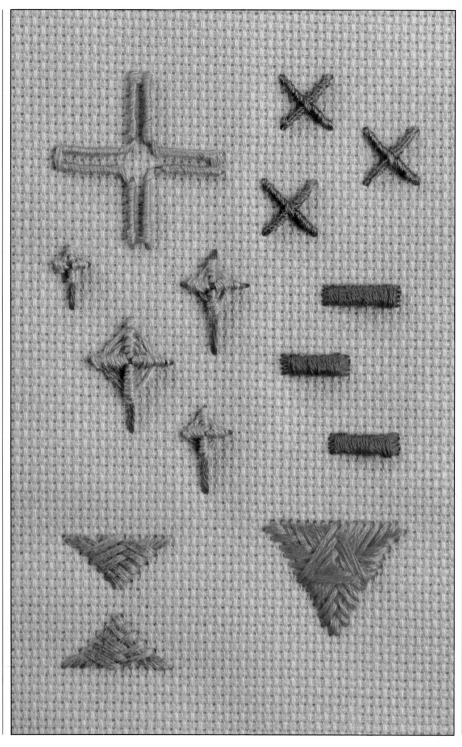

## ▌ POINT À LA MINUTE

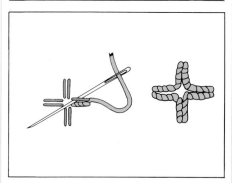

Point à la minute makes a heavy, raised cross which is worked in two colours on both plain- and even-weave fabric. It can be used to provide an accent of colour or texture, or scattered over a shape to make a rich, unusual powdering. Any type of embroidery thread can be used, and the stitch should be worked on fabric stretched taut in an embroidery hoop or frame to help prevent puckering.

Make a foundation of four vertical and four horizontal straight stitches. Arrange them in pairs to form a cross, as shown. Bring the second thread through at the end of the right-hand pair of stitches and whip each stitch around the cross in the same way as whipped back stitch (page 13).

## ▌ WRAPPED CROSS STITCH

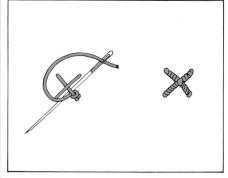

Wrapped cross stitch can be used on both plain- and even-weave fabric. It produces an individual cross with a three-dimensional appearance. Any type of embroidery thread can be used, but a round thread such as pearl cotton makes the stitch stand out most effectively. This stitch should always be worked on fabric stretched taut in an embroidery hoop or frame.

Work a large ordinary cross stitch (page 34), then bring the thread through the fabric close to the bottom right of the cross. Work across the stitch to the top of the cross, wrapping the thread as tightly as possible over it without picking up the fabric. Take the thread to the back of the fabric, bring it through at the bottom left of the cross, and repeat the wrapping.

## GOD'S EYE STITCH

God's eye stitch is worked in two colours on both plain- and even-weave fabric. The stitch is similar to ribbed spider's web (page 75) and makes a ribbed diamond with a long tail. It can be used as an accent stitch to provide extra colour or texture, or scattered over a shape to make a heavy powdering. Any type of embroidery thread can be used, and the stitch should be worked on fabric stretched taut in an embroidery hoop or frame.

Work a cross with a long tail, as shown. Bring the second thread through at the centre of the cross and work a spiral of back stitches (page 13) over the four arms of the cross, as shown, without picking up any of the ground fabric.

## CORDED BAR

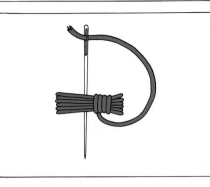

(Also known as detached bar.)

Corded bar is used on both plain- and even-weave fabric to make a raised bar. Use this stitch to add texture or colour on top of a smoothly stitched surface, or work it on a small scale scattered over a shape to make a pretty, raised powdering.

Begin by working a foundation bar of six surface satin stitches (page 114) of the required length. Position the stitches close to each other and keep the bar quite small, working several touching bars when the stitch needs to be arranged over a long stretch. Bring the thread through the fabric at the right-hand end of the bar and whip the foundation stitches together, as shown in the diagram, without picking up any of the ground fabric.

## SPRAT'S HEAD

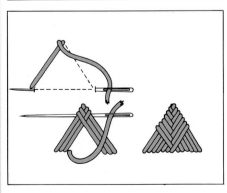

A sprat's head is actually a tailoring stitch and is normally used to strengthen a garment at a point of strain, for example, at the top of a pleat or at the edge of a pocket. Here, it is worked as a decorative surface stitch to produce a small,

solidly stitched triangular motif on plain-weave fabric. Any type of thread can be used, depending on the effect required, but a shiny, light-reflecting thread such as stranded cotton or silk enhances the light and shade effect created by the varying direction of the stitches. This stitch should be worked on fabric stretched taut in an embroidery hoop or frame.

Draw a triangular shape on the fabric with a pencil. Bring the thread through at the left of the base line, then make a tiny stitch at the top of the triangle and take the thread back through the fabric on the right. Bring the thread through on the left and repeat the sequence until the triangle is covered by the stitches.

## CROW'S FOOT

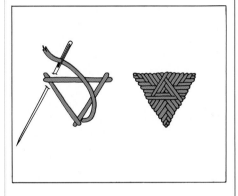

Like the previous stitch, a crow's foot is a tailoring stitch which is used to strengthen a garment. Here, it is worked as a surface stitch to produce a small, decorative triangular motif on plain-weave fabric. Any type of embroidery thread can be used to work a crow's foot, depending on the weight of the fabric and effect required, but a shiny, light-reflecting thread such as a stranded silk or synthetic thread enhances the light and shade effect created by the varying direction of the stitches. This stitch should be worked on fabric stretched taut in an embroidery hoop or frame.

To work this stitch, first draw a triangular shape, point downwards, on the fabric with a pencil. Bring the thread through at the point, then make a tiny stitch first at the left-hand point and then at the right, as shown, to produce a long stitch along each side of the triangle. Each stitch should be of an identical length. Continue around the triangle in this way, working towards the centre until the triangle is completely covered by the stitches.

# CHAPTER FIVE

# OPEN FILLING STITCHES

**T**his chapter contains stitches which are used to fill shapes with light, delicate patterns that allow the ground fabric to show through. A number of them are made up of isolated stitches which are either arranged in rows to make an attractive, regular pattern over a shape, or scattered at random over the fabric for a more informal effect. Other open filling stitches, including griffin stitch and back stitch trellis, are built up in several journeys on a threaded foundation grid.

Stretch the fabric in an embroidery hoop or frame when working these stitches to help prevent puckering of the fabric and allow the stitching to be worked evenly. When working open filling stitches across large areas of plain-weave fabric, mark guidelines with a dressmaker's pencil, tailor's chalk, or special water-soluble marker to enable the stitches to be worked in a regular manner.

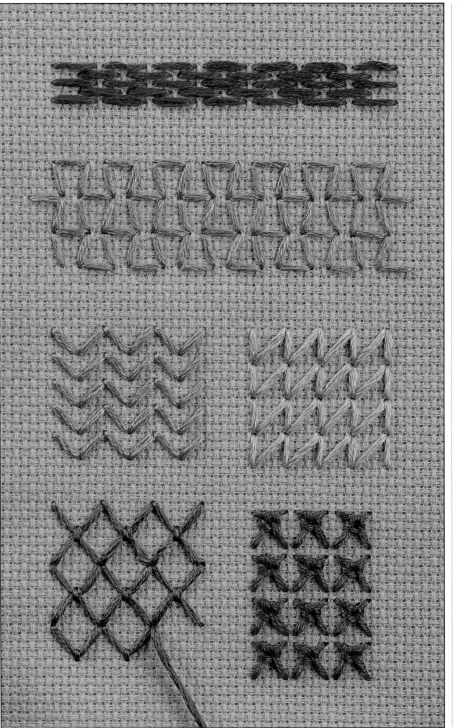

## ▌DARNING STITCH

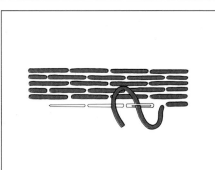

(Also known as tacking stitch.)

Darning stitch is used on both plain- and even-weave fabric. It is a variation of running stitch (page 12), but in this case the stitches are longer and fewer fabric threads are picked up with each stitch. In Eastern Europe and the Greek Islands, deep borders of darning stitch patterns are used to decorate garments and household furnishings. Interesting geometric designs can be built up by varying the arrangement of the stitches. One of the simplest arrangements, a brick pattern, is shown in the diagram.

Work this stitch by passing the needle through the fabric at regular intervals, as shown, picking up one or more threads depending on the weight of the ground fabric.

## ▌JAPANESE DARNING

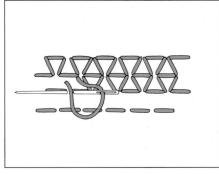

Japanese darning is a light filling stitch used on both plain- and even-weave fabric. The stitch produces a pretty, geometric effect which allows the fabric to show through, and is suitable for filling any size or shape.

Work spaced horizontal rows of ordinary darning stitches (left) over the shape to be covered. Arrange the stitches alternately on the rows, as shown in the diagram. Bring the thread through at the right of the second row and join the first two rows with slanting stitches. Work these stitches into the holes made by the darning stitches, as shown, to ensure that the geometric pattern is kept perfectly regular. Repeat this process over the shape, working all the joining rows from right to left.

## ▌ARROWHEAD STITCH

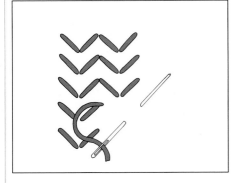

Arrowhead stitch is worked mainly as a filling on both plain- and even-weave fabric. To work it as a line stitch, group the stitches along a row. Arrowhead stitch can also be worked individually: scatter the stitches at random in pairs on plain-weave fabric to produce a light powdering. To work this stitch neatly and evenly, choose an even-weave fabric and count the threads, or mark guidelines on plain-weave fabric with tailor's chalk or a special water-soluble marker. Any type of embroidery thread can be used, depending on the weight of the fabric, stitch size and effect required.

Bring the thread through at the top left-hand corner of the shape to be covered. Insert the needle lower down to the right, then bring it out further to the right and on a level with the point where the thread first emerged. Insert the needle at the base of the first stitch and pull the thread through to complete the arrowhead.

Work the next pair of stitches directly beneath the first pair, keeping the spacing even. When filling a shape, arrange the vertical rows so that the stitches in adjacent rows touch, as shown. The pairs of stitches can also be worked in horizontal rows, with the points of the arrowheads facing to either left or right.

## ▌BOSNIA STITCH

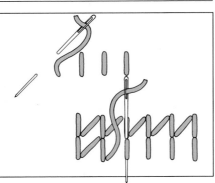

(Also known as Bosnian stitch, fence stitch and barrier stitch.)

Bosnia stitch originated in Yugoslavia, where it is used either as a filling stitch over a shape, or in multiple rows to form a deep border. On Yugoslavian embroideries, rows of Bosnia stitch are often interlaced with a second thread colour in a similar way to threaded herringbone stitch (page 61). Red thread is commonly used for the foundation stitches, blue for the interlacing, and the background is normally white. Gold or silver threads are used for special occasions.

Work this stitch in two journeys. Make upright stitches from right to left of the shape to be covered, as shown. Return in the opposite direction, filling in the spaces with slanting stitches. Arrange the rows directly underneath one another, so that the upright stitches form vertical lines.

## ▌FLY STITCH FILLING

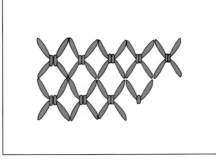

(Also known as flowing fly stitch and crossed fly stitch.)

Fly stitch filling can be used on both plain- and even-weave fabric to fill any size of shape. It is a variation of ordinary fly stitch (page 40) arranged in rows to produce an attractive trellis design.

First, work a horizontal row of fly stitches across the top of the shape to be covered. Arrange the stitches so that the V-shapes touch and keep the 'tails' quite short. Work the next row directly beneath the first row, but this time invert the stitches and arrange the tails next to those in the previous row. Repeat these two rows until the shape is covered.

## ▌SORBELLO STITCH

Sorbello stitch is an attractive Italian line stitch used on both plain- and even-weave fabric. The stitch originated in the village of Sorbello, where it is often worked in white thread on an unbleached linen background.

Work each stitch over an imaginary square of fabric. First, make a horizontal straight stitch across the top, then bring the needle through at the lower left-hand corner. Loop the thread under and over the horizontal stitch, as shown, then take it through the fabric at the lower right-hand corner. Work the stitches closely together from left to right. To use the stitch as a filling, work it in multiple rows with the stitches arranged directly underneath one another.

# OPEN FILLING STITCHES

## ▌TRIANGULAR TURKISH STITCH

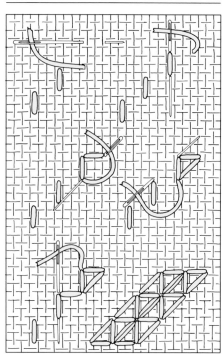

(Also known as two-sided triangular Turkish stitch.)

Triangular Turkish stitch is a delicate filling stitch which is used only on even-weave fabric. It is worked in diagonal lines and makes a regular pattern of neat triangles which is alike on both sides of the fabric. Each triangular stitch can cover three, four or five fabric threads, depending on the weight of the fabric, but the most attractive effect is produced when the stitch is worked on a fairly small scale. When using a loosely woven fabric, pull the stitches quite tightly to produce the effect of a pulled fabric stitch.

Work triangular Turkish stitch in two journeys. Begin at the bottom left and work a diagonal row of evenly spaced vertical stitches over three threads, as shown. At the top of the row, work a horizontal stitch to turn, as shown in the second diagram. Follow the sequence of stitches shown in the third, fourth and fifth diagrams to complete the triangles on both sides of the fabric, then continue in this way down the row. Work closely spaced rows above and below the first row to fill a shape, as shown in the final diagram.

## ▌SPACED BUTTONHOLE FILLING

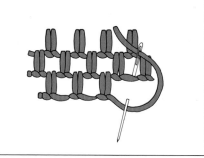

Spaced buttonhole filling is a simple but attractive filling stitch worked on both plain- and even-weave fabric. It consists of rows of ordinary buttonhole stitches (page 17) worked in groups with spaces left in between them. Any type of embroidery thread can be used, depending on the weight of the fabric, stitch size and effect required.

Begin at the top of the shape to be covered and work a row of buttonhole stitches from left to right, arranging the upright stitches in groups of two. Work the second row from right to left, filling in the spaces left in the previous row with groups of two stitches to produce a chessboard pattern. In the diagram, two stitches have been used to a group, but an equally attractive filling can be produced by working three or four stitches to a group. Spaced buttonhole filling can also be worked detached from the fabric except at the edges of the shape. When the stitch is worked in this way, some practice is needed before the tension of the stitches can be kept even.

## ▌OPEN WAVE STITCH

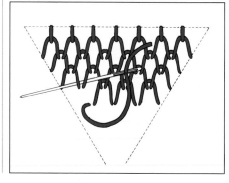

Open wave stitch is a delicate filling stitch used on both plain- and even-weave fabric. It is worked in the same way as closed wave stitch (page 101), but in this case the stitches are spaced out, allowing the ground fabric to show through and creating a light, lacy effect. The stitch is an economical one, as nearly all the working thread remains on the surface of the fabric. Each row can be worked in a different colour of thread; alternatively, a graduated thread can be used to achieve subtle colour changes. This stitch benefits from being worked on fabric stretched taut in an embroidery hoop or frame. Although this is not essential, it helps prevent puckering of the ground fabric.

Begin by working a row of widely spaced vertical satin stitches (page 102) along the top of the shape to be covered. On the next and every following row, work looped stitches, as shown in the diagram, slipping the needle under the base of the stitches in the previous row. Take a tiny stitch through the fabric at the base of the row after each loop has been completed.

## ▌CLOUD FILLING STITCH

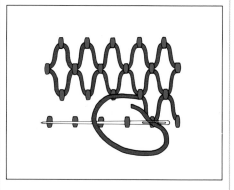

(Also known as Mexican stitch.)

Cloud filling stitch is used to fill shapes on both plain- and even-weave fabric with a light, lacy pattern. The stitches can be placed close to each other or spaced apart, but they should always be worked in a very regular manner.

To work the stitch neatly and evenly, choose an even-weave fabric and count the threads, or mark guidelines on plain-weave fabric with tailor's chalk or a special water-soluble marker. Any type of thread can be used, depending on the effect required.

Begin by working a foundation of regularly spaced vertical running stitches (page 12) over the whole shape. Bring a second thread of a contrasting colour or weight through the fabric at the top left of the shape and lace it through the running stitches. Lace alternate rows of stitches together so that the loops meet under the same stitch. The needle should enter the fabric only at the beginning and end of each row, and a blunt-ended tapestry needle should be used for this stage to avoid splitting the foundation stitches. Work an isolated stitch such as a French or Chinese knot (page 68) in the spaces in between the laced stitches to add extra decoration to the trellis pattern. Cloud filling stitch can also be shaded in bands of colour. To do this, work the rows of lacing in graduated colours.

## ▌FANCY STITCH

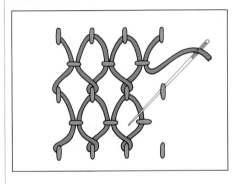

Fancy stitch is a modern stitch used on both plain- and even-weave fabric. The stitch produces a decorative, lacy trellis pattern. To work it neatly and evenly, choose an even-weave fabric and count the threads, or mark guidelines on plain-weave fabric.

Work a foundation of horizontal rows of short vertical stitches alternating with running stitches (page 12) over the whole shape, beginning at the top. Bring a second thread of a contrasting colour or weight through the fabric at the top left of the shape and lace it downwards through the foundation stitches, as shown in the diagram. Work each row of lacing separately from the top, ensuring that the needle enters the fabric only at the beginning and end of each row.

Use a blunt-ended tapestry needle for the second thread to avoid splitting the foundation stitches. Work an isolated stitch such as a French or Chinese knot (page 68) in the spaces in between the laced stitches to add decoration to the trellis pattern.

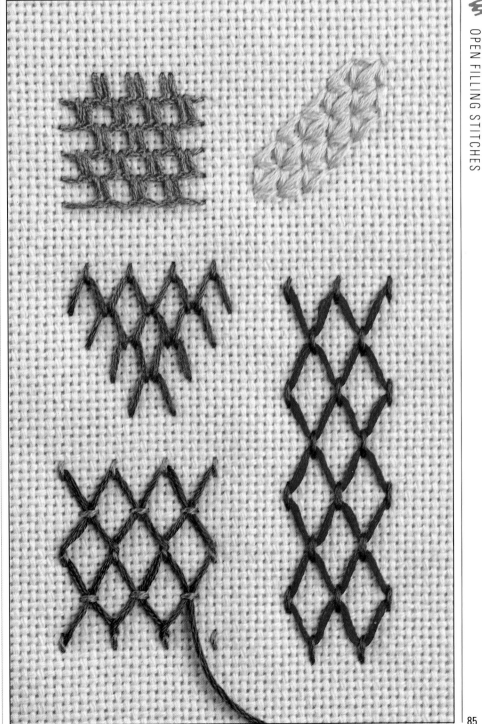

# OPEN FILLING STITCHES

## ▌SPACED CROSS STITCH FILLING

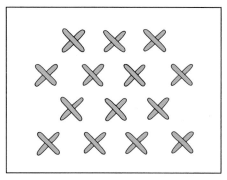

Spaced cross stitch filling can be worked on both plain- and even-weave fabric. The stitch is used as a quick and effective way of filling a large or small shape with ordinary cross stitches (page 34), and it can be worked to produce either an open or closed finish. Perfect regularity is essential when working spaced cross stitch filling, so either choose an even-weave fabric and count the threads, or mark guidelines on plain-weave fabric with tailor's chalk or a special water-soluble marker.

Any type of embroidery thread can be used, depending on the weight of the fabric, stitch size and effect required, but a round thread such as pearl or soft cotton makes the crosses stand out from the background more than a flat, stranded cotton or silk. This stitch benefits from being worked on fabric stretched taut in an embroidery hoop or frame. Although this is not essential, it helps prevent puckering of the ground fabric.

Begin at the top of the shape to be covered and work individual cross stitches at regularly spaced intervals, ensuring that all the top diagonal stitches run in the same direction. Space the stitches widely apart or closely together: in the latter case, arrange the crosses so that each corner touches diagonally.

## ▌ST GEORGE CROSS STITCH

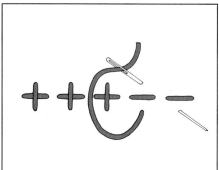

(Also known as upright cross stitch.)

St George cross stitch is an attractive filling stitch used on both plain- and even-weave fabric. It makes an upright cross which is completed in two journeys. The stitch produces a neat, geometric filling when worked in multiple rows over a shape, the effect of which can be varied by altering the spacing between the crosses. It can also be worked individually in the same way as ordinary cross stitch (page 34): scatter it at random over a shape to make an attractive, light powdering or use it as an accent stitch to add a splash of colour and texture to a flat, smoothly stitched surface.

Any type of embroidery thread can be used, depending on the weight of the fabric, stitch size and effect required, but a round thread such as pearl cotton makes the stitch stand out from the background more noticeably than a flat, stranded cotton or silk. St George cross stitch benefits from being worked on fabric stretched taut in an embroidery hoop or frame, although this is not essential.

Begin by working a row of evenly spaced horizontal stitches. On the second journey, cross these stitches with vertical stitches of an identical size.

## ▌ERMINE FILLING STITCH

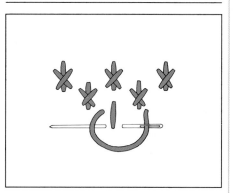

Ermine filling stitch is a versatile stitch which can be used on both plain- and even-weave fabric. When worked in black thread on a white fabric ground, the stitch has the appearance of ermine tails, hence its unusual name. It is popular for filling in shapes in blackwork, a type of traditional counted-thread embroidery from Spain. Ermine filling stitch can be used as a filling or accent stitch, or it can be worked in a straight row to produce a delicate border. When using the stitch as a filling, work it regularly on an even-weave fabric for the best results. To

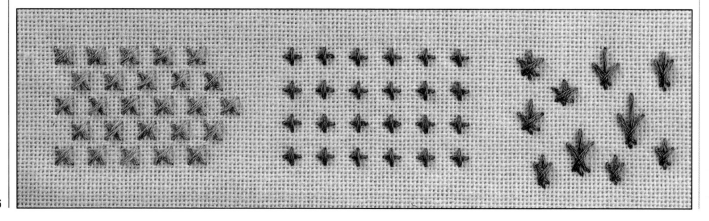

produce an attractive powdering, scatter individual stitches at random on plain-weave fabric. Any type of embroidery thread can be used, depending on the effect required.

Ermine filling stitch is simple to work. First, make a long vertical stitch, then cover it with an elongated ordinary cross stitch (page 34) about one third shorter. The cross stitch should narrow towards the base and be placed slightly above the bottom of the vertical stitch.

## STAR FILLING STITCH

Star filling stitch is used on both plain- and even-weave fabric. It is quick and easy to work and has many uses. Work it as a light filling arranged in formal rows or scattered at random over a shape. Arrange it in a straight line to make an attractive border, or use it alone as an accent stitch where extra colour is needed.

First, make a large St George cross stitch (left), then work an ordinary cross stitch (page 34) of about the same size over the top. To complete the star, work a small ordinary cross stitch across the centre to secure both the large crosses to the fabric. Work star filling stitch in one colour, or stitch each type of cross on a separate journey to allow three contrasting threads to be used.

## BRICK AND CROSS FILLING

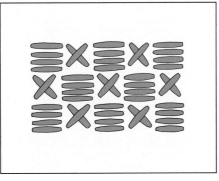

Brick and cross filling is a simple and attractive filling stitch which produces a chessboard pattern on both plain- and even-weave fabric. Any type of thread can be used, depending on the effect required.

Work the stitch downwards in vertical rows,

beginning at the top left of the shape to be covered. Make square blocks of four horizontal satin stitches (page 102), alternating them with large ordinary cross stitches (page 34) to make a chessboard pattern. A variation of this stitch can be produced by alternating square blocks of three vertical satin stitches with large St George cross stitches (left).

## CHESSBOARD FILLING STITCH

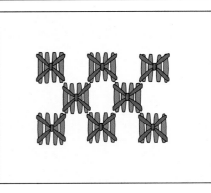

Chessboard filling stitch is used on both plain- and even-weave fabric and produces a highly decorative pattern of textured blocks. It can be worked in any type of embroidery thread, depending on the weight of the fabric, stitch size and effect required.

Work chessboard filling stitch in two journeys. On the first journey, work groups of four vertical satin stitches (page 102) arranged in a chessboard pattern. Work a large ordinary cross stitch (page 34) across each group of stitches, as shown. Anchor each cross stitch at the centre with a short vertical stitch before proceeding to the next group.

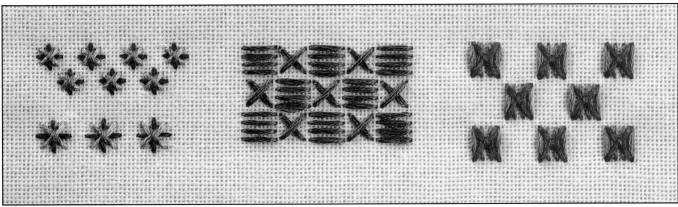

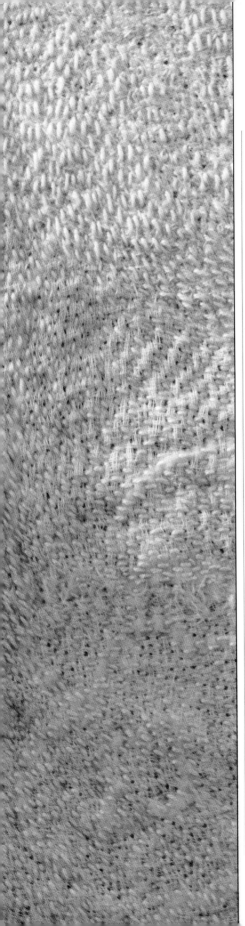

## ▌SEED STITCH

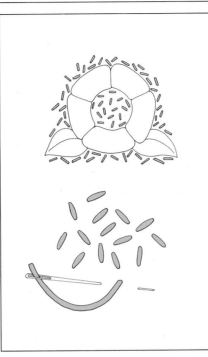

(Also known as seeding stitch, seed filling stitch, speckling stitch and isolated back stitch.)

Seed stitch is a filling stitch which is easy to work and can be used on both plain- and even-weave fabric. It can be worked as a light, speckled powdering for any size of shape and is effective for many types of embroidery. Closely worked seed stitches can also be used as a padding underneath areas of an embroidery worked in a flat stitch such as satin stitch (page 102) when a raised effect is required.

Any type of embroidery thread can be used, depending on the weight of the fabric, stitch size and effect required. Experiment by shading and blending various thread colours across a shape: mix several differently coloured strands of crewel wool or stranded cotton in the needle, and gradually change the colours of two or three of the strands as you proceed to fill the shape. Interesting effects can be achieved by adding lengths of a shiny, light-reflecting thread to matt crewel wool or Persian wool.

To work seed stitch, take minute stitches across the fabric. The stitches should be of more or less even length and can be worked in any direction over the shape to be filled. Scatter the stitches quite irregularly and do not attempt to make a pattern with them. For a similar but heavier filling, use dot stitch (page 69) worked in the same haphazard manner.

## ▌LINK POWDERING

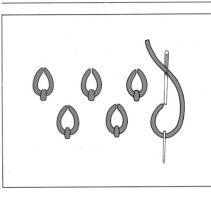

(Also known as link filling stitch and detached chain filling.)

Link powdering can be worked on both plain- and even-weave fabric. It is used as a quick and effective way of filling a large or small shape with daisy stitches (page 76). Regularity is important when working this stitch, so choose an even-weave fabric and count the threads, or mark guidelines on plain-weave fabric.

Any type of embroidery thread can be used, depending on the weight of the fabric, stitch size and effect required, but a round thread such as pearl or soft cotton makes the daisy stitches stand out from the background more effectively than a flat, stranded cotton or silk. Bear in mind that the size of the stitch depends largely on the type of thread selected: a fine crewel wool, for example, produces a smaller stitch than a heavy thread such as pearl cotton. Daisy stitch is often used in crewel embroidery, and the effect can be varied by spacing the stitches closer together or wider apart.

Begin at the top of the shape to be covered and work daisy stitches across it at regularly spaced intervals. Work the stitches in horizontal rows, positioning them alternately, as shown in the diagram.

*The striking three-dimensional embroidery on the left shows how seed stitches can be used to provide shading and texture. The stitches have been worked on a machine-embroidered background.*

## ▓ SHEAF FILLING

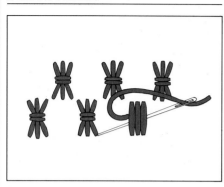

(Also known as faggot filling stitch.)

Sheaf filling can be used to fill any size of shape on both plain- and even-weave fabric. It makes an attractive, light filling which is usually worked in a regular pattern. Each stitch is worked separately and looks like a tiny sheaf of corn. The sheaves can either be arranged in formal rows, as shown in the diagram, or scattered in all directions across the fabric to create a different effect. Any type of thread can be used, depending on the effect required.

First, work three vertical satin stitches (page 102), then bring the thread through beneath them on the left. Make two overcast stitches (page 15) over the sheaf, without picking up the ground fabric. To finish, take the thread back through the fabric beneath the sheaf.

## ▓ TÊTE DE BOEUF FILLING STITCH

Tête de boeuf filling stitch is used on both plain- and even-weave fabric. It produces an attractive pattern and can be used for filling any size of shape. To work this stitch neatly and evenly, choose an even-weave fabric and count the

threads, or mark guidelines on plain-weave fabric with tailor's chalk or a special water-soluble marker.

Any type of embroidery thread can be used, depending on the weight of the fabric, stitch size and effect required, but a round thread such as pearl cotton makes the stitches stand out more effectively from the background than a stranded cotton or silk. This stitch benefits from being worked on fabric stretched taut in an embroidery hoop or frame.

Begin at the top of the shape to be covered and work single daisy stitches (page 76) set between two straight stitches worked at right angles, as shown. Position each stitch in between two of the stitches in the preceding row to form diagonal lines across the shape.

## ▓ DETACHED WHEATEAR STITCH

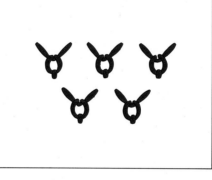

Detached wheatear stitch is a variation of ordinary wheatear stitch (page 38) which can be worked on both plain- and even-weave fabric. The stitch is used as a quick way of filling a large or small shape with a pretty powdering. To work it neatly and evenly, choose an even-weave fabric and count the threads, or mark guidelines on plain-weave fabric.

Any type of embroidery thread can be used, depending on the weight of the fabric, stitch size and effect required, but a round thread such as soft cotton makes the stitches stand out from the background more effectively than a flat, stranded cotton or silk. Bear in mind that the size of the stitch depends largely on the weight of the thread selected. Crewel wool, for example, produces a smaller stitch than a heavy thread such as pearl cotton or Persian wool. This stitch benefits from being worked on fabric stretched taut in an embroidery hoop or frame.

Begin at the top of the shape to be covered

and work two straight stitches set at right angles, as shown. Work a single daisy stitch (page 76) over the base of these stitches. Repeat over the shape, arranging the stitches in neat rows as shown.

## ▓ ROMAN FILLING STITCH

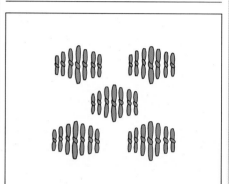

Roman filling stitch can be used on both plain- and even-weave fabric to produce an attractive filling for any size of shape. The stitch is a variation of ordinary Roman stitch (page 38).

Begin by working a group of even upright Roman stitches of different lengths, as shown. Work further groups of stitches, arranging them alternately over the shape with narrow spaces in between, as shown in the diagram. There are many variations of this stitch. For example, the groups of stitches can be positioned in such a way that the longest stitches touch at the tip and bottom. This leaves diamond shapes of fabric unworked in between the groups. Alternatively, the groups of stitches can be arranged with the edges touching to create a solidly stitched effect.

## ▓ LEAF STITCH

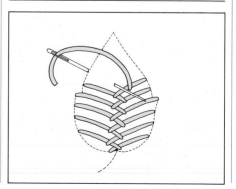

Leaf stitch is used on plain-weave and finely woven even-weave fabric. It is a light, open stitch suitable for filling small areas such as ovals and leaf shapes. The stitch can also be worked in between two lines to make a border, and the length of the stitches may be varied to produce a wavy outline. An embroidery thread with a sheen such as stranded cotton or silk shows this stitch off to best advantage, although any other type of thread is suitable. This stitch benefits from being worked on fabric stretched in an embroidery hoop or frame.

Work the stitch upwards, bringing the thread through just left of the centre. Take a slanting stitch to the right-hand margin and bring the thread through beneath the stitch, near the centre. Repeat until the shape is filled, always inserting the needle on the margin of the shape and bringing it through near the centre. An outline stitch such as back stitch (page 13) can be worked around the edge of the shape to define the outline more clearly.

## OPEN FISHBONE STITCH

Open fishbone stitch is used on plain-weave and finely woven even-weave fabric to fill small areas such as flower petals or leaf shapes. It is a variation of ordinary fishbone stitch (page 100) and is always worked downwards following the outlines of the shape. It can be worked as a border in the same way as the previous stitch.

Bring the thread through just to the left of the centre and take a slanting stitch to the right margin, as shown. Take the thread under the shape, and bring it through on the left margin ready to work the next slanting stitch. Continue in this way until the shape is filled. An outline stitch such as chain stitch (page 18) can be worked around the edge of the shape to define the outline more clearly.

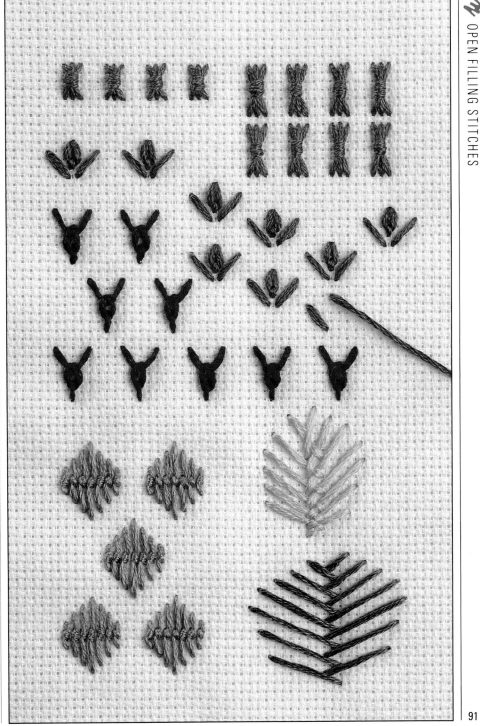

MARY THOMAS'S DICTIONARY OF EMBROIDERY STITCHES

## BURDEN STITCH

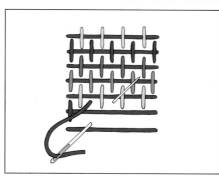

Burden stitch is a type of couching (page 23) which is used on both plain- and even-weave fabric. It dates back to the Middle Ages, when it was worked on Italian and German ecclesiastical embroideries. The stitch was rediscovered in recent times by Elizabeth Burden, a relative of William Morris who taught at The Royal School of Needlework in London.

Burden stitch produces a brick-like pattern which can be shaded in different colours of thread. It is often used to decorate ecclesiastical garments: a metallic thread is used for the long stitches, while the vertical stitches are worked in pure silk or lengths of gold and silver purl.

Begin by covering the shape with horizontal, evenly spaced long stitches. Anchor them to the fabric with rows of vertical stitches arranged to form a brick-like pattern, as shown.

## COUCHED FILLING STITCH

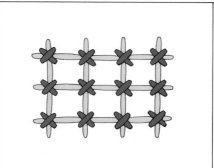

(Also known as Jacobean couching.)
Couched filling stitch is a pretty stitch which can be used to fill any size of shape on both plain- and even-weave fabric. The stitch is commonly used to work the centres of large flowers in Jacobean embroidery, and produces an attractive lattice pattern. It is often worked in more than one colour of thread. Couched filling stitch should always be worked on fabric stretched taut in an embroidery hoop or frame to enable the foundation stitches to be kept perfectly regular.

Begin by making the foundation grid. Work long horizontal stitches at regular intervals across the shape to be covered, then cross them with long vertical stitches set at right angles. Keep the grid as even as possible in order to retain the regularity of the trellis pattern. To finish, anchor the grid to the fabric at every intersection by working a tiny cross stitch (page 34) over the grid and through the fabric. The stitch can be shaded by varying the thread colour used for the cross stitches.

## TRELLIS COUCHING

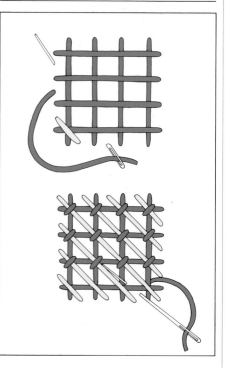

(Also known as trellis stitch.)
Trellis couching is used on both plain- and even-weave fabric and produces a delicate trellis pattern which can be worked either in one thread colour, or in several contrasting colours.

To work this stitch neatly and evenly, choose an even-weave fabric and count the threads, or mark guidelines on plain-weave fabric with tailor's chalk or a special water-soluble marker. Trellis couching should always be worked on fabric stretched taut in an embroidery hoop or frame to enable the foundation grid to be kept perfectly regular.

Begin by making the foundation grid. Work long vertical stitches at regular intervals across the shape to be covered, then cross them with long horizontal stitches set at right angles. Next, work long diagonal stitches from bottom right to top left of the foundation grid, as shown in the first diagram, arranging them so that they cross each intersection of the grid. To finish the stitch, anchor both the foundation grid and the diagonal stitches to the fabric by working a small diagonal stitch across every intersection, as shown.

## PLAID FILLING STITCH

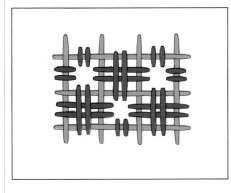

(Also known as tartan stitch.)

Plaid filling stitch is easy to work and can be used to fill any size of shape on either plain- or even-weave fabric. It is usually worked in three contrasting thread colours to produce a plaid pattern, but the effect created by working it in one colour alone can be just as attractive. To work the stitch neatly and evenly, choose an even-weave fabric and count the threads, or mark guidelines on plain-weave fabric.

Begin by making the foundation grid. Work long horizontal stitches at regular intervals across the shape to be covered, then cross them with long vertical stitches set at right angles. Interlace the stitches where they cross, just as though you were darning a sock. Keep the grid as even as you can to make a pattern of squares across the fabric. Work two horizontal

stitches across one square, as shown, using a second thread colour. Cross these stitches with two vertical stitches worked in a third thread colour to form a kind of double cross. Work the crosses in alternate squares to accentuate the plaid pattern. Small vertical and horizontal stitches can be worked on the outside edges of the shape, as shown, to fill the gaps left along the foundation stitches.

## TOROCKO STITCH

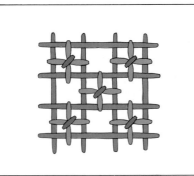

(Also known as couched filling stitch and Hungarian cross stitch.)

Torocko stitch is quick and simple to work and can be used to fill any size of shape on either plain- or even-weave fabric. The stitch is usually worked in three contrasting thread colours, but the effect created by working it in one colour alone can be just as attractive.

To work Torocko stitch neatly and evenly, choose an even-weave fabric and count the threads, or mark guidelines on plain-weave fabric with tailor's chalk or a special water-soluble marker. Any type of embroidery thread can be used, depending on the weight of the fabric, stitch size and effect required, but a round thread such as pearl cotton makes the filling stand out from the background more effectively than a stranded cotton or silk.

Begin by making the foundation grid. Work long vertical stitches at regular intervals across the shape to be covered, then cross them with long horizontal stitches set at right angles. Keep the foundation stitches as even as possible, making a regular pattern of squares across the fabric. Work a large St George cross stitch (page 86) over alternate squares, as shown in the diagram. Finally, work small diagonal stitches at the centre of each St George cross stitch to anchor it to the fabric.

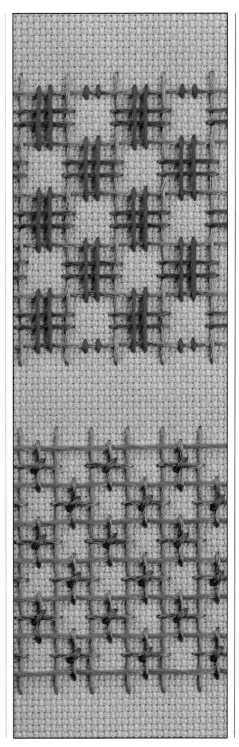

# OPEN FILLING STITCHES

## GRIFFIN STITCH

Griffin stitch is used on both plain- and even-weave fabric. It produces an attractive, fairly bold pattern which can be worked either in one thread colour, or in several contrasting colours. To work it neatly, choose an even-weave fabric and count the threads, or mark guidelines on plain-weave fabric with tailor's chalk or a special water-soluble marker. This stitch should always be worked on fabric stretched taut in an embroidery hoop or frame to enable the foundation stitches to be kept stable.

Work a square grid made up of long vertical and horizontal stitches. Cover this grid with a second grid, but this time use diagonal stitches, as shown. Next, tie down the second grid at every intersection where it does not cross the first grid, beginning at the top left of the shape. Use vertical rows of running stitches (page 12) for this stage. Finally, use a second thread to lace around the intersections at the points where the two grids cross, making a circular shape, as shown, without picking up the fabric. Take the thread through the fabric before bringing it out again to work the next circular lacing. Use a blunt-ended tapestry needle for the lacing to avoid splitting the grid stitches.

## ■ BACK STITCH TRELLIS

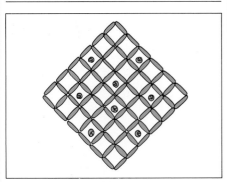

(Also known as square stitch.)

Back stitch trellis is used on both plain- and even-weave fabric. It produces an attractive trellis pattern and is quick and easy to work.

Work all the lines which run from bottom left to top right in back stitches (page 13), going up one line and returning along an adjacent one. Work the lines which run in the opposite direction in the same manner. Decorate the diamond shapes with small stitches worked in a matching or contrasting thread colour. Ordinary cross stitches (page 34), French or Chinese knots (page 68) or dot stitches (page 69) are all suitable for this purpose. Back stitch trellis can be worked diagonally, as shown in the diagram, or the lines can be stitched horizontally and vertically to form a square.

## ■ VALERIAN STITCH

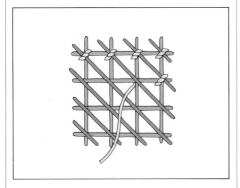

Valerian stitch is used on both plain- and even-weave fabric. It produces a similar pattern to trellis couching (page 92), but in this case bullion knots (page 69) are added to provide extra texture. This stitch should always be

worked on fabric stretched taut in an embroidery hoop or frame to enable the foundation grid to be kept perfectly even.

Begin by making the foundation grid. Work long vertical stitches at regular intervals across the shape to be covered, then cross them with long horizontal stitches set at right angles. Next, work long diagonal stitches from bottom left to top right, as shown in the diagram. These stitches should cross each intersection of the grid. To finish the stitch, anchor both the foundation grid and the diagonal stitches to the fabric by working a diagonal bullion knot across every intersection. Valerian stitch can be worked in one colour, or contrasting thread colours can be used for both the diagonal stitches and the bullion knots.

## ■ SQUARED FILLING STITCH 1

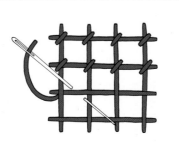

Squared filling stitch 1 is used on both plain- and even-weave fabric to produce an attractive pattern which can be worked in more than one colour of thread. To work this stitch neatly, choose an even-weave fabric and count the threads, or mark guidelines on plain-weave fabric with tailor's chalk or a special water-soluble marker.

Begin by making the foundation grid. Work long horizontal stitches at regular intervals across the shape to be covered, then cross them with long vertical stitches set at right angles. Keep the foundation grid as even as possible to ensure perfect regularity. At each intersection, secure the grid on the fabric with a small diagonal stitch, as shown. Cover the first grid with a second grid, but this time use diagonal stitches, as shown. Beginning at the top left of the shape, anchor the second grid to the fabric at every intersection where it does not cross the first grid. Use vertical rows of running stitches (page 12) for this stage.

## ■ SQUARED FILLING STITCH 2

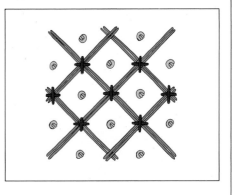

Squared filling stitch 2 is used on both plain- and even-weave fabric. It produces a pretty trellis pattern which can be worked in more than one thread colour. Any type of embroidery thread can be used, depending on the weight of the fabric, stitch size and effect required. To work the stitch neatly and evenly, choose an even-weave fabric and count the threads, or mark guidelines on plain-weave fabric with tailor's chalk or a special water-soluble marker. This stitch should always be worked on fabric stretched taut in an embroidery hoop or frame.

Begin by making the foundation grid. Work pairs of long diagonal stitches slanting from bottom left to top right at regular intervals across the shape. Cross these stitches with pairs of diagonal stitches running in the opposite direction. Keep the foundation as even as possible to ensure perfect regularity. Anchor each intersection of the grid to the fabric with a St George cross stitch (page 86) and work a French or Chinese knot (page 68) in each of the diamond shapes of fabric which show through the grid.

# CHAPTER SIX

# SOLID FILLING STITCHES

The stitches described on the following pages are used to fill designs on fabric with solid areas of embroidery. Unless otherwise specified, all these stitches can be worked on either plain- or even-weave fabric. Many of the stitches are quite straightforward to work, but some of the apparently simple ones, such as satin stitch, will require some practice before you will be able to execute them neatly. Whenever possible, the fabric should be stretched in a hoop or frame to help prevent it from distorting and pulling out of shape, and to enable you to work the stitches evenly.

Choice of thread is important; many of the stitches benefit from being worked in a lustrous thread such as stranded cotton or silk, which accentuates their rich, smooth surfaces. This type of thread also gives good fabric coverage, which is an essential consideration when working long and short stitch, fishbone stitch and damask darning. Included in this chapter are three unusual stitches; one of these makes an interesting raised pile, while the other two are used for applying beads.

# SOLID FILLING STITCHES

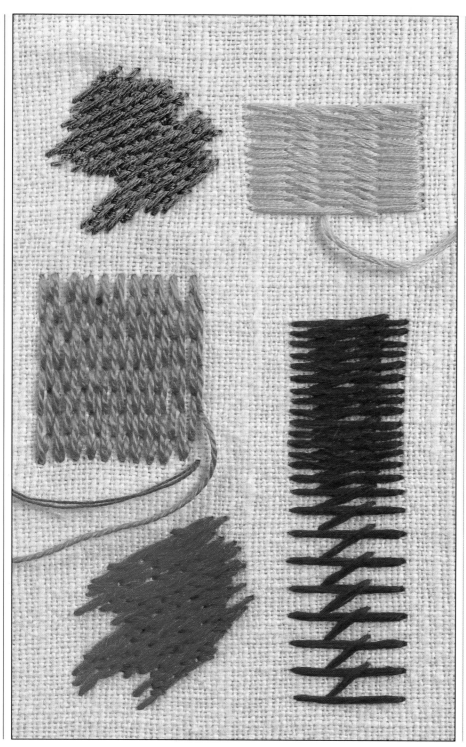

## ▌ BOKHARA COUCHING

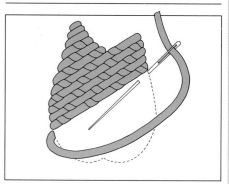

Bokhara couching is a solid filling stitch which can be used to fill any size or shape. Like Roumanian couching (below), this stitch uses the same continuous thread for both the laid stitches and the tying-down stitches. It is easy to work, but practice is needed to keep the tying-down stitches even.

Bokhara couching should always be worked with the fabric stretched taut in an embroidery hoop or frame. This helps prevent puckering of the ground fabric and enables the stitches to be worked evenly.

Lay the thread across the shape to be filled from left to right in one journey, then anchor it to the fabric on the return journey. Use small, slanting stitches set at regular intervals which form pattern lines across the whole shape. Work the tying-down stitches closely together and pull them tight, leaving the long thread slightly loose in between. Position adjacent areas of Bokhara couching with the laid threads running in opposite directions to give a pretty light and shade effect.

## ▌ ROUMANIAN COUCHING

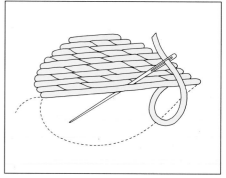

(Also known as laid Oriental stitch, antique couching, Oriental couching and figure stitch.)

Roumanian couching is worked with one continuous thread in a similar way to the previous stitch, Bokhara couching, but the effect is very different. This stitch is much smoother and flatter, without a definite pattern, and is used principally to fill large spaces and background areas.

A lustrous thread such as stranded silk or cotton accentuates the smooth, rich surface of the embroidery, which can be shaded by using graduated colours of thread. Roumanian couching should always be worked with the fabric stretched taut in an embroidery hoop or frame to help keep all the laid threads parallel and prevent the ground fabric from distorting and pulling out of shape.

To work Roumanian couching, first lay the thread by working a long stitch across the shape from left to right. Then anchor the stitch evenly to the fabric at regular intervals on the return journey, using the same thread. Work further long stitches and tying-down stitches downwards until the shape is filled. The tying-down stitches should be long, loose and slanting and should lie flat, without pulling. When Roumanian couching is worked correctly, the tying-down stitches are almost indistinguishable from the laid thread.

## UNDERSIDE COUCHING

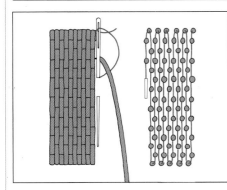

(Also known as invisible stitch.)

Underside couching is a very old stitch with a history stretching back to the Middle Ages. It is a filling stitch originally used to attach threads made from precious metals to church vestments and other textiles. Underside couching is ideal for modern metal thread embroidery and is used to fill small shapes or to cover backgrounds. The tying-down stitches are invisible on the right side and do not interrupt the shiny surface of the couched thread. Work this type of couching in any direction on a strong, finely woven ground fabric held taut in an embroidery hoop or frame. Use a strong but supple thread, preferably waxed, for the tying-down stitches and anchor it securely on the wrong side of the fabric at the beginning and end of the stitching.

First, lay the metal thread on the surface of the fabric. Bring the tying-down thread through the fabric at evenly spaced intervals, taking it over the laid thread and then back through the same hole in the fabric. After each stitch, give the thread a slight tug, so that a fraction of the laid thread is taken through the fabric and held in position. The second illustration shows the effect that is produced when the metal thread is pulled through to the reverse of the fabric by the tying-down thread. If using a fine metal thread, take the ends of it through to the wrong side of the work to secure it. A thick thread needs only to be cut short at the ends, without being taken through to the wrong side.

## NEW ENGLAND LAID STITCH

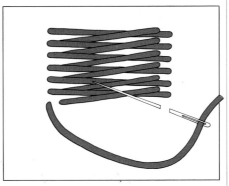

(Also known as Deerfield stitch and self couching.)

New England laid stitch is a variation of Roumanian couching (left) worked with a long crossing stitch. It is used for filling narrow shapes and borders. The stitch is an economical one, as most of the thread remains on the front of the work. It benefits from being worked on fabric stretched taut in an embroidery hoop or frame. Although this is not essential, it helps prevent distortion of the ground fabric.

The stitch is reputed to have been invented by early American settlers during a period when threads were both difficult to obtain and expensive. New England laid stitch was used mainly on the characteristic blue-and-white embroideries worked by settlers in New England, which are known as Deerfield embroideries.

To execute New England laid stitch, begin by working a long horizontal straight stitch from left to right of the shape to be filled, then make a short stitch at the edge, as shown in the diagram. Couch down the first stitch with one long diagonal stitch on the return journey. Keep the stitches close together, so that the ground fabric is completely covered.

## COLCHA STITCH

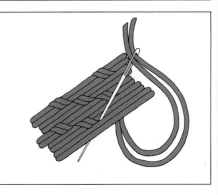

Colcha stitch is an unusual method of couching which originated in New Mexico. The name refers to the *colchas* or embroidered woollen hangings and bedcovers worked by Spanish settlers. The *colchas* were embroidered in brightly coloured woollen threads and this stitch was used to fill in the designs and completely cover the fabric. Colcha stitch gives a rough, almost woven effect and fills large shapes quickly and easily.

This stitch is worked in a similar way to Roumanian couching (far left), and looks best when it is worked in tapestry, Persian or crewel wool. It should be stitched with the fabric stretched taut in an embroidery hoop or frame to help prevent distortion and enable the stitches to be worked evenly.

Use two lengths of thread in the needle at the same time. Take a long diagonal straight stitch across the shape, then tie it down at irregular intervals with short diagonal stitches on the return journey, as shown in the diagram. Work the stitches closely together so that no ground fabric is visible.

# SOLID FILLING STITCHES

## FLAT STITCH

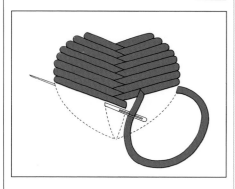

(Also known as Croatian flat stitch.)

Flat stitch, as the name implies, creates a flat, solidly worked surface. It is useful for filling small shapes such as flower petals and leaves, or it can be worked in a line where a strong outline is required. Large shapes can be filled effectively by working multiple rows of flat stitches with the edges of the rows touching. The stitches should be worked closely together, and most types of heavy thread can be used. Flat stitch should always be worked on fabric stretched in an embroidery hoop or frame.

Work slanting straight stitches from side to side of the shape to be filled, with each stitch crossing over the base of the preceding stitch. A double dotted line drawn at the centre of the shape to be filled will form a useful guide to keeping the stitches evenly spaced.

## FISHBONE STITCH

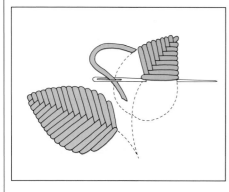

Fishbone stitch is worked in a similar way to the previous stitch, flat stitch, but the effect is different. Here, the stitches are more sharply angled and overlap at the centre of the shape,

creating an almost plaited line. This stitch is often used to fill leaf shapes, but it can also be worked between parallel lines to make a wide, rather heavy border. The stitches should be worked closely together so that they cover the ground fabric completely. A stranded thread gives the best fabric coverage. Fishbone stitch should always be worked with the fabric stretched taut in an embroidery hoop or frame. This will help to prevent distortion and puckering of the ground fabric and enable the stitches to be worked evenly.

Draw a single dotted line at the centre of the shape to be filled to help keep the stitches evenly spaced, then make a tiny straight stitch from the top of the shape down the centre line. Fill the shape with slanting straight stitches worked from side to side.

## RAISED FISHBONE STITCH

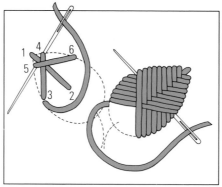

(Also known as overlapping herringbone stitch and self-padded herringbone stitch.)

Raised fishbone stitch produces a closely plaited, raised surface which looks almost padded. Use this stitch to fill small shapes but remember that it is essential to cover the ground fabric completely to achieve the correct effect. A stranded cotton or silk thread gives better fabric coverage than a twisted thread. This stitch benefits from being worked on fabric held taut in an embroidery hoop or frame, although this is not essential.

First, work a straight stitch at the top of the shape to be filled, then cover the shape with overlapping diagonal stitches worked from side to side. The stitches should slant and cross each other at the centre of the shape. Position them closely together to enhance the raised quality of the work and to ensure that the fabric is well covered.

## BUTTONHOLE STITCH SHADING

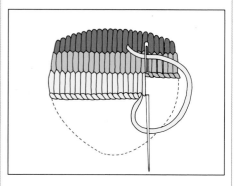

Rows of ordinary buttonhole stitches (page 17) make a useful shading stitch when a solidly embroidered shape is required. Work the rows from left to right, starting at the top of the shape to be filled. Position the second and subsequent rows so that they encroach over the base loops of the previous row. Buttonhole stitch shading benefits from being worked on fabric stretched taut in an embroidery hoop or frame, although this is not essential.

There are two methods of shading this stitch. You can change the colour of the thread on each row, or after every two rows, to give a regularly striped look, even with threads which are quite close in tone. Alternatively, work pairs of long horizontal straight stitches right across the shape, using different colours of thread. Work buttonhole stitches over this foundation, leaving small spaces in between them to allow the colour of the laid threads to show through. By varying the spacing of the buttonhole stitches over the laid threads you can control the visible colour.

## STEM STITCH SHADING

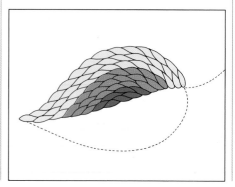

Stem stitch shading is a way of using rows of ordinary stem stitches (page 14) as a solid filling for any size of shape. It has a decorative, almost woven, appearance which is created by closely packed rows of stem stitches following the contours of the shape, and it is ideal for embroidering foliage, flowers, fruit and other similar patterns.

Any type of embroidery thread can be used to work the stitch, depending on the effect required. Graduated threads provide an attractive effect, or choose threads of different textures which are close to each other in tone. An embroidery hoop or frame need not be used when working this stitch.

Position the stitches closely together so that no ground fabric is visible and keep all the stitches of the same length. At the beginning of each row, make the first stitch a little longer or shorter than the first stitch of the previous row in order to give the effect of diagonal lines across the shape.

## ▌ CLOSED WAVE STITCH

(Also known as looped shading stitch.)

Closed wave stitch is a useful and economical stitch, as nearly all the thread remains on the surface of the fabric. Each row, or section of a row, can be worked in a different colour of thread, or you could use a graduated thread to achieve subtle colour changes. An embroidery hoop or frame should be used when working this stitch.

Begin by working a row of vertical satin stitches (page 102) along the top of the shape. On the next and every following row, work looped stitches, slipping the needle under the base of the stitches in the previous row. Take a tiny stitch through the fabric at the base of the row after each loop has been completed.

# SOLID FILLING STITCHES

## ▮ SATIN STITCH

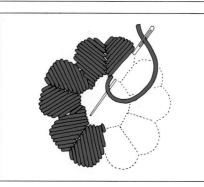

(Also known as damask stitch.)

Satin stitch is a flat stitch which looks deceptively simple to work, but practice is needed to sew it neatly. The stitches can be worked in any direction, with changes of direction giving the effect of light and shade. This effect is enhanced by the use of a lustrous thread such as stranded cotton or pure silk. Satin stitch should always be worked with the fabric held taut in an embroidery hoop or frame to prevent puckering and enable the stitches to be worked evenly.

Carry the thread right across the shape to be filled, then return it underneath the fabric close to the point where it emerged. Work the stitches closely together so that they lie evenly and make a real edge around the shape.

Satin stitch can be of any length, but long stitches tend to become loose and untidy. Large shapes can be split up into smaller, more manageable ones. Alternatively, they can be worked in encroaching satin stitch (below) or long and short stitch (page 104).

## ▮ ENCROACHING SATIN STITCH

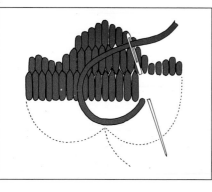

Encroaching satin stitch is used for filling large shapes on both plain- and even-weave fabric. As with all satin stitches, practice is needed to execute it correctly. It is particularly useful for shading and blending colours when working naturalistic designs. For a really subtle effect, change the colour on every row and use threads which are very close in tone. As with ordinary satin stitch, any type of thread can be used, but a lustrous cotton is probably the most sympathetic. Work this stitch with the fabric stretched in an embroidery hoop or frame to help prevent puckering and enable the stitches to be worked evenly.

First, work a horizontal row of vertical satin stitches (left) across the top of the shape to be filled. On the second and subsequent rows, work the top of each satin stitch between the bases of two stitches in the row above. The rows will then blend into each other without an obvious join.

## ▮ PADDED SATIN STITCH

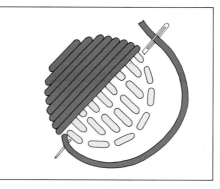

Padded satin stitch creates slightly raised shapes to contrast with flat, smooth areas of stitching. It should always be worked with the fabric stretched in an embroidery hoop or frame to prevent puckering.

Work foundation rows of stitches over and around the shape to be filled using running stitch (page 12), stem stitch (page 14) or chain stitch (page 18). Then cover these stitches with satin stitch (left).

*Satin stitch has long been used in the traditional work of many countries. The embroidery on the right is part of a sleeveless Chinese silk tunic dating from the late 19th century.*

# SOLID FILLING STITCHES

## ▮ WHIPPED SATIN STITCH

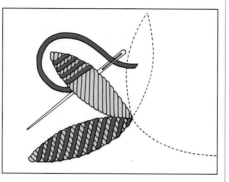

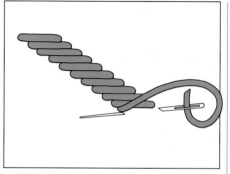

Whipped satin stitch is an attractive variation of ordinary satin stitch (page 102) used for filling narrow leaf and flower shapes and outlines where a heavy effect is required. This stitch gives a raised, corded finish and it can be worked in one or more colours of thread. Any type of embroidery thread can be used to work the stitch, but a twisted, slightly shiny thread such as pearl cotton enhances the corded quality of the stitch. Whipped satin stitch benefits from being worked on fabric held taut in an embroidery hoop or frame. Although this is not essential, it helps prevent puckering of the ground fabric and enables the stitches to be worked evenly.

Begin by filling the shape to be covered with a foundation of closely worked, slanting satin stitches. Using the same thread or one of a contrasting weight or texture, whip over the filled shape. Position the whipping stitches at right angles to the satin stitches, spacing them at regular intervals along the shape or line and inserting the needle close to the edge of the foundation stitches. The whipping stitches should be placed slightly apart.

To achieve a highly raised finish on small shapes, work a foundation of padded satin stitches (page 102) over the shape instead of ordinary satin stitches. This technique is less successful as an outline.

## ▮ JAPANESE STITCH

Examples of Japanese stitch worked in pure silk floss can be seen on antique Japanese kimonos. The stitch is an easily worked variation of satin stitch (page 102) arranged in rows and it makes an attractive filling for large areas and backgrounds. It is particularly effective when used on an even-weave fabric,

where the threads can be counted to keep the stitches of uniform size. When working Japanese stitch on a plain-weave fabric, mark guidelines with a pencil or special embroidery marker: this will enable you to keep the rows of stitching straight.

Japanese stitch looks most effective worked in a lustrous thread such as stranded cotton or silk, which shows off the smooth surface well. This stitch should always be worked with the fabric stretched in an embroidery hoop or frame to prevent puckering of the fabric and to enable the stitches to be worked evenly.

Work a series of diagonal lines consisting of equally sized horizontal satin stitches positioned directly underneath one another, slanting the lines from top left to bottom right. Place the stitches close to one another so that no ground fabric is visible.

## ▮ LONG AND SHORT STITCH

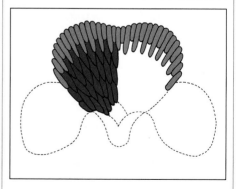

(Also known as embroidery stitch, plumage stitch, shading stitch, tapestry shading stitch, brick stitch, leaf stitch, Irish stitch, feather stitch, featherwork and Opus Plumarium.)

Long and short stitch is worked in the same way as satin stitch (page 102), and gets its name from the long and short stitches used in the foundation row. It is used for edges and outlines as well as for filling shapes. The stitch lends itself to subtle shading and is often used to work naturalistic designs. A regular outline is created by the foundation row, while the inner rows produce an irregular line which allows colours to blend gradually into one another without a strongly defined line.

Work long and short stitch in one colour to fill areas which are too large to be filled by ordinary satin stitch. This stitch benefits from being worked on fabric held taut in an embroidery hoop or frame. Although this is not essential, it helps prevent puckering of the ground fabric and enables the stitches to be worked evenly. Long and short stitch is often thought to be one of the simpler embroidery stitches, but practice is needed to keep the stitching even.

Work the foundation row in alternately long and short satin stitches, following the contours of the shape to be filled and positioning the stitches close to each other so that no ground fabric is visible. On the return journey, fit satin stitches of equal length into the spaces left in the foundation row. Continue in this way until the shape is filled.

## DOUBLE DARNING

(Also known as pessante.)

Double darning is a variation of darning stitch (page 82) which is alike on both sides of the fabric. The stitch is worked in a similar way to Holbein stitch (page 12), but double darning is always used as a filling rather than an outline stitch. It produces a flat surface with strongly norizontal lines. Work this stitch on an even-weave fabric as the beauty of the surface of the stitch lies in complete regularity. Double darning benefits from being worked on fabric held taut in an embroidery hoop or frame. Although this is not essential, it helps prevent puckering of the ground fabric.

Begin by working a row of darning stitches, making the length of the stitches equal to the spaces in between. Fill in the spaces on the return journey, pushing the needle in and out of the fabric at the holes made on the first row, as shown in the diagram. The effect of diagonal lines can be created by commencing each row one stitch further to the right or left of the previous row. Keep the stitches of an even length as before.

## DAMASK DARNING

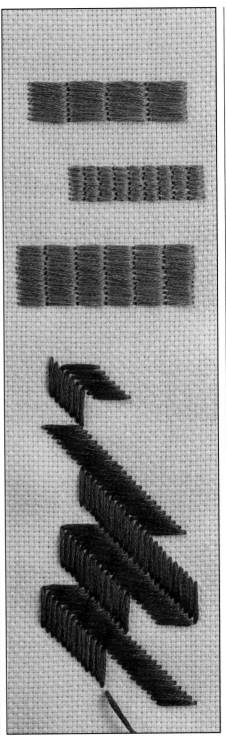

Damask darning needs to be worked evenly, and should therefore only be used on even-weave fabrics. In spite of its name, this stitch is not related to darning stitch (page 82), but is a variation of satin stitch (page 102) which resembles fabric woven with a diagonal pattern.

This stitch looks best worked in a lustrous thread such as stranded silk or cotton, which enhances the light and shade effect created by the different directions of the stitches. Damask darning benefits from being worked on fabric held taut in an embroidery hoop or frame. Although this is not essential, it helps prevent puckering of the ground fabric and enables the stitches to be worked evenly.

Work diagonal rows of short horizontal and vertical satin stitches, slanting the rows from top left to bottom right of the shape to be filled. Place the stitches closely together, as shown in the diagram, so that no ground fabric can be seen. Fill in any spaces left unworked at the edge of the shape with satin stitches of the appropriate length.

# SOLID FILLING STITCHES

## BRICK STITCH

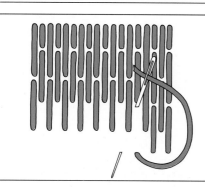

Brick stitch is simple to work and fills large spaces quickly on all types of fabric. It can be worked to give either an open or closed effect by changing the spacing of the stitches and is ideal for shading. The stitch must be sewn evenly, with the stitches worked to the same length and the rows kept parallel. When shading, choose colours which are close in tone so that they merge together gradually. Work with the fabric held taut in an embroidery hoop or frame to prevent distortion.

Begin by working a foundation row of alternately long and short straight stitches along the top edge of the shape to be filled. On the return journey, fill in the spaces with vertical straight stitches, as shown in the diagram. Work further rows of straight stitches of an identical length until the shape is filled. Work the rows alternately from left to right and from right to left, positioning the stitches so that they form a bricklike pattern. Fill in the spaces remaining at the bottom edge of the shape with straight stitches of the appropriate length.

## BASKET FILLING STITCH

(Also known as basket satin stitch.)

Basket filling stitch is simple to work and is a quick and effective way of filling a shape on both plain- and even-weave fabric. The stitch produces an attractive, flat basketweave pattern which is often used in Jacobean embroidery. Although basket filling stitch is traditionally worked only in one colour, a pretty chequerboard pattern results if alternate blocks are worked in a second colour. This stitch benefits from being worked on fabric held taut in an embroidery hoop or frame.

To execute basket filling stitch, work alternate groups of four horizontal and four vertical satin stitches (page 102) in rows to cover the shape to be filled. You can stitch the rows in a horizontal, vertical or diagonal direction, depending on your preference. Keep all the stitches evenly spaced and of equal length, as shown in the diagram.

Basket filling stitch can also be worked on single canvas in either a cotton or wool thread. On canvas, you can vary the number of stitches in each group from shape to shape, depending on the gauge of canvas and the weight of thread used. Three stitches worked over four canvas threads or five stitches worked over six threads will give a different sense of scale to the stitching.

## SPOT STITCH

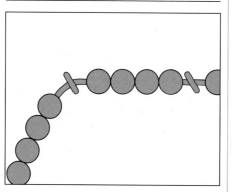

(Also known as bead couching and overlay stitch.)

Spot stitch is used to attach beads quickly to both plain- and even-weave fabric. Although this method is much simpler than the traditional one of sewing beads on individually, the resulting decoration is less durable. The stitch is a variation of couching (page 23) which has been used for many generations by the Indians of North America, particularly those of the Blackfoot, Crow and Shoshone tribes, for decorating garments.

This method of beading is good for linear designs; alternatively, a solidly beaded shape can be made by working multiple rows of the stitch close to each other. Arrange the rows side by side or have them spiralling outwards from the centre of a shape. Lazy squaw stitch (below) is another effective method of attaching beads quickly and easily to fabric.

To work spot stitch, begin by threading the beads on to a fairly strong thread which is fine enough to pass through the hole in the beads easily without fraying. A polyester or waxed linen thread is ideal for this type of work. Secure the end of the thread carefully on the wrong side of the fabric before laying it along the line to be covered. Couch it down with a second thread by making a short diagonal stitch after every group of four beads.

## LAZY SQUAW STITCH

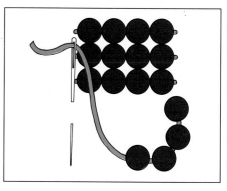

Lazy squaw stitch is a quick and easy method of beading large areas as several beads are sewn on to the fabric together. Like spot stitch (above), it is a traditional stitch used by North American Indians. Use a strong thread, which should be waxed before use, and work the stitch on closely woven fabric stretched in an embroidery hoop or frame. Fill large shapes by working several rows of the stitch.

First, draw two parallel lines on the fabric with a pencil or special embroidery marker. Secure the end of the thread, then thread several beads on to it. Take a long stitch from right to left of the guidelines, and work a small vertical stitch to anchor the beads, as shown in the diagram. Repeat, working from side to side of the row.

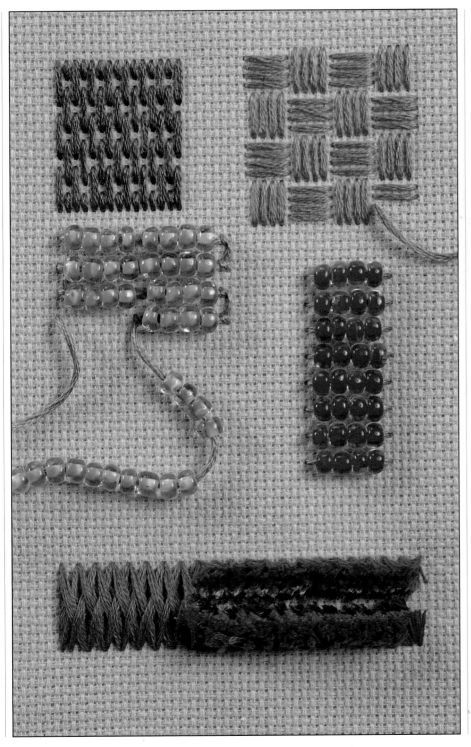

## ▮ VICTORIAN TUFTING

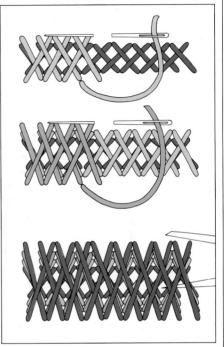

Victorian tufting is an unusual pile stitch which can be worked in a straight band or in multiple rows to fill a shape. The stitch is quite simple to work and looks very effective. It consists of several gradually widening rows of close herringbone stitch (page 47) worked on top of one another from left to right, which are cut to make a pile after the stitching has been completed. The pile forms ridges which are shallow at the centre, becoming higher towards the edges.

A soft wool thread such as Persian wool gives a soft luxuriant pile, but cotton threads – or a mixture of wool and cotton – can also be used. Work the rows of stitches in alternate colours to create an unusual striped pile.

Work the first row to form the centre of the pile using narrow stitches, then make the second and subsequent rows gradually wider. Every new row should overlap the previous row by a small amount. Work as many overlapping rows as you can fit into the space until the band is of the required width. Finally, using a sharp pair of pointed scissors, carefully cut through the centre of the band of stitches, as shown in the diagram.

# CHAPTER SEVEN

# DETACHED FILLING STITCHES

The stitches described in this chapter are, as the title suggests, detached from the fabric. These stitches are held in place either on a threaded foundation which anchors the stitching securely to the fabric, or by picking up tiny amounts of fabric at the edges of a shape. They can be used to fill shapes with lacy patterns or solid stitching, depending on the stitch. Some of the stitches described, such as Maltese cross filling stitch and battlement couching, are rather difficult to grasp at first. Spend some time studying the diagrams before working each stitch and follow the sequence of stitches carefully from the instructions.

To make stitches worked on a foundation simpler to execute, use a blunt-ended tapestry needle for the second thread to avoid picking up the ground fabric. Stretch the fabric in an embroidery hoop or frame to help prevent the fabric from puckering and to enable the stitches to be worked in a regular manner.

# DETACHED FILLING STITCHES

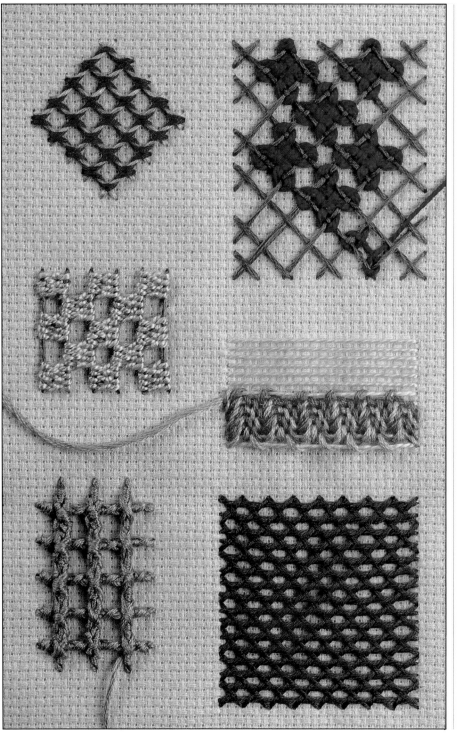

## ◼ TWISTED LATTICE STITCH

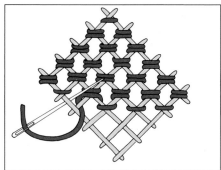

(Also known as twisted lattice filling.)

Twisted lattice stitch is used on both plain- and even-weave fabric. The stitch produces an attractive lattice pattern which is usually worked in two contrasting colours or weights of thread. It is worked in the same way as twisted lattice band (page 58).

First, make the foundation grid. Work evenly spaced long diagonal stitches in one direction over the shape to be covered. To complete the foundation, work a second set of long diagonal stitches over the first set to form a lattice. Interlace the second set of diagonal stitches with the first set by going over and under them as if you were darning a sock. Lace a second thread across the foundation grid, without picking up the fabric.

## ◼ MALTESE CROSS FILLING STITCH

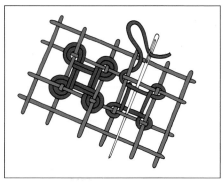

Maltese cross filling stitch is used on both plain- and even-weave fabric. It is similar to Maltese cross (page 74).

Work a foundation grid of diagonal stitches across the shape to be covered. Work one set of diagonal stitches in one direction, then work a second set in the opposite direction. Interlace the second set of stitches with the first set by going over and under them as if you were darning a sock. Arrange the grid so that it makes a plaid pattern. Bring the thread through at the top of a large square on the grid and work the interlacing as shown. Repeat to make a double interlacing. Take the thread back through the fabric before commencing to interlace the next large square.

## ▊ CRETAN OPEN FILLING STITCH

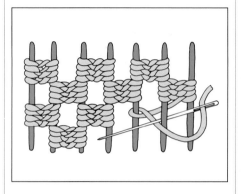

Cretan open filling stitch is a detached variation of ordinary Cretan stitch (page 30) used on both plain- and even-weave fabric. Any type of embroidery thread can be used to work it, depending on the effect required, but the foundation stitches should be worked in a heavy, firm thread. This stitch should always be worked on fabric stretched taut in an embroidery hoop or frame.

Work an evenly spaced foundation of vertical straight stitches across the shape to be covered. Bring a second, more supple thread through at the top right-hand corner and work blocks of Cretan stitches over the foundation, without picking up the fabric. Work the blocks in diagonal lines from top right to bottom left. Keep the tension of the Cretan stitches even: the blocks should make a formal chessboard pattern across the shape.

## ▊ CHEVRON STEM STITCH

Chevron stem stitch is used on both plain- and even-weave fabric. The foundation stitches must be worked in a firm thread, but any type of thread can be used for the stem stitches. To enhance the zigzag pattern, work the stitch in

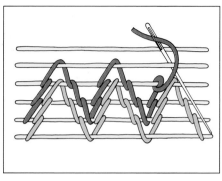

two colours of thread.

Begin by making a foundation of evenly spaced long horizontal stitches. Bring the second thread through at the bottom left and work ordinary stem stitches (page 14) in a zigzag pattern over the foundation, as shown. The needle should go through the fabric only at the beginning and end of each row. Work the stem stitches closely together to cover the foundation. Fill in the remaining V-shapes with stem stitches, keeping the pattern correct. The finished shape can be outlined with a line stitch such as pearl stitch (page 22).

## ▊ HONEYCOMB FILLING STITCH

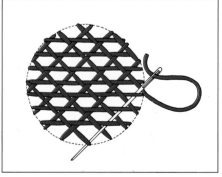

(Also known as net passing stitch.)

Honeycomb filling stitch produces a lacy, geometric pattern and can be used on both plain- and even-weave fabric. It consists of three sets of interlocking straight stitches which are often worked in more than one thread colour.

First, work a set of evenly spaced horizontal stitches across the shape to be covered. Work a set of diagonal stitches over the horizontal stitches from bottom left to top right of the

shape. Work a second set of diagonal stitches in the opposite direction, passing the needle under the horizontal stitches and over the first set of diagonal stitches so that the three sets of threads form closely interlocked triangles.

## ▊ RAISED HONEYCOMB FILLING STITCH

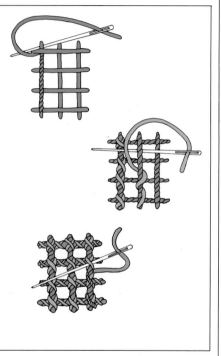

Raised honeycomb filling stitch is used on both plain- and even-weave fabric. It produces a raised trellis which looks most effective when it is worked in a lightweight thread such as coton à broder or the finest available weight of pearl cotton. Work this stitch on fabric stretched taut in an embroidery hoop or frame to help prevent puckering of the ground fabric.

Make a trellis of long vertical and horizontal stitches over the shape to be covered. Work over these stitches with overcast stitches (page 15), as shown in the first diagram. Cover all the vertical stitches first, then cover the horizontal stitches. Work the overcast stitches carefully so that they link the trellis layers together, and keep them evenly spaced. Coil a second thread around each vertical and horizontal stitch on the trellis to form crossed spirals, as shown in the second diagram. To finish, overcast the spirals again both horizontally and vertically.

# DETACHED FILLING STITCHES

## ▌HOLLIE STITCH

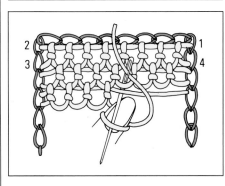

(Also known as holy stitch and holy point.)

Hollie stitch is an adaptation of an old needle-made lace technique called hollie point. It makes a pretty, lacy filling which can be used on both plain- and even-weave fabric.

Begin by outlining the shape to be covered with a row of small ordinary chain stitches (page 18), then bring the thread through the centre of the chain stitch at the top right of the shape. Make a long stitch across the shape, taking the thread through the corresponding chain stitch at the top left. Bring the thread through the next chain stitch below and make a row of looped knotted stitches, as shown, over both the long stitch and the chain loops. Repeat, following the diagram carefully.

## ▌TRELLIS FILLING STITCH

Trellis filling stitch is used as a lacy filling on both plain- and even-weave fabric.

Begin by outlining the shape to be covered with a row of evenly spaced ordinary chain

stitches (page 18). Bring the thread through at the top left of the shape. Work the first row of filling from left to right along the chain stitches by making alternate loops and knots, as shown

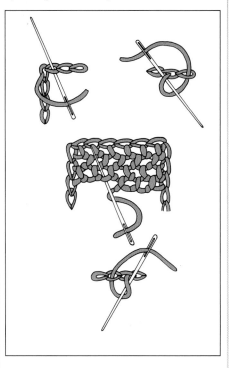

in the top two diagrams. Tighten each knot by pulling the working thread to the right. When the edge is reached, take the thread down to the next chain stitch without entering the fabric, and work the knots and loops in the opposite direction, as shown in the bottom diagrams, tightening the thread by pulling it to the left.

## ▌LACE STITCH FILLING

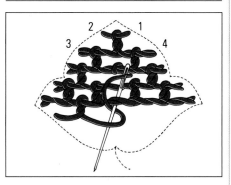

Lace stitch filling produces an attractive, twisted pattern and can be used on both plain- and even-weave fabric. A round, twisted thread such as pearl cotton makes the stitch easier to work than a stranded thread.

Make a stitch from right to left across the top of the shape to be covered. Bring the thread through lower down on the left and work a twisted loop, as shown, over the first stitch. Take the thread over to the right and make a tiny stitch at the edge, then return it to the left-hand side by winding it around the base of the previous stitch. Take the thread through the fabric at the left, bringing it out lower down ready to work the next row of twisted loops in the spaces left in the first row. On the return journey, wind the thread once around the loop in between each stitch. At the bottom of the shape, take the thread around each loop and through the fabric, pulling it taut after each stitch has been completed. Finish the edges of the shape with an outline of stem stitches (page 14) or back stitches (page 13).

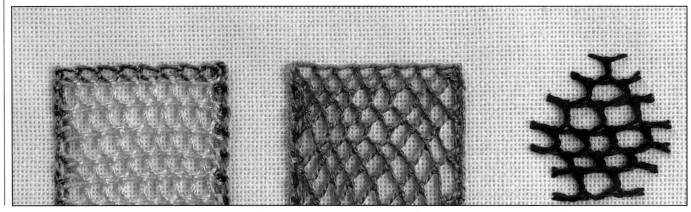

## ▌CEYLON STITCH

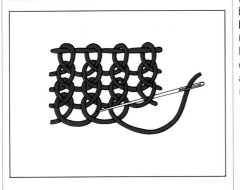

Ceylon stitch is used on both plain- and even-weave fabric. The stitch can be worked to produce two different effects: space the stitches widely apart to create a light, lacy filling or work them closely together to make a surface which looks like knitted stocking stitch. Try to keep the tension of the stitches even.

Make a horizontal straight stitch across the top of the shape to be covered, then work a row of looped stitches of an equal size from left to right over this foundation, as shown, without picking up the fabric. At the end of the row, take the thread through the fabric, and bring it out on the left-hand side. Work the next row of loops through the previous row.

## ▌DIAMOND FILLING STITCH

Diamond filling stitch makes a pretty, knotted filling and can be used on both plain- and even-weave fabric. It is worked as a detached filling over a foundation of long horizontal stitches. Work each row of stitches in two journeys.

First, make a horizontal foundation stitch from right to left of the shape to be covered, bringing the thread back through the fabric just below the left-hand corner. Make a coral knot (see coral stitch, page 21) at the corner, leave a loop of thread, then work a second coral knot over the foundation stitch. Continue in this way along the row, making knots and loops at regular intervals. At the end of the row, take the

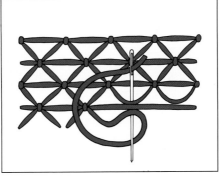

thread through the back of the fabric and bring it out a little lower down in line with the depth of the loops. Make another long stitch across the shape and repeat the process, anchoring the loops made on the previous journey when working the knots, as shown.

## ▌BATTLEMENT COUCHING

Battlement couching is a detached form of ordinary couching (page 23) which is used on both plain- and even-weave fabric. It makes an unusual filling for simple shapes. The stitch looks rather complicated at first sight, but it is actually quite simple to work once the

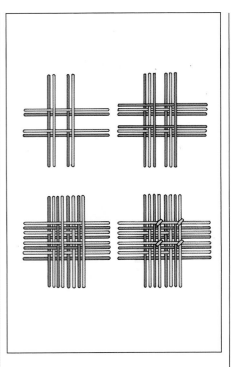

sequence of foundation stitches has been mastered. Any type of thread can be used, but a twisted thread gives the best results. This stitch should be worked on fabric stretched taut in an embroidery hoop or frame.

First, work long vertical and horizontal stitches as shown in the first three diagrams. Follow the sequence carefully, making sure that the stitches are arranged alternately on the fabric to create an overlapping lattice. When the foundation is complete, secure the top stitches with small diagonal stitches, as shown.

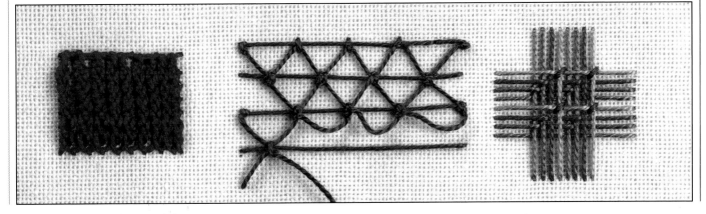

# DETACHED FILLING STITCHES

## SURFACE SATIN STITCH

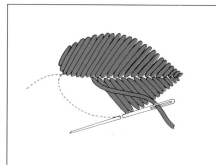

Surface satin stitch is an alternative method of working ordinary satin stitch (page 102) on both plain- and even-weave fabric. When satin stitch is worked in the normal way, as much thread lies below the fabric as above it, which is rather wasteful, particularly when an expensive silk thread is used. Utilize this method instead for large areas of stitching.

Bring the thread through the fabric and take a stitch across in the usual way. Pick up a tiny amount of fabric at the edge and bring the needle through ready to work the next satin stitch, as shown in the diagram. If you find it difficult to keep the stitches close to each other when working a large shape, work the stitch in two journeys. Leave a small space in between each stitch on the first journey, then fill it in on the return journey.

## SURFACE DARNING

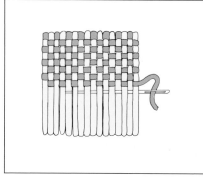

Surface darning is used on both plain- and even-weave fabric. The stitch is actually an ordinary stocking darn which has been adapted for embroidery. It produces a closely woven surface which looks attractive when it is worked in more than one thread colour. Use this stitch to fill small shapes.

First, work a foundation of vertical satin stitches (left) over the shape to be covered. Arrange the stitches closely together. Using a second thread, weave the needle regularly in and out of the foundation stitches, as shown. The second thread picks up the fabric only at the sides of the shape so the filling is quite detached, except at the edges. Use a blunt-ended tapestry needle for the second thread to avoid splitting the foundation stitches.

## PLAITED STITCH

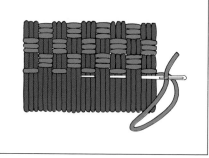

Plaited stitch is a variation of surface darning (left) used on both plain- and even-weave fabric. The stitch makes a pretty basket-work pattern and looks most attractive when it is worked in more than one colour of thread.

First, work a foundation of vertical surface satin stitches (left) over the shape, arranging the stitches closely together. Weave a second thread regularly in and out of the foundation stitches, as shown, going over three and under three vertical stitches alternately. The second thread picks up the fabric only at the sides of the shape. Work three rows, as shown, then reverse the sequence of 'unders' and 'overs' for the next three rows. Continue in this way, reversing the sequence each time three rows have been completed. Use a blunt-ended tapestry needle for the second thread.

*Detached stitches are economical to use as most of the thread remains on the surface of the fabric. Surface satin stitch has been worked on this 19th-century Chinese embroidery.*

# DETACHED FILLING STITCHES

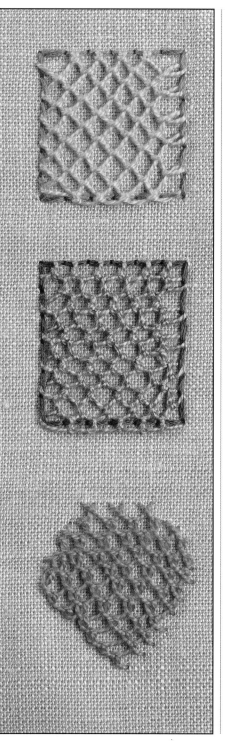

## FANCY BUTTONHOLE FILLING

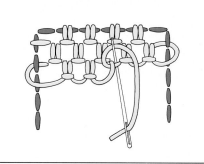

Fancy buttonhole filling is used on the surface of both plain- and even-weave fabric, and also in cutwork. When working it as a surface stitch, outline the shape with back stitches (page 13); for cutwork, arrange buttonhole edging stitches (page 172) around the raw edges.

Bring the needle through just to the left of the top stitch in the left-hand row, then work a buttonhole stitch (page 17) into the top line. Make another buttonhole stitch close to the first one, but this time work it upside-down, as shown. Pull the working thread through the stitch towards you. Repeat along the row, leaving a small loop in between each pair of stitches. Arrange subsequent rows in alternate directions, working each pair of stitches into the loops in the previous row.

## KNOTTED BUTTONHOLE FILLING

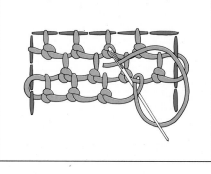

Knotted buttonhole filling is used on the surface of both plain- and even-weave fabric, and also in cutwork. Outline it in the same way as the previous stitch. Bring the needle through just to the left of the top stitch in the left-hand row.

Work a buttonhole stitch (page 17) into the first back stitch in the top row. Work a second buttonhole stitch at an angle over the first stitch, as shown by the needle in the diagram, to make a knot. Pull each knot tight before proceeding to work the next stitch. Work the first row in this way along the back stitch foundation. Work subsequent rows in alternate directions, taking the stitches into the loops in the row above. Secure the final row of stitches by working the loops through the back stitch foundation.

## OPEN BUTTONHOLE FILLING

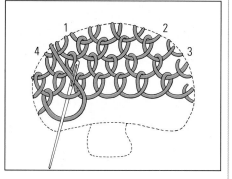

Open buttonhole filling is used mainly as a detached filling on both plain- and even-weave fabric. It can also be used to fill a space in cutwork, but is less successful for this purpose than fancy buttonhole filling or knotted buttonhole filling (left). The stitch has a rather attractive, lacy appearance.

Bring the thread through at the top left of the shape to be covered and make a row of loose buttonhole stitches (page 17), taking the top of each stitch through the fabric, as shown, and picking up a small amount of fabric at the side of the shape. On the return journey, reverse the stitches and work them through the loops in the previous row. Continue in this way, picking up a little fabric when working the bottom row of stitches. Keep the stitches quite small to prevent them from pulling out of shape.

## DETACHED BUTTONHOLE STITCH

Detached buttonhole stitch is used on both plain- and even-weave fabric. It is useful where a raised, solidly stitched shape is needed and should be worked in a firm, twisted thread for the best results.

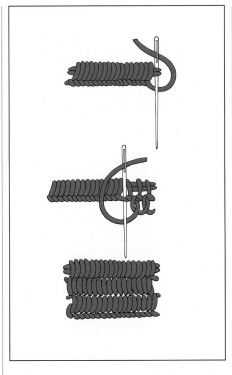

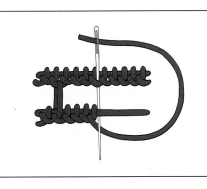

longer stitch over the previous row, as shown. Decorate the shapes of fabric showing through the filling with an isolated stitch such as daisy stitch (page 76) worked in a contrasting or matching thread colour.

## VENETIAN FILLING STITCH

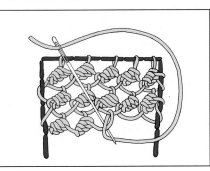

Work two horizontal straight stitches across the top of the shape to be covered, then work a row of ordinary buttonhole stitches (page 17) from left to right over the first stitches without entering the fabric. Arrange the buttonhole stitches closely together. At the end of the row, take the needle through the fabric and bring it out ready to work the next row from right to left. Work subsequent rows of buttonhole stitches into the loops in the row above, as shown. The needle should enter the fabric only at the beginning and end of the rows.

## RICH BUTTONHOLE STITCH

(Also known as loop buttonhole filling stitch.)

Rich buttonhole stitch produces an attractive honeycomb pattern on both plain- and even-weave fabric.

Begin by making a foundation of parallel horizontal straight stitches across the entire shape. Work a row of ordinary buttonhole stitches (page 17) from left to right over the top stitches, without picking up the ground fabric. In subsequent rows, work buttonhole stitches in alternate directions over the straight stitches, but at regular intervals along each row, work a

Venetian filling stitch is an adaptation of a needle-made lace filling and is used on both plain- and even-weave fabric. It has a heavy texture which shows up best when the stitch is worked in a firm thread such as pearl cotton. Use stranded cotton for a softer effect.

Outline the shape with large back stitches (page 13). Work the first row of filling from left to right over the back stitch outline. Make a loose buttonhole loop, as shown, then work a group of four buttonhole stitches (page 17) into it. Continue in this way until the right-hand side is reached, then take the thread behind the back stitch line to anchor it. On the return journey make loose loops in between each group of buttonhole filling (left). Alternate these two rows to fill the shape, taking the thread behind the outline stitches at the end of every row. At the lower edge, pick up the back stitches with the last row of loops.

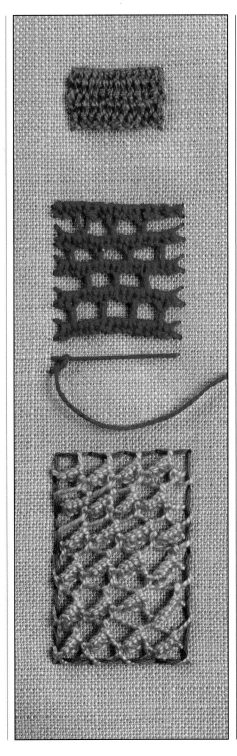

# STRAIGHT AND SLANTED CANVAS STITCHES

**A**ll the stitches in this chapter are made up of straight stitches worked either vertically, horizontally or diagonally across the canvas. They produce a variety of patterned surfaces, many of which are ideal for large shapes and backgrounds. For a flat, smoothly stitched surface, select from twill stitch, Florentine stitch or one of the Gobelin stitch variations. Byzantine stitch, diagonal stitch and Jacquard stitch make zigzag patterns, while mosaic stitch and Hungarian stitch are worked in small, neat blocks.

The majority of these stitches can be worked on single canvas, but some are suitable only for double canvas. Choose the best quality of canvas that you can afford and work with it stretched in an embroidery frame or stretcher for the best results. Select your embroidery threads carefully, and make sure that they are compatible with the size of stitch and gauge of canvas you are using to ensure good canvas coverage. Choice of a suitable thread is particularly important when working on double canvas.

# STRAIGHT AND SLANTED CANVAS STITCHES

## ▮ ALGERIAN EYE STITCH

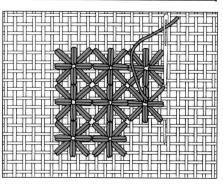

(Also known as star stitch and star eyelet stitch.)

Algerian eye stitch is used only on single canvas. It produces a neat block of stitching with a central hole, rather like a square eyelet. Work the blocks either in diagonal rows, beginning at the top left of the shape to be covered, or downwards in vertical rows. To make a chessboard pattern, leave alternate squares unworked, then fill them with tent stitches (page 125) worked in a contrasting thread colour.

Any type of embroidery thread can be used to work this stitch, providing it is compatible with the gauge of the canvas selected. Use a strong thread on heavy canvas: too fine a thread could snap when the stitches are pulled.

Work Algerian eye stitch over a square of four canvas threads. Begin at any point around the square and work eight pairs of straight stitches into the centre, as shown in the diagram, to make a star shape within the square. Pull the stitches tightly while working them to make the square eyelet at the centre of the block.

## ▮ FLORENTINE STITCH

(Also known as bargello stitch, cushion stitch, flame stitch, Irish stitch and Hungary stitch.)

Florentine stitch is used to work a type of embroidery called Florentine work or bargello which produces a characteristic wavy pattern. It is always worked on single canvas in a selection of toning thread colours or different shades of a single thread colour. Florentine work is often used to cover cushions, chair seats and stool tops. The second diagram shows an alternative, less-known way of working the stitch.

First, work vertical straight stitches, usually

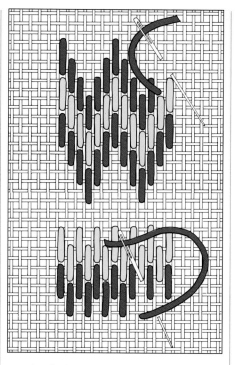

over four horizontal canvas threads, arranged in a step sequence to form zigzag rows. Work subsequent rows of stitches in different colours to fill the canvas above and below the first row, following the contours carefully. The stitching can be varied to create different effects.

## ▮ LONG STITCH

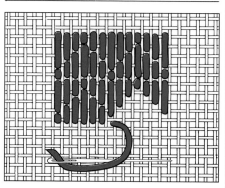

Long stitch is used on single canvas to produce an attractive pattern of triangles arranged in double rows. When worked on a small gauge canvas in an embroidery thread with a sheen such as stranded cotton or silk, the finished

result resembles silk brocade.

Work each row of long stitches in two journeys. On the first journey, work groups of vertical straight stitches of graduated length arranged in triangles, as shown. Reverse the triangles on the second journey, filling in the spaces left on the first journey. For an effective result, use a different shade of the same thread colour for each journey. Work the double row of triangles over five horizontal threads, as shown, or make the row deeper by adding extra graduated stitches to each triangular group.

## ▮ PARISIAN STITCH

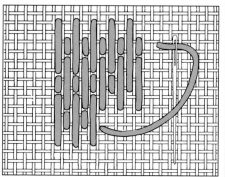

Parisian stitch is used only on single canvas. It produces a smooth surface which is ideal for filling large shapes and backgrounds. This stitch is useful when a gradually shaded area is required: choose close tones of the same thread colour and work the stitching in narrow bands. Any type of embroidery thread can be used, providing it is compatible with the gauge of canvas selected.

Begin at the top and work rows of vertical straight stitches in either direction across the shape to be covered. Alternate long stitches worked over six canvas threads with short stitches worked over two threads, as shown in the diagram. Each row of stitches should interlock and overlap the previous row by two horizontal threads.

## ▮ TWILL STITCH

Twill stitch is used only on single canvas. It is quick to work and produces a diagonal pattern which looks rather like the woven fabric, twill. Use this stitch to fill any size of shape and large background areas when a smooth surface is needed. Wool or cotton threads give equally

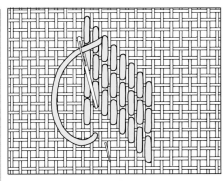

attractive results, but a lustrous stranded cotton or silk enhances the smoothly stitched surface most effectively.

Arrange twill stitch in diagonal rows slanting from top left to bottom right of the shape to be covered. Work rows of vertical straight stitches over three canvas threads, as shown in the diagram. Vary the direction of the rows to produce a different effect.

## ▍DOUBLE TWILL STITCH

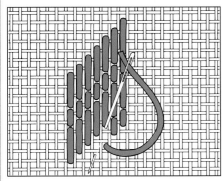

Double twill stitch is a variation of ordinary twill stitch (above) which is also worked only on single canvas. The stitch creates a striking diagonal pattern, and is useful for filling large shapes and backgrounds. Work the rows of stitches in two contrasting or toning thread colours to produce an attractive, diagonally striped pattern.

Arrange this stitch in diagonal rows slanting from top right to bottom left of the shape to be covered. First, work a row of vertical straight stitches over four canvas threads, then work a row of shorter vertical straight stitches over two canvas threads, as shown. Vary the direction of the rows to create a different effect.

MARY THOMAS'S DICTIONARY OF EMBROIDERY STITCHES

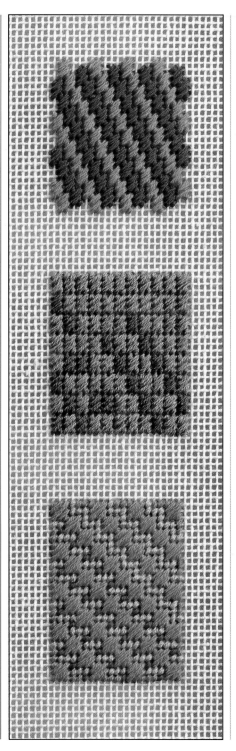

## CASHMERE STITCH

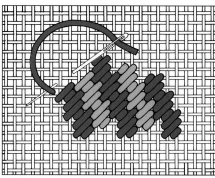

Cashmere stitch is used only on single canvas. It produces a regular pattern with a steep slant, rather like a woven fabric. The stitch is often used for filling large shapes and backgrounds as it is quick to execute and covers the canvas well when the appropriate thread, which matches the canvas gauge, is selected. When worked in more than one thread colour, this stitch makes an attractive striped pattern.

Work this stitch up and down the shape to be covered, beginning at the bottom right-hand corner. Make a short stitch over one intersection of the canvas, then work two stitches over two vertical and two horizontal canvas threads. Repeat along the row, moving the group of stitches one thread to the left, as shown in the diagram.

## STRAIGHT CASHMERE STITCH

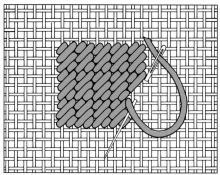

Straight Cashmere stitch is a variation of ordinary Cashmere stitch (above) used on single canvas. The stitch makes a regular pattern of small, rectangular blocks across the canvas. It is quick and easy to work, and is used for filling large shapes and backgrounds. Any type of embroidery thread can be used, but care should be taken to match the weight of thread to the gauge of canvas so that the canvas is completely covered by the stitching.

To work straight Cashmere stitch, begin at the top left of the shape to be covered. Make a block of four diagonal straight stitches, as shown in the diagram. These stitches should cover a rectangle of two vertical canvas threads by three horizontal canvas threads. Work the blocks in either vertical or horizontal rows to cover the shape.

## MOORISH STITCH

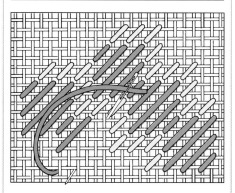

Moorish stitch can be used on both single and double canvas to fill any size of shape. It produces a flat, smoothly stitched surface with an attractive, diagonal zigzag pattern. Moorish stitch is usually worked in two colours of thread to enhance the zigzag pattern. A matt wool thread combined with a shiny, light-reflecting cotton thread provides an extremely attractive effect. Try using strands of Persian or crewel wool with stranded cotton or the heaviest available weight of pearl cotton. Any type of embroidery thread can be used, but care should be taken to match the weight of thread to the gauge of canvas so that the canvas is completely covered by the stitching.

To work Moorish stitch, first make stepped rows of graduated diagonal stitches worked over two, four, six and four vertical and horizontal canvas threads, as shown in the diagram. Work the rows from top left to bottom right of the shape to be covered, then work rows of small diagonal stitches over two vertical and horizontal canvas threads, following the stepped outlines of the first rows, as shown in the diagram.

## DIAGONAL STITCH

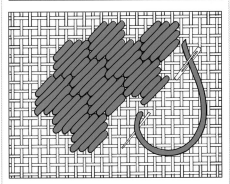

Diagonal stitch is used only on single canvas. The stitch produces a flat, patterned surface with the appearance of a brocaded fabric, and is used for filling large shapes and backgrounds. For an attractive effect, work it in a lustrous, light-reflecting thread such as stranded cotton. Use two or more thread colours to produce a diagonally striped pattern. Arrange back stitches (page 13) worked in a contrasting thread colour in between the rows of diagonal stitches to enhance the stripes.

Work this stitch in diagonal rows from top left to bottom right of the shape to be covered. Make a group of diagonal straight stitches over two, three, four, and three vertical and horizontal canvas threads, as shown in the diagram. Repeat the stitches to form a stepped row. Work each row of stitches to fit into the stepped outline of the previous row.

## BYZANTINE STITCH

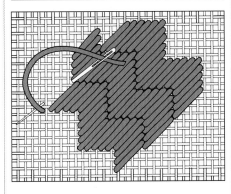

Byzantine stitch is used only on single canvas. It is quick and easy to work and is used for covering large areas and backgrounds. The stitch produces a regular, brocade-like pattern similar to the formal geometric patterns found in Byzantine art. This effect is enhanced when it is worked on a small gauge canvas in a shiny, light-reflecting thread such as stranded cotton. Any type of embroidery thread can be used to work the stitch, but care should be taken to match the weight of thread to the gauge of canvas.

Work groups of five diagonal straight stitches arranged in equally sized steps, as shown in the diagram. Each stitch should cover four vertical and four horizontal canvas threads. Work the stepped rows diagonally across the shape, beginning at the top left. Fill in any small spaces left unworked at the edges of the shape with graduated diagonal stitches.

## JACQUARD STITCH

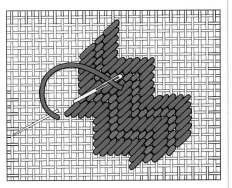

Jacquard stitch is used on both single and double canvas for covering large shapes and backgrounds. Like the previous stitch, Jacquard stitch produces a regular zigzag pattern which looks rather like brocade, but in this case the stitches are shorter. Jacquard stitch is usually worked in more than one colour and weight of thread to create an attractive, diagonally striped zigzag pattern. Any type of embroidery thread can be used, providing it is compatible with the gauge of canvas selected, but a combination of Persian or crewel wool for the first row and stranded or pearl cotton for the second row is very effective.

First, work a row of evenly sized diagonal stitches covering two vertical and two horizontal canvas threads. Arrange the stitches in steps of six. Work a row of tent stitches (page 125), following the stepped outline. Work alternate rows of the two stitches in diagonal rows across the shape to be covered.

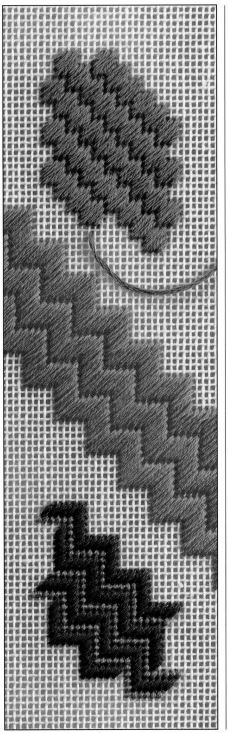

## ▌ HALF CROSS STITCH

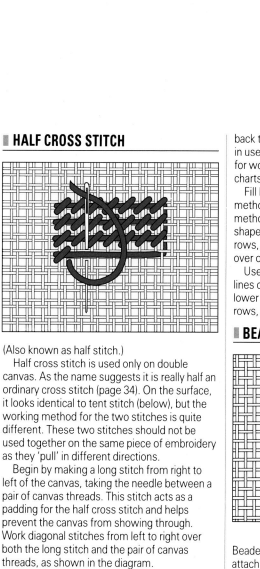

(Also known as half stitch.)

Half cross stitch is used only on double canvas. As the name suggests it is really half an ordinary cross stitch (page 34). On the surface, it looks identical to tent stitch (below), but the working method for the two stitches is quite different. These two stitches should not be used together on the same piece of embroidery as they 'pull' in different directions.

Begin by making a long stitch from right to left of the canvas, taking the needle between a pair of canvas threads. This stitch acts as a padding for the half cross stitch and helps prevent the canvas from showing through. Work diagonal stitches from left to right over both the long stitch and the pair of canvas threads, as shown in the diagram.

## ▌ TENT STITCH

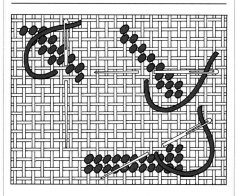

(Also known as needlepoint stitch, petit point, canvas stitch, perlen stitch, cushion stitch and continental stitch.)

Tent stitch is a small diagonal stitch used mainly on single canvas. The stitch can be dated back to the sixteenth century, but was probably in use much earlier. Its small size makes it ideal for working detailed, figurative designs from charts or over designs painted on to canvas.

Fill large shapes by using the diagonal method shown in the first diagrams. This method is less likely to pull the canvas out of shape. Work up and down the shape in diagonal rows, as shown, making small diagonal stitches over one intersection of the canvas.

Use the second method for working single lines or small, isolated shapes. Begin at the lower edge of the shape and work in horizontal rows, as shown in the bottom diagram.

## ▌ BEADED TENT STITCH

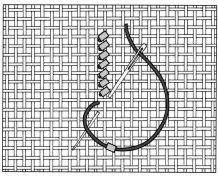

Beaded tent stitch is used as a method of attaching beads to a piece of canvas embroidery. Use this stitch for working details and highlights as a contrast to flat, smooth areas of stitching. Make sure that the thread you use passes easily through the centre of the bead without fraying or breaking.

Work beaded tent stitch downwards in vertical rows. Bring the thread through to the front of the canvas and thread a single bead on to it. Secure the bead to the canvas by working a tent stitch (left).

Choose your beads with care: they should be small enough to sit neatly on the stitched surface. If using larger beads, work ordinary tent stitch alternately with beaded tent stitch to allow extra space for the beads.

*The late-Victorian embroidered tray shown opposite is worked entirely in beaded tent stitch and features an attractive design of a teapot, covered sugar bowl and cream jug.*

125

### FANCY BRICK STITCH

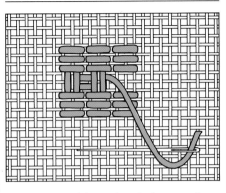

Fancy brick stitch is used on single canvas for filling large shapes and backgrounds. The stitch should be worked in one thread colour or in two shades of a single thread colour for the best result. Use one thread for the blocks and a second thread for the row containing the smaller stitches.

Work in horizontal lines, beginning at the top of the shape to be covered. Work blocks of three horizontal straight stitches over three canvas threads. Arrange the blocks in rows across the shape, as shown. Fill in the spaces left in between the rows of blocks with smaller horizontal stitches worked over two canvas threads and vertical stitches worked over three canvas threads, as shown in the diagram.

### MOSAIC STITCH

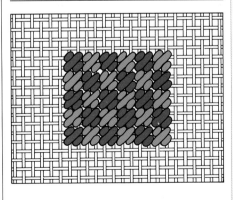

Mosaic stitch is used on both single and double canvas to make a regular pattern of tiny square blocks. It is a delightful stitch to use and can be built up quickly into intricate, multicoloured designs in much the same way as mosaics are created. To keep the mosaic pattern well-

defined, use a thread with a smooth surface such as stranded or pearl cotton.

Each mosaic stitch block consists of a diagonal stitch worked over two vertical and two horizontal canvas threads at the centre of two short diagonal stitches, as shown in the diagram. Stitch the blocks individually when embroidering a multicoloured design. Work the areas in the predominating colour first, then fill in with the remaining colours. To work mosaic stitch in one colour, work each horizontal row of squares in two journeys for the best result. Begin at the top left and work the first short stitch and the long stitch of each block. On the second journey, complete each block by working the remaining short stitch.

### REVERSED MOSAIC STITCH

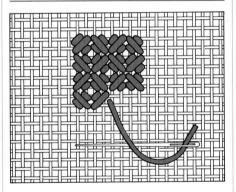

Reversed mosaic stitch is used on single and double canvas. It is a variation of ordinary mosaic stitch (left) which also produces a pattern of small square blocks, but in this case the diagonal stitches slant in the opposite direction on alternate squares.

The light and shade effect created by the slant of the stitches is enhanced when the stitch is worked in a shiny, light-reflecting thread such as pearl cotton. Work the stitch in one colour, as a contrast to raised and textured stitches, or use it to work multicoloured designs in the same way as mosaic stitch.

Each reversed mosaic stitch block consists of a diagonal stitch worked over two vertical and two horizontal canvas threads at the centre of two short diagonal stitches, as shown in the diagram. Work the blocks individually, changing the slant of the stitches on alternate blocks. Complete each block before proceeding to the next one and arrange the blocks in horizontal rows across the canvas.

### REVERSED CUSHION STITCH

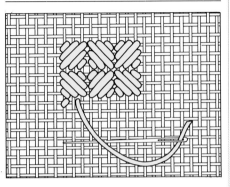

Reversed cushion stitch is a variation of ordinary cushion stitch (page 152) which is worked without the framing of tent stitches. It can only be used on single canvas. The stitch produces a neat pattern of regular square blocks over the canvas and can be used for filling any size of shape and for backgrounds. The varying slant of the stitches produces an attractive light and shade effect. To enhance this effect, use a thread with a sheen such as stranded or pearl cotton. Tapestry or Persian wool also produce good results.

Each reversed cushion stitch block consists of diagonal straight stitches of graduated length worked over a square of three canvas threads. Arrange the blocks in horizontal rows and reverse the slant of the stitches on alternate blocks, as shown in the diagram.

### HUNGARIAN STITCH

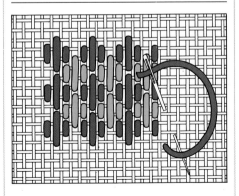

Hungarian stitch is used on both single and double canvas. The stitch produces a pattern of small, diamond-shaped blocks. Work the blocks alternately in two thread colours or arrange

126

them to create intricate geometric patterns in the same way as mosaic stitch (left). To provide a flat, smoothly stitched background, work the stitch in one colour of thread. Experiment with different thread types: mix multiple strands of crewel wool in the needle and use this to stitch alternate blocks; fill in the spaces left in between the blocks with the heaviest available weight of pearl cotton.

Each Hungarian stitch block consists of three vertical stitches worked over two, four and two horizontal canvas threads, as shown in the diagram. Complete each block of stitches before proceeding to work the next one and arrange the blocks in horizontal rows, leaving two vertical threads in between each block. In each row, arrange the blocks to fit into the spaces left in the previous row, as shown. Work the blocks individually when embroidering an intricate design. Stitch the areas in the predominating colour first, then fill in the spaces with the remaining colours.

## ▌DIAMOND STRAIGHT STITCH

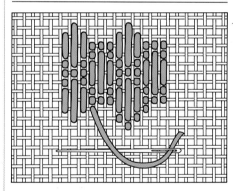

Diamond straight stitch is used only on single canvas. It fills large shapes and backgrounds with a regular pattern of diamond-shaped blocks. Any type of embroidery thread can be used, providing it is compatible with the gauge of canvas selected.

Each block consists of five vertical straight stitches worked over one, three, five, three and one horizontal canvas threads. Work the blocks in horizontal rows across the shape to be covered. Set the blocks alternately in subsequent rows so that each row fits neatly into the row above, leaving an unworked gap of one thread separating the blocks. Fill in the gaps with small vertical stitches, as shown, using the same or a contrasting colour of thread.

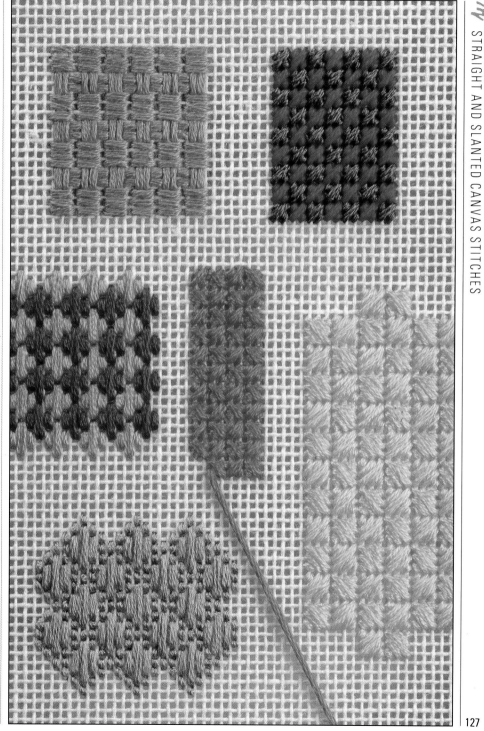

MARY THOMAS'S DICTIONARY OF EMBROIDERY STITCHES

## ▊ GOBELIN STITCH

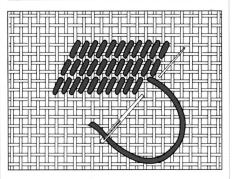

(Also known as oblique Gobelin stitch.)

Gobelin stitch is used only on single canvas. The stitch produces a flat, smoothly stitched surface which is useful when a plain area of embroidery is needed as a contrast to a more textured stitch. Any type of embroidery thread can be used, providing it is compatible with the gauge of canvas selected.

Work rows of small diagonal stitches over one vertical and two horizontal canvas threads. Work the first row from left to right, then return in the opposite direction. Work the second row below the first row in the same way, but this time insert the needle downwards. The stitches must be formed correctly to obtain an evenly stitched surface.

## ▊ ENCROACHING GOBELIN STITCH

(Also known as interlocking Gobelin stitch.)

Encroaching Gobelin stitch is a variation of ordinary Gobelin stitch (above) used on single canvas. The stitch produces a flat, smoothly stitched surface and is excellent for shading and

blending colours over large shapes and backgrounds. Any type of embroidery thread can be used, but care should be taken to match

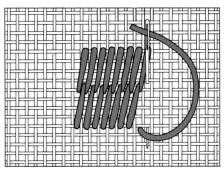

the weight of thread to the gauge of canvas so that the canvas is well covered.

Work this stitch in closely spaced horizontal rows. Begin at the top of the shape to be covered and work the rows in alternate directions. The stitches are longer than ordinary Gobelin stitches: work them over five horizontal canvas threads, and make them slant diagonally across one vertical thread, as shown in the diagram. Arrange each row so that it overlaps the previous row by one horizontal canvas thread, as shown.

## ▊ WIDE GOBELIN STITCH

(Also known as oblique Slav stitch.)

Wide Gobelin stitch is a larger variation of ordinary Gobelin stitch (left), which is used on single canvas. It is quick and simple to execute and produces a smoothly stitched, banded surface which is useful when a plain, flat area of embroidery is needed as a contrast to a raised

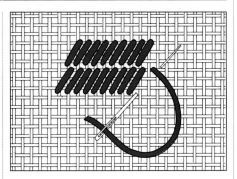

or heavily textured stitch. Any type of thread can be used, but care should be taken to match the weight of thread to the gauge of canvas so that the canvas is completely covered by the stitching. An attractive effect is produced when the stitch is worked in shaded bands: always choose your threads with care, as several close shades of a single colour can often look more effective than a random arrangement of bright colours. Different threads of a similar weight can be used to work alternate bands: experiment by using a shiny, light-reflecting cotton thread such as stranded or pearl cotton with several strands of crewel or Persian wool. A combination such as this enhances the smooth, banded pattern produced by the stitch.

Work wide Gobelin stitch in a similar way to ordinary Gobelin stitch, but in this case give the stitches a greater slant by working them over two vertical canvas threads instead of one. Work rows of diagonal stitches over two vertical and three horizontal canvas threads. Arrange the second row directly below the first row, as shown in the diagram. Working downwards, repeat the two rows until the shape is completely covered by the stitches.

## STRAIGHT GOBELIN STITCH

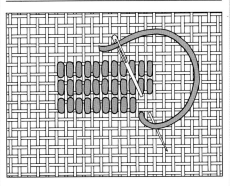

(Also known as upright Gobelin stitch.)

Straight Gobelin stitch is used on single and double canvas. It produces a closely stitched, ridged surface which is ideal for filling small, intricate shapes.

Work this stitch in horizontal rows. Begin at the top of the shape to be covered and work rows of small vertical stitches over two horizontal canvas threads as shown.

To use straight Gobelin stitch on double canvas, work each row in two journeys. Make a long stitch across the canvas from right to left in exactly the same way as for half cross stitch (page 125). Work straight Gobelin stitches from left to right over both the long stitch and the pair of canvas threads.

## PLAITED GOBELIN STITCH

Plaited Gobelin stitch produces an attractive, plaited surface and is used on both single and double canvas. It is a variation of ordinary Gobelin stitch (left) which is quick to work, and is ideal for filling large shapes and backgrounds. Any type of embroidery thread can be used to work plaited Gobelin stitch, but care should be taken to match the weight of thread to the gauge of canvas so that the canvas is completely covered by the stitching.

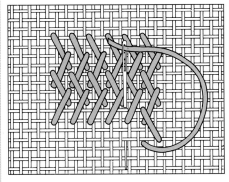

Begin by working the first row of stitches from left to right, taking each stitch over two vertical and four horizontal canvas threads. Work the next row as shown, making the stitches slant in the opposite direction. Arrange the stitches so that they overlap the stitches in the previous row by two vertical and two horizontal canvas threads.

## RENAISSANCE STITCH

Renaissance stitch is used on both single and double canvas. The stitch produces a solidly worked surface of small vertical stitches arranged in horizontal rows. Use this stitch to fill shapes, work intricate details and build up geometric designs in a range of thread colours. Renaissance stitch makes a durable surface

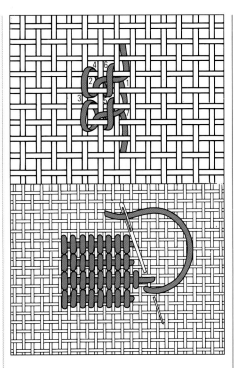

and can be used to cover chair seats and stool tops when worked in tapestry wool. It looks like straight Gobelin stitch (left), but the stitches are worked differently.

Work the stitches in blocks of four, as shown in the first diagram. Begin by working a horizontal stitch over two canvas threads, then work two vertical stitches of the same length over the top. Repeat this stage to make a block of four vertical stitches, as shown. Work the blocks in vertical rows, beginning at the top left of the shape to be covered.

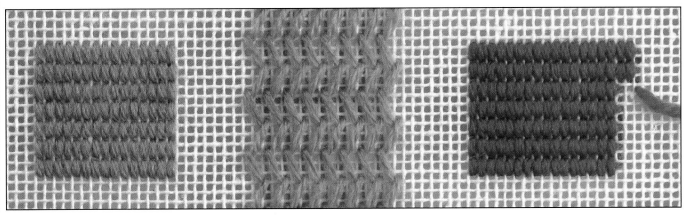

# STRAIGHT AND SLANTED CANVAS STITCHES

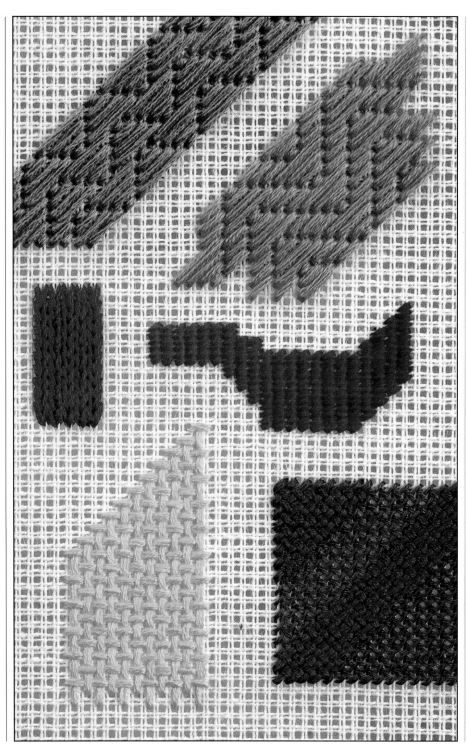

## ▊ MILANESE STITCH

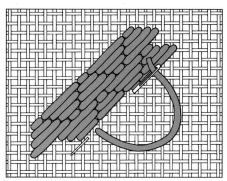

Milanese stitch is used on both single and double canvas. The stitch produces an attractive surface with a triangular pattern and is ideal for working backgrounds. Its brocaded appearance is enhanced when it is worked in a shiny, light-reflecting thread, but a matt wool thread produces an equally attractive result.

Each triangle consists of four stitches of graduated length. Work rows of back stitches diagonally across the shape to be covered, beginning at the top right. In the first row, the stitches are worked alternately over one and four canvas intersections. In the second row, they are worked over two and three intersections, in the third row, over three and two, and in the fourth row, over four and one. Repeat the four rows until the shape is filled.

## ▊ ORIENTAL STITCH

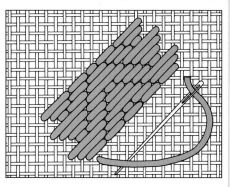

Oriental stitch is a variation of Milanese stitch (above) used on both single and double canvas. The stitch produces a larger pattern than the previous stitch, with the appearance of brocade woven with an attractive zigzag design. Use this stitch to fill large shapes and backgrounds. Any type of embroidery thread can be used, providing it matches the gauge of the canvas.

Work this stitch in the same way as Milanese stitch, using back stitches (page 13) worked in diagonal rows across the shape from bottom left to top right. Follow the sequence of stitches carefully from the diagram. Work subsequent rows in alternate directions across the shape, taking care to keep the pattern correct.

## ▌KNITTING STITCH

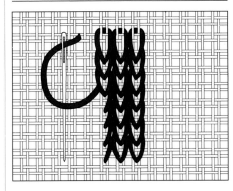

(Also known as tapestry stitch and kelim stitch.)
Knitting stitch is used only on double canvas. It produces a solidly stitched surface and can be worked in various threads to produce different effects. Use a fine thread on a small gauge canvas for working small shapes, or a heavy wool thread on a coarse canvas for filling large shapes and backgrounds.

Work each row in two journeys, beginning at the bottom right. On the first journey, work the right-hand set of stitches, slanting them upwards over two horizontal canvas threads and bringing the needle through in between a pair of threads. Work the second set of stitches downwards with a reverse slant.

## ▌LINEN STITCH

Linen stitch is used on both single and double canvas. The stitch produces a neatly woven surface rather like an even-weave linen fabric and provides an unusual way of covering large shapes and backgrounds. Linen stitch looks equally effective when it is worked in tapestry wool, multiple strands of crewel wool, or soft cotton, providing the weight of thread is compatible with the gauge of canvas selected. Begin at the top right and work a stepped

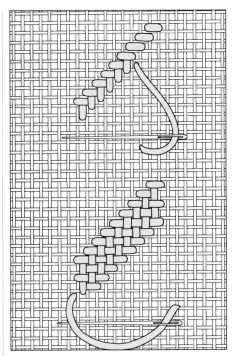

diagonal row of horizontal stitches over two canvas threads. Arrange the next row to interlock with the first, but this time work vertical stitches over two canvas threads. Repeat until the shape is filled.

## ▌REP STITCH

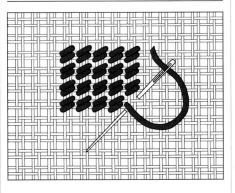

(Also known as Aubusson stitch.)
Rep stitch is used only on double canvas. It is a minute diagonal stitch which produces a ridged texture and is used mainly for working detailed designs and small shapes. The stitch takes its name from a fabric called rep, which

has a similar ridged surface. The stitches in the diagram have been drawn very openly to show their construction, but rep stitch should cover the canvas ground completely.

Work rep stitch downwards, in a similar manner to tent stitch (page 125). Take diagonal stitches over a pair of canvas threads, as shown, working them not only into the usual spaces but also in between the pairs of horizontal canvas threads, as shown, to produce the characteristic appearance.

## ▌WEB STITCH

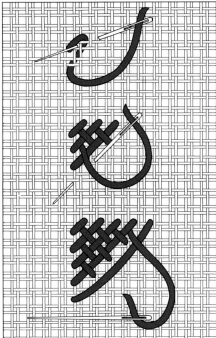

Web stitch is used only on double canvas. It produces a solidly stitched surface and can be used for filling any size of shape or background. It is actually a form of couching (page 23) which consists of long diagonal stitches tied down at regular intervals with short stitches.

Arrange long stitches slanting from bottom left to top right across the shape to be covered. Work the stitches into the normal holes in between the pairs of canvas threads and tie them down at right angles with short crossing stitches worked into the tiny holes at the intersections of the canvas, as shown. Arrange the short stitches alternately in each row.

# CHAPTER NINE

# CROSSED CANVAS STITCHES

**A**ll the canvas stitches in this chapter produce a textured surface of one kind or another. Stitches such as upright cross stitch and plait stitch are worked on a small scale and have a delicate texture, while waffle stitch, double cross and octagonal Rhodes stitch are much larger, with a strongly textured appearance. Select the bolder stitches with care as they can easily overwhelm an area of fine embroidery when used in the same piece of work.

All the stitches can be worked on single canvas, and some are also suitable for double canvas. Choose the best quality of canvas you can afford and work with it stretched in a frame to give the best possible results. Select your embroidery threads carefully, ensuring that they are compatible with the size of stitch and the gauge of canvas you are using. Good coverage of the canvas ground is an important step towards achieving a neat, well-worked piece of embroidery.

# CROSSED CANVAS STITCHES

## ■ PLAIT STITCH

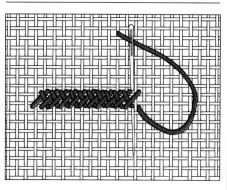

(Also known as Spanish stitch.)

Plait stitch is used on both single and double canvas. It makes a dense, slightly raised and plaited surface, which is similar in appearance to plaited Algerian stitch (right), although the working method is slightly different. This stitch should be worked in a fairly heavy thread, such as tapestry or Persian wool, or several strands of crewel wool, which accentuates the raised surface and ensures adequate canvas coverage. It can be used for outlines, or for filling large areas and backgrounds with a single colour, and it is quick and easy to work.

Work plait stitch in horizontal rows from left to right over two horizontal canvas threads. Make a series of irregular cross stitches, inserting the needle vertically through the canvas, and travelling forwards to make one stitch and then backwards to make the next, as shown in the diagram. The back of the stitch should consist of a row of evenly spaced, single upright stitches. Work the second and subsequent rows directly beneath the first row.

## ■ LONG-ARMED CROSS STITCH

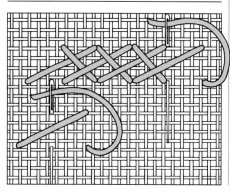

(Also known as long-legged cross stitch, plaited Slav stitch, Portuguese stitch and twist stitch.)

Long-armed cross stitch is usually worked on single and double canvas, but it can also be stitched successfully in a fine thread on an even-weave fabric. Plain-weave fabric is not suitable, as the stitches need to be worked perfectly evenly. The stitch can be used either as a border, or as a textured filling with a pretty, plaited appearance.

Long-armed cross stitch is extremely straightforward to work and looks equally effective on fabric or canvas. Any type of embroidery thread can be used to work it, providing the weight of thread is compatible with the fabric or canvas. If worked on a small scale in pearl or stranded cotton, the effect of long-armed cross stitch is completely different to that created by using a wool thread.

Work long-armed cross stitch in rows from left to right. Begin by working a long diagonal stitch over eight vertical and four horizontal canvas threads, then cross this with a shorter diagonal stitch which spans a square of four canvas threads. Repeat these two stitches along the row. The back of the stitch should consist of single upright stitches spaced at regular intervals.

You can change the size of the stitch to achieve a finer or coarser effect, but keep the proportions correct by working the long stitches over twice the number of vertical threads used for the short stitches.

## ■ GREEK STITCH

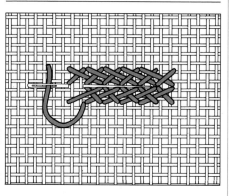

(Also known as Greek cross stitch.)

Greek stitch is used on both single and double canvas. The stitch produces a raised, plaited pattern arranged in horizontal bands, and is ideal for filling large shapes and background areas on canvas with a single colour. It is worked rather like herringbone stitch (page 47), but in this case the stitches are spaced asymmetrically.

Unlike most crossed canvas stitches, Greek stitch is worked from side to side of the shape to be filled, with the long arm of the crosses slanting in the opposite direction on alternate rows. This method of working gives the stitch its characteristic plaited surface. Greek stitch should always be worked in a fairly thick thread, such as tapestry or Persian wool, so that the canvas ground is adequately covered. Multiple strands of crewel wool can also be used.

To execute this stitch, work the first row from left to right by making a series of irregular crossed stitches which are two canvas threads high, as shown in the diagram. Work the second row of stitches in the same way, but this time commence stitching at the right-hand side and work in the opposite direction. Repeat these two rows until the entire area is filled.

## ■ PLAITED ALGERIAN STITCH

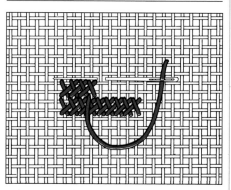

Plaited Algerian stitch is used on both single and double canvas and is worked in a similar way to a fabric stitch, close herringbone stitch (page 47). The stitch produces a dense, plaited surface and is useful for working small areas in a single colour. On the surface, it closely resembles plait stitch (left), but it is more economical, with the working thread forming neat channels of back stitch on the reverse of the canvas. Plaited Algerian stitch looks best when worked on small gauge canvas in a lustrous thread such as coton à broder or the lightest weight of pearl cotton. A different effect is achieved if multiple strands of crewel wool are used in the needle and if the stitch is worked on larger gauge canvas.

To work plaited Algerian stitch, begin at the bottom left of the shape to be filled and work a series of interlocking crossed stitches, as shown in the diagram. Take small horizontal stitches through the canvas at the top and then at the base of the row to make each stitch. Work the second and subsequent rows directly above the first row.

## ▌KNOTTED STITCH

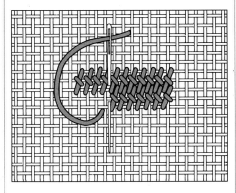

(Also known as pangolin stitch and Persian cross stitch.)

Knotted stitch can be used on either single or double canvas, but the embroidered surface is more hard-wearing when the stitch is worked on the latter. It has a closely packed, ridged appearance with a dense surface. Knotted stitch is very quick and easy to work, and is ideal for filling backgrounds and large areas on cushion covers, chair seats and stool tops, where a durable surface that is subject to heavy daily wear is needed. If using the stitch for this purpose, choose a thread which is mothproof and resistant to fading.

This stitch can be worked in any type of embroidery thread, providing it is compatible with the canvas gauge, but a loosely twisted wool thread such as tapestry or Persian wool gives the best canvas coverage. Stitch alternate rows in a contrasting or toning thread colour to produce an attractive pattern of broken stripes.

Work knotted stitch in horizontal rows from side to side of the shape to be filled. Begin by working a long diagonal stitch over one vertical and three horizontal threads of canvas, then tie this stitch down with a short diagonal crossing stitch, as shown. Arrange the rows so that the stitching overlaps by one horizontal canvas thread, and work the second and subsequent rows directly under the first row.

# CROSSED CANVAS STITCHES

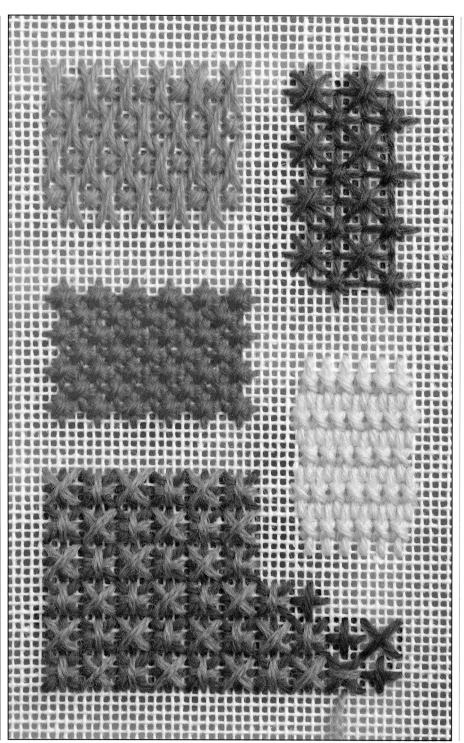

## ▌ DOUBLE STITCH

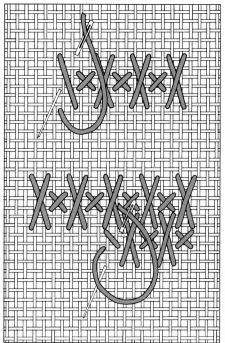

(Also known as alternating cross stitch.)

Double stitch is a neat, slightly textured stitch which is used on single canvas. It makes an ideal background stitch as it is quick and easy to work and covers the canvas ground extremely well. To achieve an unusual speckled effect, double stitch can be worked in two colours. Choose two threads which are close to each other in tone and work the differently sized crosses in two threads over two journeys instead of one.

Any type of embroidery thread can be used for double stitch, but care should be taken to match the weight of thread to the gauge of canvas so that the canvas is adequately covered by the stitching.

To work double stitch, begin by making a row of ordinary cross stitches (page 34) over a square of two canvas threads. Alternate these stitches with oblong cross stitches (page 143), worked over two vertical and six horizontal threads. Arrange the rows of crosses so that they overlap one another by positioning the oblong cross stitches neatly under the ordinary cross stitches in the previous row, as shown in the diagram.

## DOUBLE CROSS STITCH

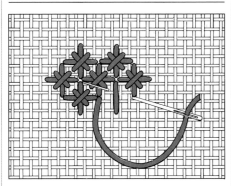

(Also known as double straight cross stitch.)

Double cross stitch is a very decorative stitch used on single canvas. It produces a pattern of raised diamond shapes which have a distinctive, almost crunchy appearance, and it can be used to fill any size of shape and for backgrounds. Any type of embroidery thread can be used to work double cross stitch, but care should always be taken to match the weight of thread to the gauge of canvas to ensure that the canvas ground is completely covered by the stitching.

First, work a large upright cross stitch (page 148) over four vertical and four horizontal canvas threads. Then overstitch this cross with an ordinary cross stitch (page 34) worked over two canvas threads. This completes one diamond. Follow the sequences of stitches shown in the diagram.

Always commence stitching at the top left of the shape to be filled, working the rows of diamonds from left to right and then from right to left across the canvas.

## REVERSED CROSS STITCH

Reversed cross stitch is worked in two journeys on single canvas. The stitch has a dense, closely worked texture and is equally useful for filling any size of shape or for backgrounds. It is made by combining ordinary cross stitch (page 34) with upright cross stitch (page 148).

The first set of stitches can be worked in any type of embroidery thread, but care should be taken to match the weight of thread to the gauge of canvas so that the canvas is well covered by the stitching. The second set of stitches, which is worked on top of the first set, is usually worked in a contrasting colour and

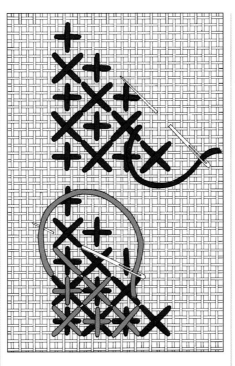

weight of thread, including supple metallic and iridescent synthetic threads. Reversed cross stitch can also be shaded by choosing a selection of threads in graduated colours for the second journey.

Starting at the bottom left of the shape to be filled, work alternate diagonal rows of ordinary cross stitches and upright cross stitches over four vertical and four horizontal canvas threads. Repeat the stitches in reverse sequence on the second journey, working them directly over the first set of stitches, as shown in the diagram.

## STAR STITCH

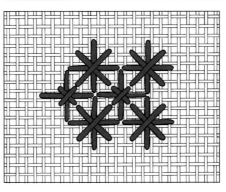

Star stitch is worked in two journeys on single canvas. It makes an attractively textured pattern of star shapes, and can be used to fill any size of shape. If desired, the second journey can be stitched in a contrasting colour and weight of thread to add interest to the work.

Commence working star stitch by making a grid on the area to be filled consisting of upright cross stitches (page 148) which span six vertical and six horizontal canvas threads. Arrange the stitches in horizontal rows, as shown in the diagram, with the four arms of adjacent crosses sharing the same hole in the canvas. On the second journey, overstitch the upright cross stitches with two sizes of ordinary cross stitch (page 34). Use rows of small stitches worked over two canvas threads alternately with larger stitches worked over four canvas threads to achieve the correct result.

## CROSSED GOBELIN STITCH

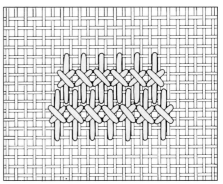

Crossed Gobelin stitch is an adaptation of a pulled fabric stitch, Gobelin filling stitch (page 193), used on single canvas. It has a ribbed surface and can be worked in any type of embroidery thread, but care must be taken to match the weight of thread to the gauge of canvas so that the canvas is adequately covered by the stitching.

To execute crossed Gobelin stitch, work vertical straight stitches over six horizontal canvas threads into alternate holes along the canvas. After each straight stitch is formed, work an ordinary cross stitch (page 34) over the centre before proceeding to work the next stitch. Work the stitches in horizontal rows, from side to side of the shape to be filled. On the second and subsequent rows, overlap the previous row by two horizontal threads, arranging the stitches as shown in the diagram.

# CROSSED CANVAS STITCHES

## PLAITED STITCH

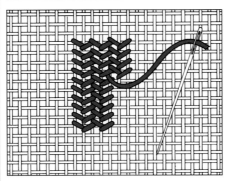

Plaited stitch is used on both single and double canvas. It has an attractive, ridged surface which looks almost plaited and it can be used for filling any size of shape or background. Plaited stitch is worked in a similar way to canvas fern stitch (below), but here the rows of stitches overlap closely, giving the stitch its characteristic interwoven appearance.

Any type of embroidery thread can be used for working plaited stitch, but care should be taken to match the weight of thread to the gauge of canvas so that the canvas is adequately covered by the stitching. A soft wool thread such as tapestry or Persian wool looks most attractive, as well as providing excellent canvas coverage.

To execute plaited stitch, work rows of top-heavy crosses, beginning at the top left of the area to be filled. The top of each cross should span three vertical canvas threads. Arrange the second and subsequent rows so that the stitches overlap those in the previous row, as shown in the diagram.

## CANVAS FERN STITCH

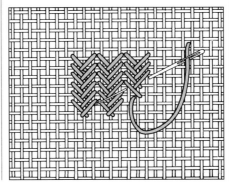

Canvas fern stitch is worked in a similar way to the previous stitch on both single and double canvas. It has a strongly ridged surface, and is useful for filling large shapes and backgrounds. The ridged appearance of this stitch can be accentuated by the use of two or more toning or contrasting thread colours.

Any type of embroidery thread can be used for canvas fern stitch, but care should be taken to match the weight of thread to the gauge of canvas so that the canvas is adequately covered by the stitching.

To work canvas fern stitch, make rows of top-heavy crosses, beginning at the top left of the area to be filled. The crosses should span three vertical and two horizontal canvas threads, and should be worked directly underneath each other. Work the rows side by side across the shape, as shown in the diagram.

## RIDGE STITCH

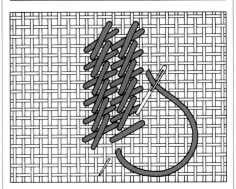

Ridge stitch makes a distinctive, vertically ridged pattern on single canvas. Use this stitch for filling any size of shape or background where a strongly textured effect is required.

Ridge stitch can be striped by using a contrasting or toning colour of thread on every alternate row. The most attractive effect is provided when the stitch is worked in a heavy thread such as tapestry or Persian wool, which covers the canvas well and accentuates the ridged surface of the work.

To work ridge stitch, commence at the left-hand side of the area to be filled and work vertical rows of oblique cross stitches over four vertical and four horizontal canvas threads. On the second and subsequent rows, overlap the previous row of stitches by one vertical canvas thread, as shown in the diagram, so that the rows interlock.

## FISHBONE STITCH

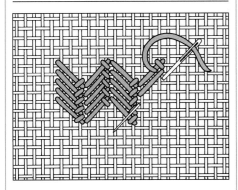

Fishbone stitch is used on both single and double canvas for filling large areas and backgrounds. It makes an attractive chevron pattern and can be worked in more than one colour and texture of thread. Alternatively, fishbone stitch can be worked in two weights of thread, combined in alternate rows with tent stitch (page 125). In this case, position the fishbone stitches so that the long diagonals point in the same direction.

Work vertical rows of diagonal straight stitches over three canvas threads with a short crossing stitch, as shown. Work the rows alternately upwards and downwards, changing the direction of the diagonal stitches to create the chevron pattern.

## DUTCH STITCH

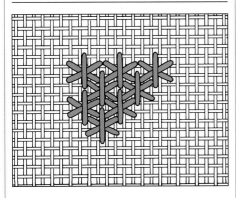

(Also known as Dutch cross stitch.)

Dutch stitch is used on single canvas for filling large shapes and backgrounds. It makes a bold pattern of raised crosses with an attractive texture. The stitch is worked in two journeys and a contrasting thread can be used for the vertical stitches made on the second journey. For an attractive effect, use tapestry or Persian wool for the first set of stitches and a lustrous stranded cotton or silk for the overstitching.

First, work oblong cross stitches (page 143) over the entire area to be filled. Position each cross on its side and work it over four vertical and two horizontal canvas threads. The stitches should fit neatly into each other, as shown in the diagram. In a second journey over the filled area, use the same thread or one of a contrasting colour and weight to overstitch the centre of each cross stitch with a vertical straight stitch worked over four horizontal canvas threads.

## DOUBLE DUTCH STITCH

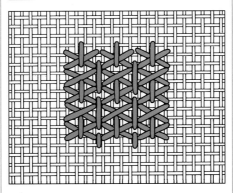

(Also known as double Dutch cross stitch.)

Double Dutch stitch is a variation of the previous stitch worked on single canvas. It makes a textured surface with strong vertical lines and gives better canvas coverage than Dutch stitch. Any type of embroidery thread can be used to work the stitch, but care should always be taken to match the weight of thread to the gauge of canvas.

First, work vertical rows of oblong cross stitches (page 143) over the entire area to be filled, beginning at the top left-hand corner. Position each cross on its side and work it over four vertical and two horizontal canvas threads. Tie down each alternate cross with a vertical straight stitch worked over three canvas threads, as shown in the diagram, so that the tied crosses line up next to each other. In a second journey over the filled area, use the same thread or one of a contrasting colour and weight to work vertical rows of large back stitches (page 13) between the rows of oblong cross stitches.

# CROSSED CANVAS STITCHES

## RHODES STITCH

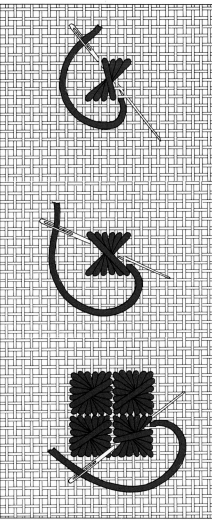

Rhodes stitch is used on single canvas for filling large areas and backgrounds. It makes a pattern of three-dimensional square blocks and can be worked over five, six or more canvas threads. The blocks are arranged in rows and two colours can be used to give a chequerboard effect. Rhodes stitch looks equally effective worked in tapestry or crewel wool, stranded or pearl cotton, but match the weight of the thread to the gauge of the canvas to ensure that the canvas is adequately covered by the stitching.

To work Rhodes stitch, take straight stitches across the block to be filled, following each other in an anti-clockwise direction. Begin by working the first stitch from the bottom left-hand corner to the top right-hand corner. Continue in this way, filling every hole around the square.

When working over an even number of threads, you can also add a short vertical stitch spanning two threads at the centre of the block. On large blocks worked over an even number of threads, work a straight stitch at each corner from the mid-point of one side of the square to the mid-point of an adjacent side, to hold the long stitches in place.

## HALF RHODES STITCH

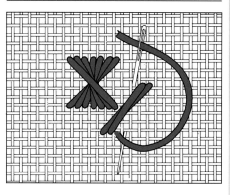

Half Rhodes stitch is a variation of Rhodes stitch (left) worked on single canvas. This stitch is excellent for covering large areas and backgrounds when a textured surface is required and it can be worked in any type of thread. Match the weight of thread to the gauge of canvas to ensure good canvas coverage.

Work vertical rows of half-formed Rhodes stitches over six vertical and six horizontal canvas threads, from left to right across the area to be covered. Begin the first stitch in the same way as for Rhodes stitch and continue stitching across the square in an anti-clockwise direction until all the holes at the top and bottom of the square are filled. Work the subsequent stitches directly underneath until the first row has been completed. For clarity, only the top stitch of the first row is shown in the diagram. Position further rows so that each one interlocks with the preceding one.

This stitch can also be worked in horizontal rows with the edges of the stitches touching. The diamond shapes of unworked canvas left showing in between the stitches can then be filled with tent stitches (page 125).

## PLAITED RHODES STITCH

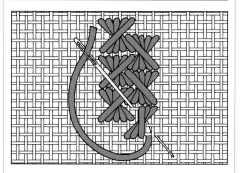

Plaited Rhodes stitch is a variation of half Rhodes stitch (left) used on single canvas. It gives an attractive plaited effect which is shown off to best advantage over a small shape worked in a colourful lustrous thread such as stranded or pearl cotton.

Plaited Rhodes stitch can alternatively be worked in a heavy weight of thread to fill large shapes and background areas where a bold texture is required. Use tapestry wool, or mix multiple strands of crewel wool in the needle to produce a stitched surface with the texture of woven fabric. Always match the weight of thread to the gauge of canvas to ensure that the canvas is adequately covered.

Work each plaited Rhodes stitch over four vertical and four horizontal canvas threads in a similar manner to a half Rhodes stitch. Arrange the stitches in interlocking vertical rows, as shown in the diagram, changing the direction of the stitches on alternate rows from anti-clockwise to clockwise. This change of direction gives the stitch its characteristic plaited effect.

## OCTAGONAL RHODES STITCH

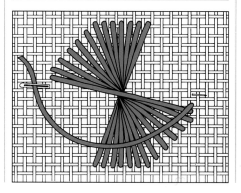

Octagonal Rhodes stitch is a variation of Rhodes stitch (left) used on single canvas to make a raised octagon. Care should be taken when using this stitch, as the pattern created by it is very dominant and may swamp a smaller, more delicate stitch used on the same item.

As in Rhodes stitch, arrange the straight stitches to follow each other in an anti-clockwise direction, crossing at the same central point. Each stitch should span sixteen threads. Follow the sequence of the stitches carefully from the diagram, beginning at the bottom left. Position the blocks so that they touch at the vertical and horizontal edges, leaving squares of unworked canvas which can then be filled with ordinary Rhodes stitch.

## ▉ WAFFLE STITCH

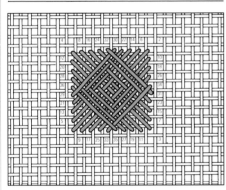

(Also known as Norwich stitch.)

Waffle stitch is a large stitch worked on single canvas to make a bold pattern of square blocks with superimposed raised diamond motifs. Use waffle stitch to fill large shapes and backgrounds, in any type of embroidery thread, but match the weight of thread to the gauge of canvas so that the canvas is completely covered by the stitching. The blocks can be worked over various sizes of square, but they must contain an odd number of canvas threads. The diagram shows a waffle stitch worked over a nine-thread square.

Work diagonal straight stitches across the square, following the sequence shown in the diagram. For this size of square, you will need to work eighteen stitches. Take each stitch over the previous one, until seventeen stitches have been worked. Bring the last straight stitch under the straight stitch it crosses, instead of over the top of it.

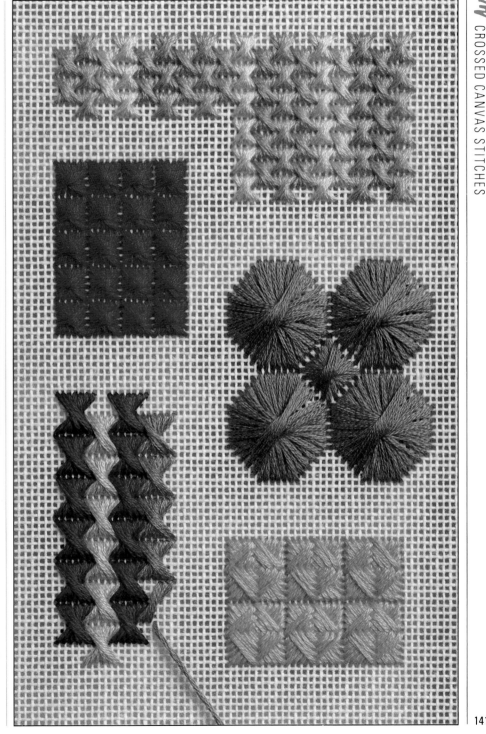

# CROSSED CANVAS STITCHES

## DIAGONAL CROSS STITCH

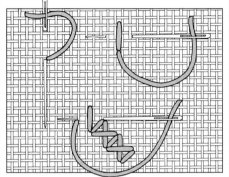

Diagonal cross stitch is an attractive stitch which is used for filling large shapes and background areas on single canvas. The stitch is quite quick to work and covers the canvas ground extremely well. Any type of embroidery thread can be used, providing its weight matches the gauge of the canvas. Worked in two or more colours or weights of thread, this stitch produces an attractive, diagonally striped pattern. Diagonal cross stitch can also be worked as a filling stitch in fine thread on an even-weave fabric.

Position the stitches in diagonal rows from bottom right to top left of the area to be filled, as shown in the diagram. Begin by working an upright cross stitch (page 148) over four vertical and four horizontal canvas threads, then work a short diagonal straight stitch across two of the arms. Repeat this sequence of stitches along the row being covered.

## UNDERLINED STITCH

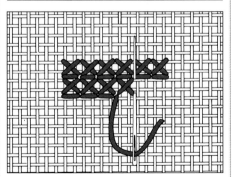

Underlined stitch is used on both single and double canvas to fill any size of shape or background. It is a variation of ordinary cross stitch (page 34) which is equally suited to being worked on canvas or on an even-weave fabric.

Any type of embroidery thread can be used when working the stitch on canvas, but care should be taken to match the weight of thread to the gauge of canvas so that the canvas is completely covered by the stitching. When working underlined stitch on an even-weave fabric, choose a fine thread such as crewel wool, coton à broder or two strands of stranded cotton.

Arrange underlined stitch in horizontal rows from left to right, starting at the top of the area to be filled. Work rows of ordinary cross stitches over two vertical and two horizontal canvas threads, underlining each cross with a horizontal straight stitch before working the next cross stitch. Position the rows of stitches directly underneath one another.

## ▌ITALIAN CROSS STITCH

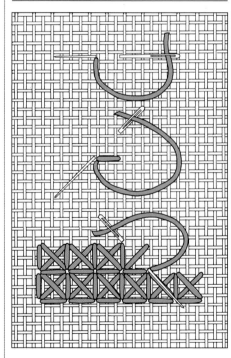

(Also known as two-sided Italian cross stitch, two-sided Italian stitch and arrowhead cross stitch.)

Italian cross stitch is used primarily on canvas, and produces a rather densely worked surface with a close texture. It can be worked on both single and double canvas, but also looks

attractive on an even-weave fabric if a fine thread is used to stitch it. Worked on a loosely woven even-weave fabric, an open effect similar to pulled fabric work (pages 186-205) can be created when the stitches are pulled tightly. The stitch produces an identical result on both sides of the fabric.

Any type of fine embroidery thread can be used when working Italian cross stitch on an even-weave fabric. When stitching it on canvas, care should be taken to choose a loosely twisted thread which matches the gauge of the canvas so that the canvas ground is adequately covered by the stitching.

Work this stitch in rows from left to right, starting at the lower edge of the area to be filled. First, work an ordinary cross stitch (page 34) covering a square of three canvas threads. Then surround the cross with a border of four straight stitches, as shown in the diagram, before proceeding to work the next cross stitch. Position each row of stitches directly above the preceding row.

## ▌MONTENEGRIN STITCH

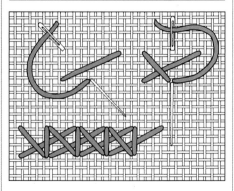

(Also known as Montenegrin cross stitch and two-sided Montenegrin cross stitch.)

Montenegrin stitch is used on both single and double canvas. The stitch is similar in appearance to long-armed cross stitch (page 134) with the addition of vertical bars, and it is formed in a similar way. Worked in the correct sequence, it is reversible, with a regular pattern of ordinary cross stitches (page 34) divided by vertical straight stitches appearing on the reverse of the canvas.

This stitch can also be used on an even-weave fabric as a border or filling, with the stitching worked in a fine thread such as coton à broder. It is quick to work on canvas and can be

used for filling any size of shape, but use a heavy thread to ensure good coverage of the canvas ground.

Work Montenegrin stitch in horizontal rows, starting each row at the left-hand edge of the area to be filled. Begin by working a long diagonal stitch over eight vertical and four horizontal canvas threads, then cross this with a diagonal stitch spanning a square of four canvas threads. Next, work a vertical straight stitch, as shown in the diagram. Repeat these stitches along the row. Position the rows of stitches directly underneath one another.

## ▌OBLONG CROSS STITCH

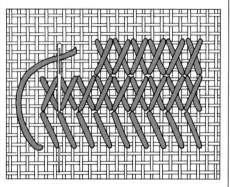

(Also known as long cross stitch, economic long cross and Czar stitch.)

Oblong cross stitch is a variation of ordinary cross stitch (page 34) used on both single and double canvas. The two stitches are made in the same way, but here the stitches are elongated. Use oblong cross stitch for working straight outlines and wide borders, and for filling large areas. It is quick to work and produces an attractive, ridged surface.

Any type of embroidery thread can be used to work oblong cross stitch, but care should be taken to match the thread to the gauge of canvas, particularly when using double canvas, so that the canvas is adequately covered by the stitching.

This stitch can be worked over four, six or more horizontal canvas threads, but it is usually kept at the width shown in the diagram. Work each row of stitches in two journeys. On the first journey, work one set of diagonals from right to left across the shape, as shown. Complete the crosses by working in the other direction. Position each row of stitches directly under the preceding row.

# CROSSED CANVAS STITCHES

## ▌LEVIATHAN STITCH

## ▌DOUBLE LEVIATHAN STITCH

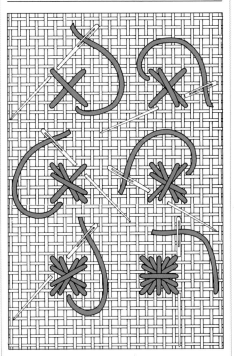

(Also known as double cross stitch, Smyrna cross stitch and railway stitch.)

Leviathan stitch is used on single canvas to fill any size of shape or background. It produces a neat, raised pattern of square blocks which can be worked in more than one colour or weight of thread, giving a chequerboard effect.

Work leviathan stitch in tapestry wool to produce a durable surface suitable for covering cushions, stool tops, chair seats and other areas that are subject to heavy wear. Where a less hard-wearing surface is required, for the background of a picture, for example, use any type of embroidery thread, taking care to match the weight of thread to the gauge of canvas to ensure that the canvas is adequately covered by the stitching.

Work leviathan stitch in horizontal rows from right to left, beginning at the lower edge of the shape to be filled. First, work an ordinary cross stitch (page 34) over four vertical and four horizontal canvas threads. Then work an upright cross stitch (page 148) of the same size directly over the top. Repeat the two stitches along the row. Position each row of stitches directly above the preceding row.

Double leviathan stitch is used on single canvas and is a complex variation of leviathan stitch (left). The stitch makes a large, highly raised pattern of square blocks which can look almost three-dimensional when worked in a shiny, light-reflecting thread such as pearl or stranded cotton. Like ordinary leviathan stitch, the double version can be worked in more than one colour to produce a chequerboard design. This stitch is also suitable for covering chair seats and stool tops when worked in tapestry wool.

Begin by working a large cross stitch (page 34) over a square of four canvas threads. Work a series of crossing stitches over the top, following the sequence shown and finishing with an upright cross stitch (page 148). The sequence of stitches shown in the diagram should be followed carefully to ensure that the correct result is achieved.

*The two types of leviathan stitch both produce raised surfaces which contrast well with smooth stitches. The embroidery shown on the right illustrates this contrast of texture.*

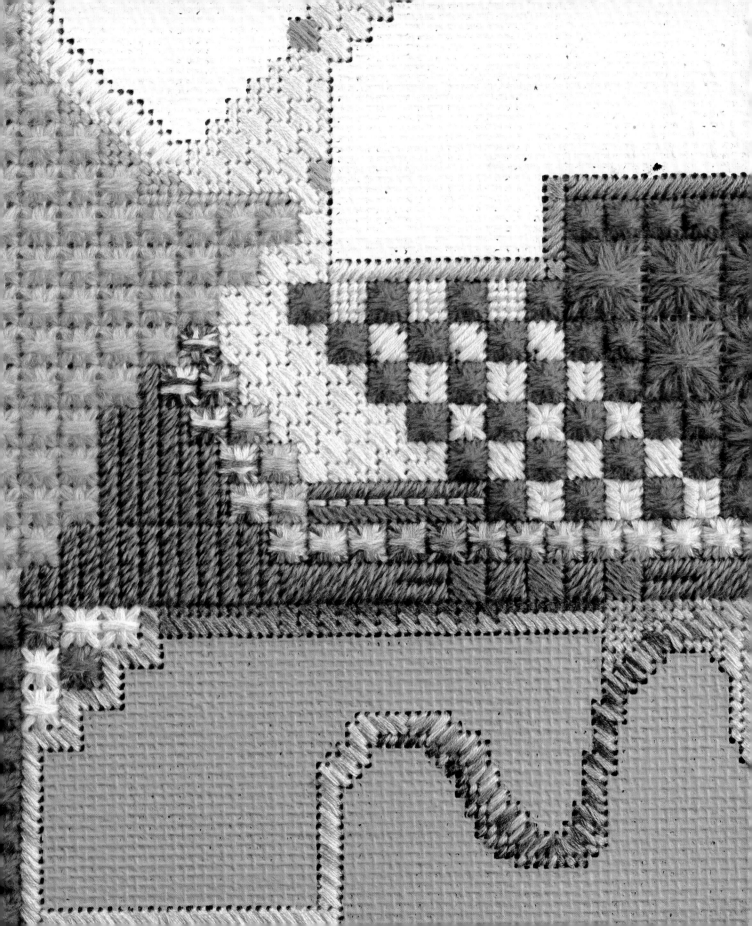

# CROSSED CANVAS STITCHES

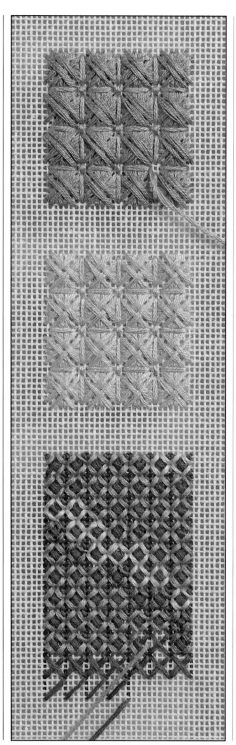

## DOUBLE CROSS

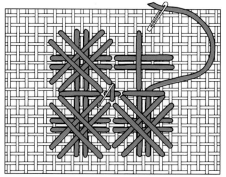

Double cross is used on single canvas to produce a distinctive pattern of raised square blocks. Choice of a suitable thread and gauge of canvas is important; the stitch should preferably be worked on a small scale, since its effect can be rather dominant. Each block covers a square of seven canvas threads and is worked in two journeys.

First, cross the square with two horizontal and two vertical straight stitches to make an upright cross. Work a second cross over this, made up of four diagonal straight stitches, the first two running from top right to bottom left and the remaining two in the opposite direction. Complete all these blocks on the first journey, then frame them with vertical and horizontal straight stitches. Work a tiny upright cross stitch (page 148) over two canvas threads where the corners of the blocks meet.

## PLAITED DOUBLE CROSS

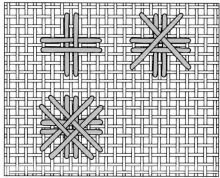

Plaited double cross is a variation of double cross (above) which makes a similar pattern of raised blocks, but with a woven effect. Both stitches are worked in a similar way, with two journeys needed to work the blocks and the framework of straight stitches. The difference lies in the arrangement of the stitches which make up the blocks.

As with double cross, this stitch should preferably be worked on a small scale because of its dominant effect. Care should be taken to match the weight of thread to the gauge of canvas so that the canvas ground is completely covered by the stitching.

Begin by working two horizontal and two vertical straight stitches over a seven-thread square. Plait the stitches over and under each other, following the sequence shown in the diagram, then work the sequence of four diagonal straight stitches, as shown. Work all the blocks on the first journey, then frame them with straight stitches worked in a matching or contrasting thread. To complete the stitch, work a tiny upright cross stitch (page 148) where the corners of the blocks meet.

## RICE STITCH

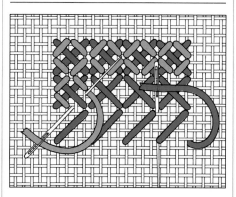

(Also known as crossed corners cross stitch and William and Mary stitch.)

Rice stitch is used on single or double canvas and covers the canvas ground well. It is suitable for any size of shape and for backgrounds, and is often worked in two thicknesses of thread, usually a heavy thread for the large crosses and a fine one for the corner stitches.

Begin by covering the area to be filled with large cross stitches (page 34) worked over four vertical and four horizontal canvas threads, as shown at the bottom of the diagram. Then work small diagonal stitches over each corner at right angles to the arms of the cross. Position each row of rice stitches directly under the preceding row.

## TRIPLE RICE STITCH

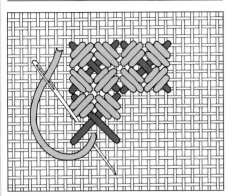

Triple rice stitch is used on either single or double canvas. It is worked in a similar way to ordinary rice stitch (left) but gives a heavier effect. The stitch can be worked in one or more colours and is excellent for filling large shapes and backgrounds.

Any type of embroidery thread can be used for working this stitch, providing that it is compatible with the gauge of the canvas. However, a thread with a sheen such as stranded cotton enhances the light and shade effect created by the slant of the stitches.

Begin by covering the area to be filled with large cross stitches (page 34) worked over six vertical and six horizontal canvas threads. Then work three graduated diagonal stitches over each corner at right angles to the arms of the cross. Position each row of stitches directly under the preceding row. The cross stitch can be made larger, with more diagonal stitches at the corners; it is then known as multiple rice stitch. Work alternate diagonal stitches in contrasting colours of thread to give a pretty, striped effect.

## CAPTIVE RICE STITCH

(Also known as framed rice stitch and boxed rice stitch.)

Captive rice stitch is a variation of rice stitch (left) which can be used on both single and double canvas. It makes a strong geometric pattern with a distinctive texture. The stitch can be worked in either one or several different colours of thread and it is useful for filling large areas and backgrounds.

Any type of embroidery thread can be used to work captive rice stitch, but take care to match the weight of thread to the gauge of canvas so

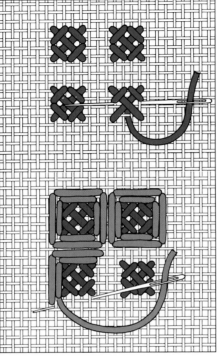

that the canvas is completely covered by the stitching. This stitch benefits from being worked on canvas stretched taut in an embroidery frame. Although not essential, using a frame helps to keep the stitches perfectly regular and prevents the canvas ground from pulling out of shape.

Captive rice stitch can look very effective when the framing straight stitches are worked in a different colour and weight of thread to that used for the rice stitches. Experiment by mixing lustrous stranded silk or pearl cotton with soft cotton or several strands of crewel wool on a medium gauge canvas.

Work each stitch over a square of six canvas threads. Begin by working an ordinary rice stitch over four threads, then surround it with a frame of straight stitches. Make the frame by working four straight stitches around the rice stitch, sharing the same holes, then work four more stitches over six threads. Arrange the stitches side by side, as shown in the diagram, leaving a small gap of canvas showing at the point where the corners of four stitches meet. This is usually left unworked, but it can be filled by an ordinary cross stitch (page 34) worked in the same thread.

# CROSSED CANVAS STITCHES

## ▌UPRIGHT CROSS STITCH

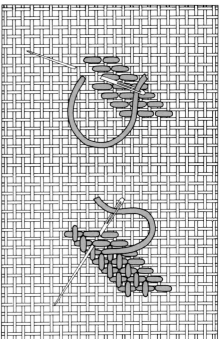

Upright cross stitch is worked on both single and double canvas. It creates a closely worked surface with an attractive, almost crunchy texture. It is a useful stitch for filling small shapes and details because of the tiny scale of each stitch, which is worked over two vertical and two horizontal canvas threads. Any type of embroidery thread can be used for upright cross stitch, but care should always be taken to match the weight of thread to the gauge of canvas so that the canvas ground is completely covered by the stitching.

Worked in a durable thread such as tapestry wool, this stitch produces a hard-wearing surface suitable for covering cushions, stool tops, chair seats and other areas that are subject to a considerable amount of daily wear. Upright cross stitch also looks very effective when it is worked in a fine thread on an even-weave fabric. Choose coton à broder, stranded cotton or a delicate linen thread.

Work upright cross stitch diagonally in two journeys, stitching from bottom right to top left of the shape to be filled, and then back in the opposite direction. Work horizontal stitches over two canvas threads on the first journey, then cross them with vertical stitches of the same length on the second journey, as shown in the diagram. To work upright cross stitch across a very small shape, work each of the crosses individually.

## ▌WOVEN CROSS STITCH

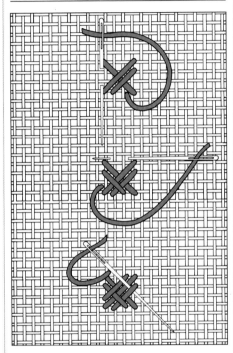

(Also known as plaited cross stitch.)

Woven cross stitch is used on both single and double canvas to make an unusual pattern of neat square blocks with a textured, almost woven appearance. It can be used for large shapes and backgrounds where a geometric effect is required.

This stitch can be worked in two contrasting or toning shades of thread, with the blocks arranged to make a chequerboard design. A further contrast of colour, weight and texture can be introduced by framing each woven cross stitch with a border of back stitches (page 13) worked in a contrasting thread.

Any type of embroidery thread can be used to work woven cross stitch, but take care to match the weight of thread to the gauge of canvas so that the canvas ground is completely covered by the stitching.

Work the blocks in horizontal rows, starting at the lower edge of the shape to be filled. First,

work a large ordinary cross stitch (page 34) over four vertical and four horizontal canvas threads. Overstitch the cross with four diagonal straight stitches, which should be woven over and under each other as they are worked. Follow the weaving sequence shown in the diagram. Position each row of stitches directly above the preceding row.

## ▌BROAD CROSS STITCH

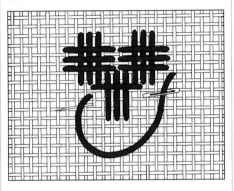

Broad cross stitch is used on single canvas for filling large shapes and makes a raised geometric pattern which is quite bold and striking in appearance. It is a quick and easy stitch to work.

To execute broad cross stitch, first take three vertical straight stitches across a six-thread square, then cross them with three horizontal stitches of the same length. Work the blocks in horizontal rows, beginning at the top left-hand corner of the shape to be filled. Fit the subsequent rows of blocks into the spaces at the bottom of the preceding row, as shown in the diagram.

## ▌BROAD DIAGONAL CROSS STITCH

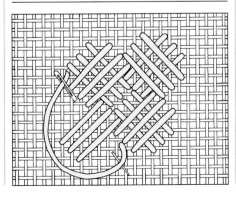

Broad diagonal cross stitch is an attractive and useful stitch which can be used on single canvas for filling large shapes and backgrounds. It produces a raised surface with a strong diagonal feel. The stitch is worked in a similar way to broad cross stitch (left), but here the blocks which make up each stitch are arranged on the diagonal.

Any type of embroidery thread can be used to work the stitch, but care should always be taken to match the weight of thread to the gauge of canvas so that the canvas is adequately covered by the stitching.

Stitch each block over a square of seven canvas threads. First, work three straight stitches slanting from bottom left to top right, crossing them with three stitches of identical length. Interlock the blocks of stitches as shown in the diagram.

## ▌QUICK STITCH

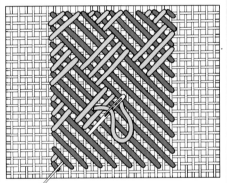

Quick stitch is used on single canvas. It covers the canvas extremely rapidly with a diagonally woven pattern and is an adaptation of an embroidery technique used on fabric called laidwork. Quick stitch should not be worked on an item which will be subject to heavy daily wear, such as a cushion cover or chair seat, as the stitches are long and will soon snag and look untidy.

Take care to select an embroidery thread which will cover the canvas adequately, and first work a small sample to test the compatibility of the thread with the canvas.

Begin by working long stitches diagonally from top left to bottom right across the area to be filled. These stitches follow the canvas intersections closely. Cross the long stitches at right angles with groups of three diagonal stitches, as shown in the diagram.

# CHAPTER TEN

# COMPOSITE CANVAS STITCHES

The stitches described in this chapter produce decorative, highly patterned surfaces on canvas. Some, like quodlibet stitch, perspective stitch and vault stitch, create strong, boldly textured patterns across the canvas and are excellent for filling large areas. Others, such as tweed stitch, rapid stitch and compact filling stitch, are much smaller, with a neat appearance. This chapter also includes three interesting stitches which form dense, three-dimensional piles that can be sculpted with a sharp pair of scissors.

All composite canvas stitches are quite easy to work despite their complex appearance. Study the working instructions and diagrams in detail and work a small test sample on a spare piece of canvas when using a stitch for the first time. Always choose the best quality of canvas and work with it stretched in a frame to keep the tension of the stitches even. Select your embroidery threads with care to ensure that the canvas is adequately covered by the stitching.

# COMPOSITE CANVAS STITCHES

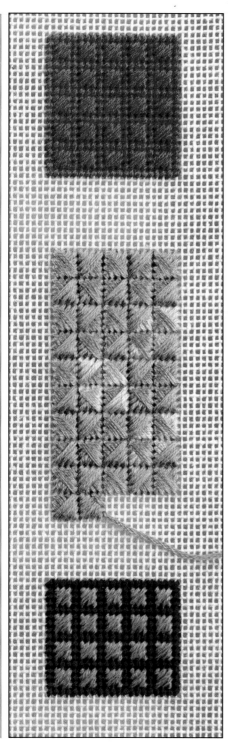

## CUSHION STITCH

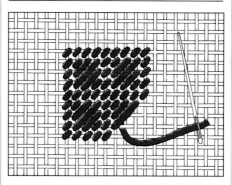

Cushion stitch is used on single canvas to produce a stitched surface which looks like woven or brocaded fabric. It makes a neat, geometric pattern across the canvas and is ideal for filling large shapes and backgrounds. Any type of embroidery thread can be used, providing its weight is compatible with the gauge of canvas selected. However, the embroidered surface looks most effective when the stitch is worked in a thread with a sheen such as pearl or stranded cotton. Work the stitch in two journeys, using the same thread for each journey.

First, work blocks of five graduated diagonal stitches over three vertical and three horizontal canvas threads. Slant all the stitches in the same direction and leave a gap of one canvas thread around each block. On the second journey, work a border of tent stitches (page 125) slanting in the same direction around the blocks. If preferred, the blocks of long stitches can be worked closely together without the border of tent stitches.

## CROSSED CORNERS CUSHION STITCH

Crossed corners cushion stitch is a variation of ordinary cushion stitch (above) worked on single canvas. The stitch produces a neat, geometric pattern of square blocks across the canvas and fills large shapes and backgrounds quickly and easily.

Any type of embroidery thread can be used, but care should be taken to match the weight of thread to the gauge of canvas so that the canvas is completely covered by the stitching. A lustrous thread such as stranded cotton enhances the light and shade effect created by the varying direction of the stitches.

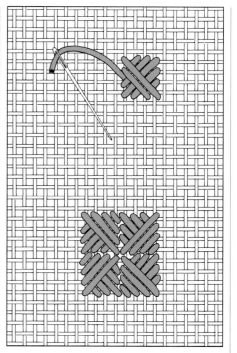

Work seven diagonal stitches of graduated length over a square of four canvas threads, then work three diagonal stitches over one half of the block, as shown in the diagram. Arrange the blocks either as shown, or alternately, so that the overstitched corners meet to form a diamond shape.

## SCOTTISH STITCH

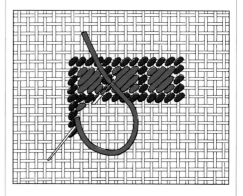

Scottish stitch is worked on single canvas in two contrasting colours of thread. The stitch makes a regular pattern of square blocks set within a trellis and is worked in the same way as cushion stitch (left). Use a combination of a lustrous cotton thread and a matt wool thread for the most effective result.

First, work blocks of five graduated diagonal stitches over three vertical and three horizontal canvas threads. Slant all the stitches in the same direction and leave a gap of one canvas thread around each block. On the second journey, work a border of tent stitches (page 125) in a contrasting colour slanting in the same direction around the blocks.

## ▌CHEQUER STITCH

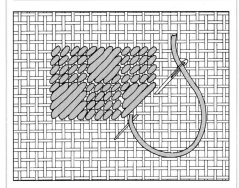

Chequer stitch is used only on single canvas. The stitch looks rather like brocade, and is often worked in one colour as a filling for backgrounds. The brocade effect is enhanced if the stitch is worked in a lustrous, light-reflecting thread such as stranded cotton or silk. Two colours of tapestry, Persian or crewel wool can alternatively be used to produce an attractive chessboard pattern.

Work blocks of stitches over four vertical and four horizontal canvas threads. Alternate blocks of sixteen tent stitches (page 125) with blocks of diagonal stitches, as shown, making all the stitches slant in the same direction. Work the blocks in diagonal rows from top left to bottom right of the shape to be covered.

## ▌FOLIAGE STITCH

Foliage stitch is used only on single canvas. The stitch produces a neat pattern of square blocks which look like tiny diagonal leaves, and can be used to fill any size of shape or background. It is quick to work and covers the canvas ground extremely well. Use a soft wool thread such as Persian wool for the best result. Work each block of stitches over four vertical and four

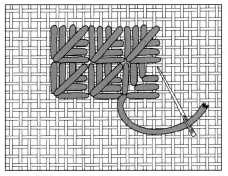

horizontal canvas threads and repeat the blocks in horizontal rows. Make three vertical and three horizontal straight stitches of graduating length, as shown in the diagram. Work a long diagonal stitch over the block from bottom left to top right. The diagonal stitch makes the central vein of the leaf.

## ▌RAY STITCH

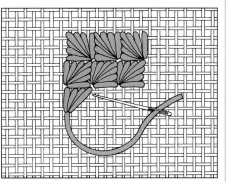

(Also known as fan stitch.)

Ray stitch makes a regular pattern of square blocks on single canvas. The stitch is usually worked over a square of three canvas threads, as shown in the diagram, and makes an effective filling for small shapes. To make the pattern larger, work the blocks over six or eight canvas threads and add further stitches.

Work seven straight stitches radiating from the same hole at the bottom right-hand corner of the square. Pull the stitches quite tightly to make a hole at the corner of the block. Arrange the blocks in horizontal rows and reverse the direction of the stitches in alternate rows. To vary the effect, work all the stitches in one direction, or work diagonally facing pairs of blocks into the same central hole.

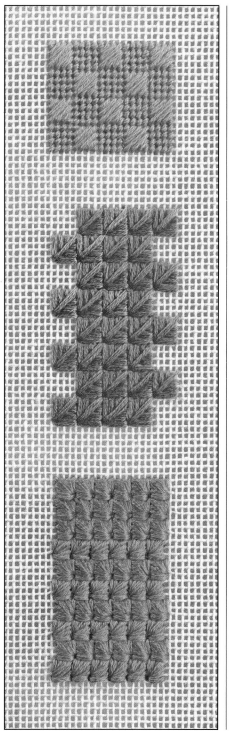

# COMPOSITE CANVAS STITCHES

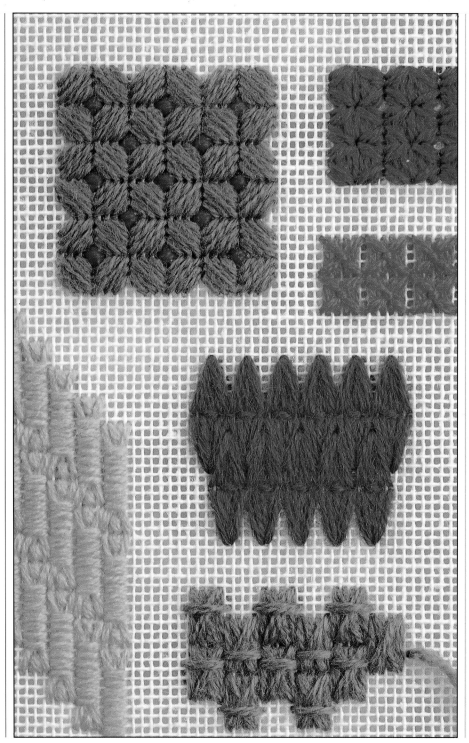

## ▌ BRIGHTON STITCH

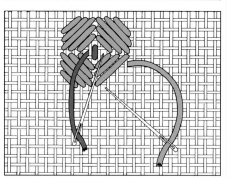

Brighton stitch makes an attractive, geometric pattern when embroidered in two thread colours on single canvas. The stitch is normally worked in tapestry or crewel wool to produce a strongly patterned background, but it looks equally effective when stitched on a small gauge canvas in a thread with a sheen like coton à broder or the finest available weight of pearl cotton. Make sure that the weight of thread matches the gauge of canvas.

To execute Brighton stitch, work blocks of five diagonal stitches of graduated length. Arrange the blocks in rows, as shown in the diagram, changing the direction of the slant in alternate rows. Each new row of blocks should be the mirror image of the row above to achieve the correct effect. After the blocks have been worked right across the shape, work a St George cross stitch (page 86) in a toning or contrasting thread colour in the gap in between each block, as shown in the diagram.

## ▌ ENGLISH STITCH

English stitch is a fairly new stitch used on single canvas. It produces a bold, textured surface of rectangular blocks and is ideal for filling large shapes and backgrounds. Any type of embroidery thread can be used, but care should be taken to match the weight of thread to the gauge of canvas so that the canvas is completely covered by the stitching.

Work this stitch in vertical or horizontal rows, depending on your preference. Each rectangular block covers six vertical and four horizontal canvas threads. The blocks can be made larger, but they should always be worked over an even number of canvas threads. Begin by working five vertical straight stitches to fill

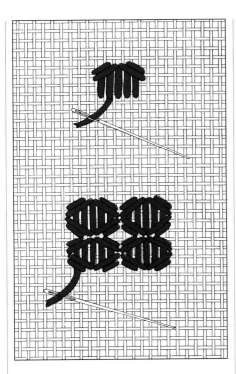

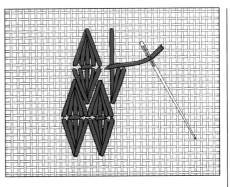

stitches and another for both the cross stitch and the short horizontal stitch.

First, work a block of four vertical straight stitches over four horizontal canvas threads. Work an ordinary cross stitch (page 34) spanning four threads over this block. Make sure that the top diagonal stitch crosses from bottom right to top left. Finally, anchor the cross at the centre with a short horizontal stitch worked over the middle thread of the canvas.

### ▌SPRING STITCH

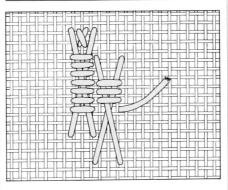

(Also known as coil stitch.)

Spring stitch produces an attractive pattern of springs on single canvas and is ideal for filling large areas and backgrounds.

Each spring stitch is worked over a rectangle of three vertical and twelve horizontal canvas threads. First, work a large oblong cross stitch (page 143) spanning the rectangle. Work seven horizontal straight stitches over the cross, as shown. Arrange the stitches in diagonal rows, working from top left to bottom right of the area to be covered. Position the rectangles in each row three threads lower than those in the preceding row. Finally, work small oblong cross stitches at each end of the springs on a separate journey.

### ▌QUODLIBET STITCH

Quodlibet stitch is used only on single canvas. The stitch covers large shapes and backgrounds with a double-pointed arrowhead pattern.

First, work a long vertical stitch over twelve canvas threads, then work four diagonal stitches over six threads radiating from the same hole to form the lower arrowhead. Anchor the long stitch with a short horizontal stitch before proceeding to make the upper

arrowhead in the same way. Arrange the stitches in horizontal rows across the canvas, interlocking each row with the preceding row, as shown in the diagram.

### ▌GATE STITCH

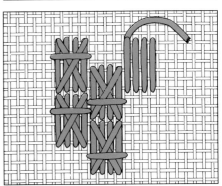

Gate stitch is used only on single canvas. The stitch produces a pattern of rectangular, textured blocks which are set with a half drop. It is quick and easy to work, and is used to fill large shapes and backgrounds. The stitch looks most effective when worked in a soft, thick thread such as tapestry or Persian wool.

Each gate stitch spans five vertical and six horizontal canvas threads. First, work four vertical straight stitches, as shown. Work an elongated ordinary cross stitch (page 34) over these stitches. To finish the block, work a horizontal crossing stitch over five threads, placing it two threads from the top or from the bottom. Fill the shape to be covered by working the stitch in vertical rows, dropping the blocks in the second and subsequent rows by three threads. Position the crossing stitches alternately at the upper and lower ends of the blocks, as shown in the diagram.

the rectangle. Work two diagonal stitches of different lengths across each corner, as shown in the diagram, before proceeding to work the next block.

### ▌PINEAPPLE STITCH

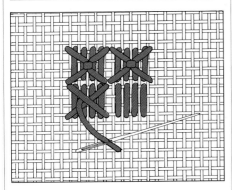

Pineapple stitch is worked only on single canvas. It produces a regular pattern of textured blocks which look rather like the outside of a pineapple. The stitch is quick and easy to work and is suitable for covering large shapes and background areas. It can be worked in two thread colours: use one thread for the straight

# COMPOSITE CANVAS STITCHES

## ■ PERSPECTIVE STITCH

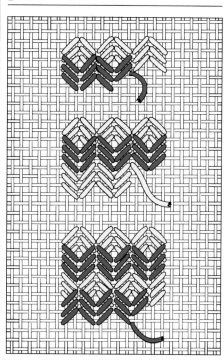

Perspective stitch is used only on single canvas. It produces a strong, three-dimensional pattern which is usually worked in two shades of the same thread colour. Care should be taken when using this stitch, as the pattern created by it is dominant enough to overwhelm more subtle stitches used on the same item. The stitch can either be worked on a small scale in stranded cotton, or on a larger scale in a heavy thread such as tapestry or Persian wool.

Work one complete pattern in four journeys. On the first journey, work groups of three diagonal stitches from left to right over two vertical and two horizontal canvas threads. Alternate the slant of the stitches, as shown. Work the remaining three journeys in the same way, but reverse the direction of the stitches on the second and fourth journeys, as shown in the diagram, overlapping the stitches over those in the previous row.

## ■ BROAD STEM STITCH

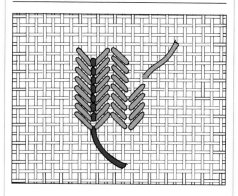

(Also known as canvas stem stitch.)

Broad stem stitch is used on both single and double canvas. In spite of its name, it is not a variation of the stem stitch used on fabric. This stitch produces an attractive, ridged surface, and can be used either as a border, or in multiple rows to fill any size of shape.

A lustrous, light-reflecting thread such as pearl or stranded cotton enhances the light and shade effect created by the varying direction of the stitches. Broad stem stitch combines well with canvas fern stitch (page 138): work the

two stitches in alternate rows in two different thread colours.

Work this stitch in two journeys. First, work two vertical rows of diagonal stitches over two vertical and two horizontal canvas threads. Arrange the stitches to form V-shapes. Finish by working a row of back stitches (page 13) down the centre of the row.

## ■ COMPACT FILLING STITCH

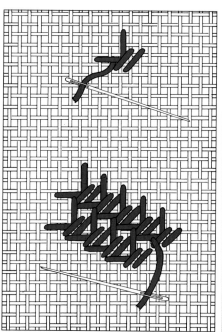

Compact filling stitch is used only on single canvas. It is quick and easy to work and covers the canvas ground well. Use it to fill any size of

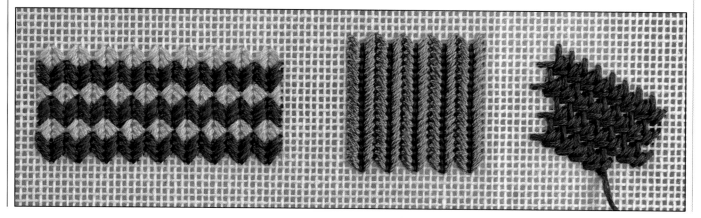

shape or background with a neat, closely worked texture. Any type of embroidery thread can be used, but care should be taken to match the weight of thread to the gauge of canvas so that the canvas is completely covered by the stitching. The stitch looks equally attractive worked on a large or small scale, in tapestry or Persian wool, or in stranded cotton or silk.

To execute compact filling stitch, begin by working one vertical and one horizontal straight stitch over three canvas threads. Arrange the stitches at right angles to fill two sides of a square, as shown in the diagram. Work two diagonal stitches over two vertical and two horizontal canvas threads at the bottom right of the straight stitches, as shown. Position the stitches in diagonal rows running from top left to bottom right of the shape to be covered, arranging the rows as shown.

## RAPID STITCH

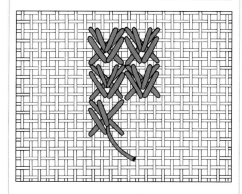

Rapid stitch is used only on single canvas. It is extremely quick to work and makes a regular texture across the canvas. Use the stitch to fill

any size of shape or background. A soft wool thread such as tapestry or Persian wool gives better canvas coverage than a firm, round thread such as pearl cotton.

Each rapid stitch covers a square of four vertical and four horizontal canvas threads. Begin by working an ordinary cross stitch (page 34) right across the square. Next, work four diagonal stitches across the square, arranging one pair of stitches to the right and one pair to the left, as shown in the diagram. An extra stitch can be worked down the centre of the square to prevent the canvas from showing through, and each square can be framed with back stitches (page 13) to give a more solidly stitched effected. Work the back stitches in a matching or contrasting thread colour.

## VAULT STITCH

(Also known as fan vaulting and church roof stitch.)

Vault stitch is used on single canvas for filling large areas and backgrounds. It produces a regularly textured surface composed of a pattern of alternating vertical and horizontal rectangles. Any type of embroidery thread can be used, providing its weight matches the gauge of the canvas, but the surface looks most effective when the stitch is worked in a soft wool thread such as tapestry or Persian wool.

Work each rectangular vault stitch individually. Begin by working a vertical vault stitch. First, work a central straight stitch over eight horizontal canvas threads. Cover this stitch with a large oblong cross stitch (page 143) worked over two vertical and eight horizontal canvas threads. Next, work a wide oblong cross stitch covering four vertical and six

horizontal canvas threads over the top of the previous stitches to complete the rectangle, as shown in the diagram. Repeat the rectangles until the shape is covered, working them vertically and horizontally so that they interlock, as shown. Small, unworked patches of canvas may be left in between the rectangles at this stage, depending on the weight of thread used. Fill these patches with tent stitches (page 125) or small ordinary cross stitches (page 34) worked in either a matching or contrasting thread colour.

# COMPOSITE CANVAS STITCHES

## █ VELVET STITCH

(Also known as Astrakhan stitch, Berlin plush stitch, plush stitch, raised stitch, rug stitch and tassel stitch.)

Velvet stitch produces a surface which looks like carpet pile and is used on both single and double canvas. A soft wool thread or multiple strands of fine wool provide the best result.

Begin at the bottom left-hand corner and work a diagonal stitch over one canvas intersection. Bring the thread through at the base of this stitch, and take the needle under one horizontal canvas thread, as shown in the first diagram. Leave the thread loose to form a loop, as shown. Work another diagonal stitch over the first one, but with the opposite slant. This stitch anchors the loop firmly to the canvas. Repeat along the row. Cut and trim the loops to the desired length after all the stitching has been completed.

## █ TURKEY RUG KNOT

(Also known as Ghiordes knot, quilt knot stitch, single knotted Smyrna rug stitch, tufted knot stitch and Turkey stitch.)

Turkey rug knot is used on both single and

double canvas. It produces a series of closely worked loops which can be cut and trimmed to make a thick, rich pile. Use this stitch to form raised areas as a contrast to a flat, smoothly stitched area of canvaswork. Work the stitch in a soft, thick wool thread or multiple strands of fine wool for the best result. Use strands of several different thread colours in the needle at the same time and change some of the colours in each row of stitches to give an attractive, shaded appearance.

Work a row of back stitches (page 13) over three vertical canvas threads. Alternate these stitches with loops, as shown in the diagram.

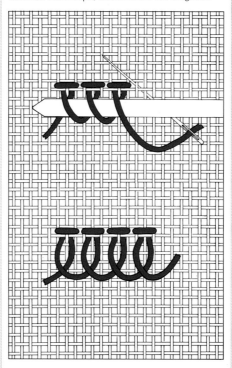

Work the loops around a pencil or large knitting needle to keep them of an identical size. Arrange each row of stitches above the preceding row, keeping the rows as close together as possible.

## █ SURREY STITCH

Surrey stitch is used on both single and double canvas. It produces a series of closely worked loops which can be cut and trimmed to make a thick, rich pile. Use this stitch to work three-dimensional shapes as a contrast to a flat,

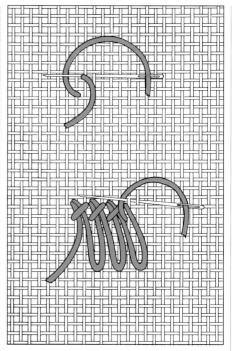

smoothly stitched area of canvaswork. Any type of thread can be used, providing its weight is compatible with the gauge of canvas selected, but a soft, thick wool thread or multiple strands of fine wool provide the best result. Use strands of several different colours of crewel wool in the needle at the same time, changing a proportion of the colours in each row of stitches to give a shaded effect.

Bring the thread through at the bottom left-hand corner. Make a diagonal stitch over two vertical and two horizontal canvas threads, as shown, bringing the needle through in front of the working thread. Pull the working thread gently downwards and repeat along the row, leaving a long loop of thread in between each stitch, as shown. Work the loops around a pencil or large knitting needle to keep them of an identical size. Arrange each row of stitches above the preceding row, keeping the rows as close together as possible.

*Both the cut and uncut loops of velvet stitch produce an attractive tufted surface. This embroidery illustrates the effect of the two variations of the stitch.*

158

# COMPOSITE CANVAS STITCHES

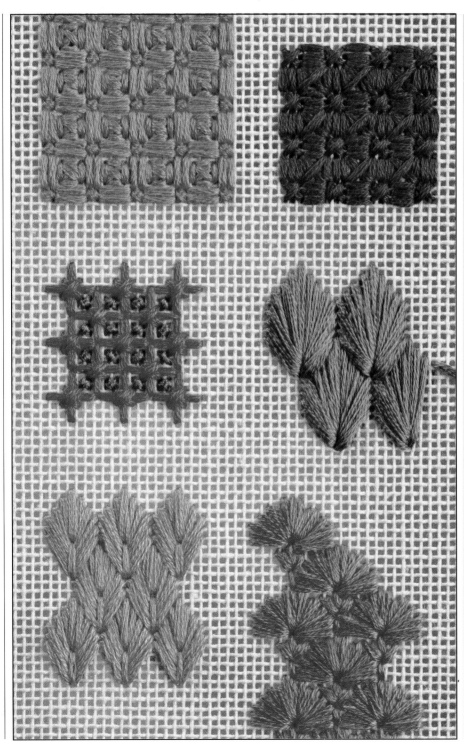

## FLOWER STITCH

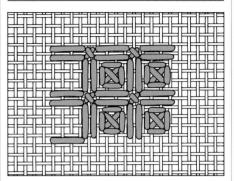

Flower stitch is used on both single and double canvas. The stitch looks rather like floral stitch (below), but in this case the regular pattern is larger. Use flower stitch to fill any size of shape or background area with a decorative pattern.

Work flower stitch in horizontal rows, starting at the top left of the shape to be covered. First, work a row of blocks of two horizontal straight stitches over four canvas threads, alternating them with ordinary cross stitches (page 34) spanning one intersection of the canvas, as shown. Then, proceeding from right to left, work blocks of two vertical straight stitches over four canvas threads below the crosses in the previous row. Alternate them with large cross stitches worked over two vertical and two horizontal canvas threads. Frame each large cross stitch with four straight stitches.

## FLORAL STITCH

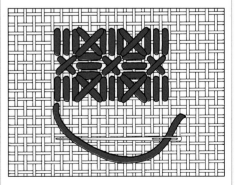

Floral stitch is used on both single and double canvas. It produces a decorative pattern which can be worked over any size of shape or background. A soft wool thread such as Persian wool is the best choice for this stitch. Work floral stitch in horizontal rows, beginning at the top left of the shape to be covered. First, work a row of blocks of three vertical straight stitches over three canvas threads, alternating them with ordinary cross stitches (page 34) worked over three vertical and three horizontal threads, as shown. Then, proceeding in the opposite direction, work blocks of three horizontal straight stitches over three canvas threads underneath the crosses in the previous row. Alternate these blocks with cross stitches worked over two vertical and two horizontal threads, as shown in the diagram. Repeat the two rows until the shape is covered.

## TWEED STITCH

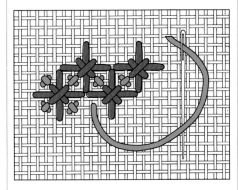

Tweed stitch is used on both single and double canvas. It produces a tweedy looking texture and is useful for filling all sizes of shape. The stitch looks best when worked in a soft wool thread such as tapestry or Persian wool, and a mixture of thread colours can be used.

Begin by covering the shape with large St George cross stitches (page 86). Work each cross over six vertical and six horizontal canvas threads and arrange the crosses so that the arms touch, as shown. Work ordinary cross stitches (page 34) spanning two vertical and two horizontal canvas threads over the first cross stitches. To finish, work ordinary cross stitches in the areas of unworked canvas, alternating the top diagonals, as shown.

## SCALLOP STITCH

Scallop stitch is used only on single canvas. The stitch produces a bold pattern of interlocking scallop shapes and is used to fill large areas. Work each scallop stitch individually over eight

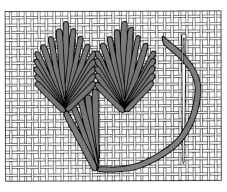

vertical and twelve horizontal canvas threads. Begin by working a central vertical straight stitch over twelve canvas threads. Next, work sixteen diagonal straight stitches of graduating length, arranged so that they radiate from the base of the centre stitch, as shown in the diagram. Begin by working the eight stitches at the left, then work the stitches at the right. Arrange the stitches in horizontal rows across the shape to be covered, and interlock each row with the preceding row.

## FAN STITCH

(Also known as expanded ray stitch and fantail stitch.)

Fan stitch is used only on single canvas. The stitch produces an attractive pattern of fan shapes and can be used when a strongly patterned background is required.

Work the fan shapes individually, arranging them in horizontal rows and setting the fans alternately in the second and subsequent rows. Each fan spans ten vertical and five horizontal canvas threads. Begin at the bottom left of the fan and work fifteen straight stitches of different lengths radiating from the same hole

at the centre of the fan. Directly beneath the fan, work a group of five radiating stitches spanning four vertical and three horizontal canvas threads, as shown in the diagram. To finish, work a vertical straight stitch over two horizontal canvas threads underneath the group of five stitches.

## FIR STITCH

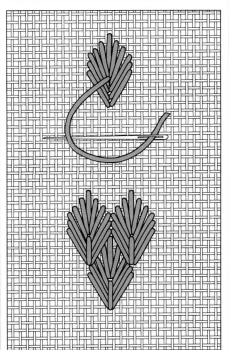

(Also known as leaf stitch.)

Fir stitch is used only on single canvas. It produces a strongly patterned surface and is used for filling large areas and backgrounds. Use this stitch to create a subtly shaded background by choosing a selection of threads in close tones of a single colour.

First, work a central vertical straight stitch over six canvas threads. At the left of this stitch work five diagonal stitches of varying lengths, as shown. Repeat the stitches at the right of the vertical stitch. These stitches should be worked in a row of five spaces under the vertical stitch, as shown in the diagram. To finish, work a vertical stitch over the five spaces. Work the fir stitches in horizontal rows from the top of the shape to be covered, arranging each row to interlock with the preceding row.

# COMPOSITE CANVAS STITCHES

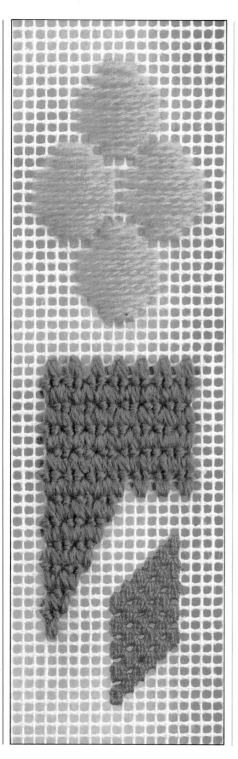

## ▮ BEETLE STITCH

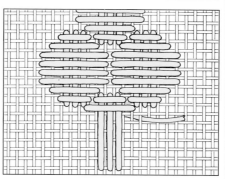

Beetle stitch is used only on single canvas. It produces a striking pattern of raised oval shapes and can be used to fill large shapes and backgrounds when a strong pattern is required for a design.

Work three vertical straight stitches over nine canvas threads at the centre of the oval. Take eight horizontal stitches of varying lengths over these three stitches, as shown in the diagram. When a fine thread is used, patches of unworked canvas may show through in between the ovals. Fill these patches with tent stitches (page 125) or back stitches (page 13) worked in the same thread.

## ▮ FRENCH STITCH

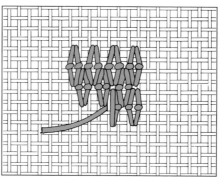

French stitch is used on both single and double canvas. The stitch produces a solidly stitched, textured surface and is ideal for filling large shapes and backgrounds. French stitch looks most effective when worked in a soft wool thread such as tapestry or Persian wool.

First, work two vertical straight stitches over four canvas threads. These stitches should share the same holes at the top and bottom. Anchor the stitches to the canvas at each side with two short horizontal stitches, as shown in the diagram. Work French stitch in diagonal or horizontal rows, from top to bottom of the shape to be covered, arranging each row so that it interlocks with the previous row.

## ▮ EASTERN STITCH

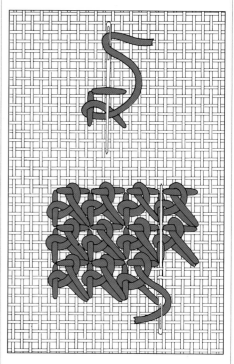

(Also known as Eastern buttonhole stitch.)

Eastern stitch is used only on single canvas. It produces an attractive, lacy pattern.

Work each stitch over a square of four canvas threads. Begin at the left-hand side and work two straight stitches along the top and left-hand side of the square. Bring the thread through at the bottom right-hand corner and make two loops over the foundation. Take the thread back through the same hole, as shown. Work Eastern stitch downwards in horizontal rows from left to right of the shape to be covered.

## ▮ ROCOCCO STITCH

(Also known as queen stitch.)

Rococco stitch is used on single canvas and on wide-meshed double canvas. It produces an

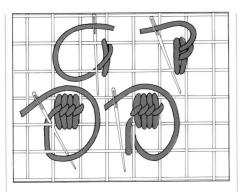

unusual, rather beautiful surface dotted with a regular series of holes.

Work a group of four vertical stitches over two canvas threads. These stitches should share the same holes at the top and bottom. Cross each stitch with a small horizontal stitch, as shown. The two outside vertical stitches are anchored to the canvas by the crossing stitch and curve slightly. Arrange the groups in alternate holes, as shown, and work them in diagonal rows, from top right to bottom left of the area to be covered.

## SHELL STITCH

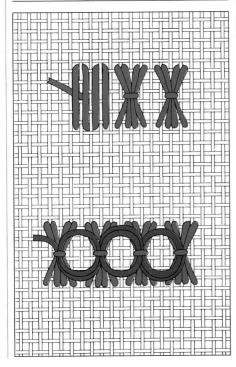

Shell stitch is used only on single canvas. It can be worked as a decorative border or as a filling for any size of shape. Work the stitch downwards in horizontal rows from right to left in two journeys, using a contrasting thread colour for the second journey.

Work blocks of four vertical straight stitches over six canvas threads, positioning them one thread apart. Tie each block of stitches together around the centre with a short horizontal stitch worked over one canvas thread, as shown. Lace the second thread in a circular pattern through the horizontal stitches, as shown.

## ARROW STITCH

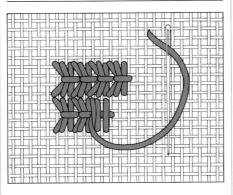

Arrow stitch is used only on single canvas. Any type of embroidery thread can be used, providing its weight is compatible with the gauge of canvas selected. This stitch looks effective when it is worked in shaded bands, but always choose your threads carefully, as close shades of a single colour can look better than a mixture of bright colours. Contrasting thread types of a similar weight can also be used to work alternate bands for an attractive effect. Experiment by using a shiny, light-reflecting thread such as pearl cotton with several strands of crewel wool.

Begin by working three vertical straight stitches over four canvas threads. Bring the needle through the canvas one thread to the right, as shown, loop it underneath the stitches and take it back through the canvas in the same place, pulling it tightly. This makes the vertical stitches curve gently. If any small gaps of unworked canvas show around the edges of the shape, cover them with tent stitches (page 125). Work arrow stitch downwards in horizontal rows from left to right of the shape to be covered.

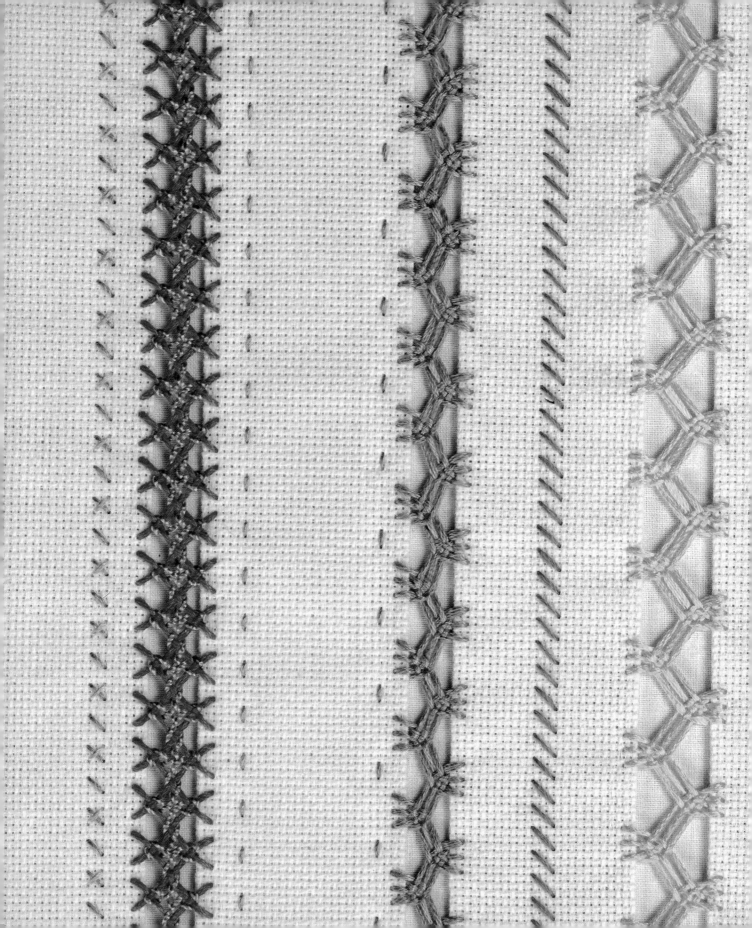

# INSERTION STITCHES

nsertion stitches are used to join together two pieces of fabric to make a decorative seam. The technique, which is also known as faggoting, was originally developed as a means of joining pieces of narrow, hand-woven fabric to produce large items of household linen such as tablecloths and sheets. Traditionally, insertion stitches are always worked in white thread on white plain- or even-weave fabric and the effect is very attractive.

With the exception of laced insertion stitch, the fabric pieces are first hemmed, then tacked on to a strip of fairly stiff brown paper. This ensures that the gap in between the pieces remains constant and enables the stitches to be worked evenly. Choose your embroidery threads with care and for the best results use a strong cotton or linen thread which is slightly heavier than the ground fabric. Avoid using a very heavy thread, as this will be difficult to pull easily through the fabric.

# INSERTION STITCHES

## ■ BUTTONHOLE INSERTION STITCH

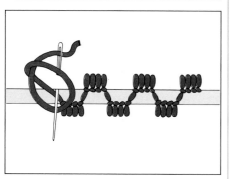

(Also known as buttonhole faggot stitch.)
Buttonhole insertion stitch is used to join together two pieces of plain- or even-weave fabric. It makes a strong, narrow join with a pretty, open appearance, and can be worked in either ordinary buttonhole stitches (page 17) or tailor's buttonhole stitches (page 27), depending on the effect required. To accentuate the stitching, use a cotton or linen thread which is slightly heavier than the ground fabric.

First, prepare the fabric. Hem each piece of fabric along the edge to be joined, then tack the pieces down on to a strip of brown paper, leaving an even gap of approximately ¼ inch (5mm) in between the pieces. Use quite stiff paper to ensure an even result.

Buttonhole insertion stitch is simple to execute. Begin at the right-hand side and work groups of four tailor's buttonhole stitches alternately on the upper and lower edges of the the fabric, as shown in the diagram. Different effects can be achieved by altering the spacing between the groups or by working groups of three ordinary buttonhole stitches with the centre stitch slightly longer. After the stitching has been completed, remove the tacking stitches and brown paper and press the join lightly on the wrong side.

## ■ ITALIAN BUTTONHOLE INSERTION STITCH

(Also known as Italian faggot stitch.)
Italian buttonhole insertion stitch is used to join together two pieces of plain- or even-weave fabric. It makes a wide, decorative join which is a little difficult to work at first. To accentuate the stitching, use any type of strong cotton or linen thread which is slightly heavier than the fabric.

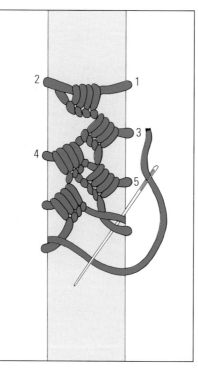

Begin by hemming each piece of fabric along the edge to be joined, then tack the pieces down on to a strip of stiff brown paper, leaving an even gap of approximately 1 inch (2.5cm) in between the pieces.

Work this stitch downwards, beginning at the top right. Bring the needle through at the top right and take a stitch across the gap to make a crossbar, inserting the needle exactly opposite, as shown, and bringing it through underneath the fabric edge, as if you were making an ordinary buttonhole stitch (page 17). Work four buttonhole stitches over the crossbar and make a buttonhole loop into the right-hand edge, as shown. Carry the thread across the gap and make another buttonhole loop on the left-hand side, slightly lower down. Next, work a group of four buttonhole stitches over the first buttonhole loop, working from the centre to the right. Repeat from side to side along the row.

*Insertion stitches can be used in an informal manner, as well as in the more traditional way. This contemporary embroidery uses strong colours and heavy threads to bring the technique up to date.*

# INSERTION STITCHES

## ▍TWISTED INSERTION STITCH

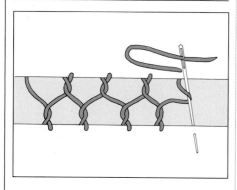

(Also known as faggoting and twisted faggot stitch.)

Twisted insertion stitch is used to join together two pieces of plain- or even-weave fabric. The stitch is quick and easy to work and produces an attractive join with an open, rather lacy appearance. To emphasise the stitching, use any type of strong cotton or linen thread which is slightly heavier than the ground fabric.

First, prepare the fabric. Hem each piece of fabric along the edge to be joined, then tack the pieces down on to a strip of brown paper, leaving an even gap of approximately ¼ inch (5mm) in between the pieces, or slightly more when working on a heavy fabric. Use stiff paper to ensure an even result.

Beginning at the left-hand side, bring the needle through on the upper edge and take a stitch across to the lower edge, as shown. Take a stitch to the upper edge, passing the needle under and over the previous stitch to make the twist and inserting it through the fabric from behind, as shown in the diagram. Continue

along the row in this way, working the twisted stitches from edge to edge. After the stitching has been completed, remove the tacking stitches and brown paper and press the join lightly on the wrong side.

## ▍KNOTTED INSERTION STITCH

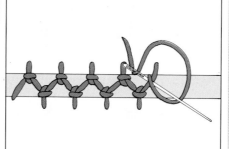

(Also known as knotted faggot stitch.)

Knotted insertion stitch is used to join together two pieces of plain- or even-weave fabric. It produces a narrow join with a pretty, knotted finish. To emphasise the stitching, use any type of strong cotton or linen embroidery thread which is slightly heavier than the ground fabric. Avoid using a heavy thread, as this will be difficult to pull easily through the fabric.

First, prepare the fabric. Hem each piece of fabric along the edge to be joined, then tack the pieces down on to a strip of brown paper, leaving an even gap of approximately ½ inch (1cm) in between the pieces. Use strong, firm paper to ensure an even result.

To execute knotted insertion stitch, work Antwerp edging stitches (page 173) from left to

right, setting the stitches alternately on the upper and lower pieces of fabric. After the stitching has been completed, remove the tacking stitches and brown paper and press the join lightly on the wrong side.

## ▍LACED INSERTION STITCH

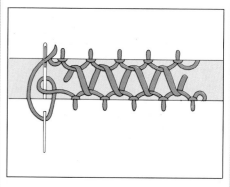

(Also known as laced faggot stitch.)

Laced insertion stitch is used to join together two pieces of plain- or even-weave fabric. The stitch produces a lacy join and looks particularly decorative when it is worked in more than one thread colour. An edging stitch is worked along each of the edges to be joined before the two pieces of fabric are tacked in position. To accentuate the stitching, use any type of strong cotton or linen embroidery thread which is slightly heavier than the ground fabric. Use a contrasting colour, weight and texture of thread for the lacing.

Begin by working a row of braid edging stitches (page 174) along the fabric edges to be joined. Next, tack the fabric pieces down on to a strip of brown paper, leaving an even gap of

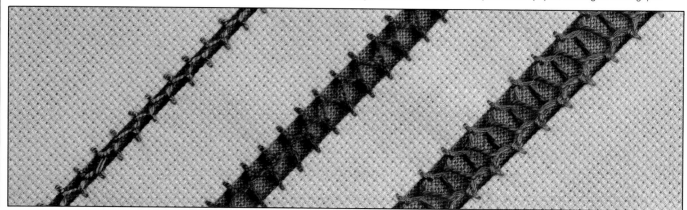

approximately 1¼ inches (3cm) in between the pieces. Arrange the pieces of fabric so that the loops of the edging stitches on the upper edge alternate with the loops on the lower edge, as shown. Use firm, rather stiff paper to ensure that the gap in between the fabric pieces remains perfectly even.

Finally, using a contrasting thread, lace the two rows of loops together, working from right to left. Use a blunt-ended tapestry needle for the lacing to avoid splitting the braid edging stitches. After the stitching has been completed, remove the tacking stitches and brown paper and press the join lightly on the wrong side.

## ▮ INTERLACING INSERTION STITCH

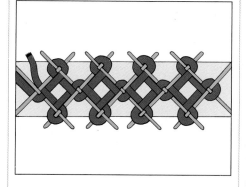

(Also known as interlaced faggot stitch and interlaced insertion stitch.)

Interlacing insertion stitch is a wide, decorative insertion stitch used to join together two pieces of plain- or even-weave fabric. The attractive appearance of this stitch is enhanced when it is worked in more than one thread

colour. Use a contrasting weight and colour of thread to work the interlacing.

First, hem each piece of fabric along the edge to be joined, then tack the pieces down on to a strip of brown paper, leaving an even gap of approximately 1 inch (2.5cm) in between the pieces. Use stiff paper to ensure than the gap in between the pieces remains perfectly even.

First, work a foundation row of double herringbone stitches from left to right, using the second method shown on page 60, and taking the stitches into the edges of the fabric. Work the interlacing in two journeys, following the sequence shown in the diagram. Use a blunt-ended tapestry needle for the second thread to avoid splitting the herringbone stitches. After the stitching has been completed, remove the tacking stitches and paper and press the join lightly on the wrong side.

## ▮ PLAITED INSERTION STITCH

(Also known as interlaced insertion stitch.)

Plaited insertion stitch is a wide, rather ornate insertion stitch used to join together two pieces of plain- or even-weave fabric. The stitch was popular during the Victorian period, when it was used for decorating bed linen, undergarments and ecclesiastical vestments. It produces a bold, plaited join. Use a thick, firm cotton or linen thread which is slightly heavier than the ground fabric to emphasise the plaited line.

First, prepare the fabric. Hem each piece along the edge to be joined, then tack the pieces down on to a strip of brown paper, leaving an even gap of approximately ¾–1¼ inches (2–3cm) in between the pieces, according to the weight of the ground fabric. Use firm, rather stiff paper to ensure that the

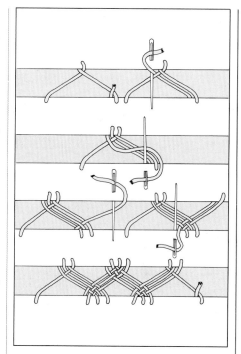

gap in between the fabric pieces remains perfectly even.

Bring the needle through at the left-hand end of the lower edge and carefully follow the sequence of stitches shown in the diagram. Repeat the stitches shown in the first five diagrams to complete the row, keeping the spaces in between the groups of stitches regular to achieve the correct effect. After the stitching has been completed, remove the tacking stitches and brown paper and press the join lightly on the wrong side.

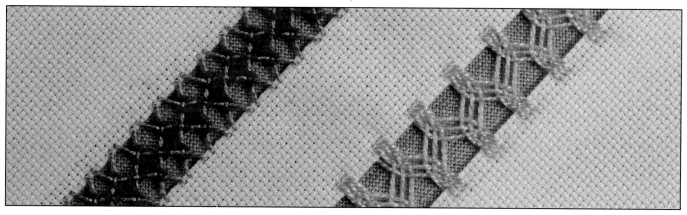

# CHAPTER TWELVE

# EDGING STITCHES

The edging stitches described in this chapter are used in a variety of ways. Buttonhole edging stitch and the looped edging stitches are used to finish raw edges in cutwork, particularly in the forms known as Renaissance and Richelieu embroidery; cord stitch is used to join together two pieces of fabric, while other edging stitches make a decorative row of knots and loops on a plain hemmed edge.

Picots consist of loops of thread or little bumps of stitches and are attached to an embroidered edging. With the exception of woven picot, which is worked directly into the edge of the fabric, all picots are worked into the buttonhole edging without entering the fabric. They are usually used as a decoration on an ordinary buttonhole stitch edge, but can also be worked as an ornament on embroidered bars in cutwork and needle-made lace, or on a plain row of surface buttonhole stitches, for example around an appliquéd shape.

# EDGING STITCHES

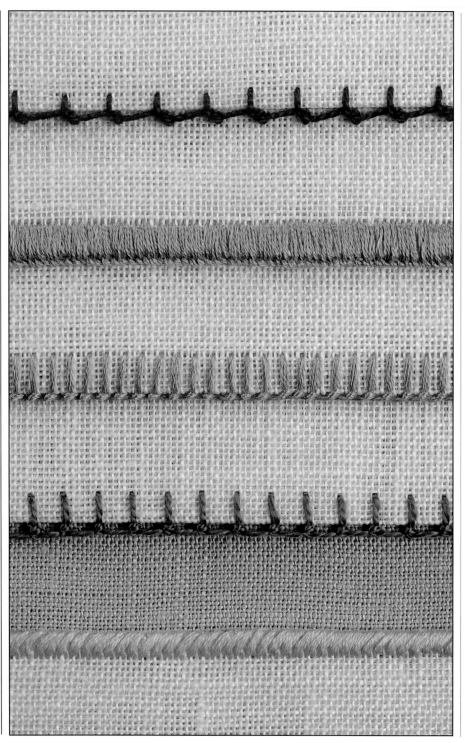

## ▌ARMENIAN EDGING STITCH

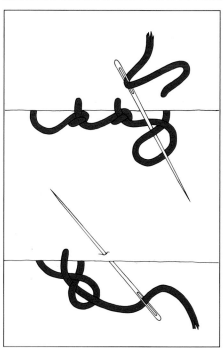

Armenian edging stitch is used as a decoration on plain-weave fabric. It produces a neat row of small loops and knots along a plain hemmed edge. Any type of embroidery thread can be used, but a round, smooth thread such as soft cotton or the heaviest available weight of pearl cotton provides the most effective result. Keep the stitches quite small and even.

Work Armenian edging stitch from left to right along the fabric edge. First, bring the needle through from under the edge of the fabric, then insert it from below a little further along the edge, as shown in the second diagram. Before pulling the thread through completely, twist it into a loop and slip the needle through, as shown in the first diagram. Pull the working thread tightly to form a knot before working the next stitch.

## ▌BUTTONHOLE EDGING STITCH

Buttonhole edging stitch is used to finish raw edges in Renaissance and Richelieu embroidery and in other types of cutwork.

Begin by outlining the shape with evenly worked running stitches (page 12), then cut

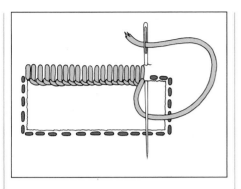

away the fabric close to this line with a small pair of sharp scissors. Work a row of ordinary buttonhole stitches (page 17) over the running stitches and the raw edge, arranging the loops close to the edge, as shown in the diagram. Position the stitches closely together so that no ground fabric is visible. When working on a fabric which is liable to fray, work both the running stitch outline and the buttonhole edging stitch before cutting away the surplus fabric. Always use very sharp scissors and take care not to cut the running stitches when cutting away the fabric.

## PLAITED EDGE STITCH

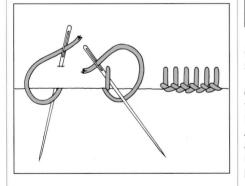

Plaited edge stitch is used on both plain- and even-weave fabric. Work this stitch on a plain hemmed edge to produce a decorative finish, or use it along a raw edge to prevent it from fraying. The stitch is extremely durable and can be used to finish hemmed edges on household linen and garments which will be laundered. Any type of embroidery thread can be used to work plaited edge stitch. Keep the stitches quite small and space them evenly along the row, as shown.

Work plaited edge stitch from left to right. Secure the thread as neatly as possible on the back of the fabric, a little way from the edge. Bring the needle downwards to the front of the work and insert it at right angles to the edge and a short distance above, as shown in the first diagram. Pull the working thread through to leave a straight stitch on both sides of the fabric. Slip the needle under the straight stitch from left to right, as shown in the second diagram, and pull it through over the working thread to complete the stitch. The needle should not enter the fabric when this second stage is being worked. Repeat along the row, arranging the stitches either closely together or slightly apart, as shown in the third diagram.

## ANTWERP EDGING STITCH

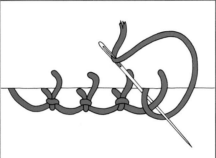

(Also known as knot stitch and knotted blanket stitch.)

Antwerp edging stitch is a decorative edge decoration worked on plain-weave fabric. Use this stitch to produce a row of evenly worked loops and knots along a plain hemmed edge. Any type of embroidery thread can be used, but a round, thick thread such as soft cotton or the heaviest available weight of pearl cotton produces the most effective result.

Work Antwerp edging stitch from left to right. Bring the needle through from beneath the fabric, insert it a little way to the right, then pull it through over the working thread as if working an ordinary buttonhole stitch (page 17). Make a stitch over the buttonhole loop, then pull the thread tightly to form a knot. Repeat this sequence along the edge. Add more rows to create a deep, lacy edging, working through the loops in the previous rows, or whip the outer row of loops with a contrasting thread colour, as in whipped back stitch (page 13).

## CORD STITCH

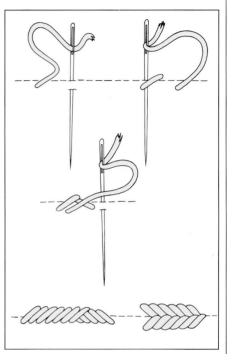

Cord stitch is a decorative joining stitch used on both plain- and even-weave fabric. It produces a solidly stitched, plaited line which should cover the fabric ground completely. Use cord stitch to finish cushion covers, purses and other small items. Any type of embroidery thread can be used, but a flat thread such as stranded cotton or silk gives the best fabric coverage.

Begin by turning under and pressing the raw edges of the two pieces of fabric to be joined. Position the fabric pieces with the wrong sides facing, then tack them together to hold them in place. Secure the thread neatly between the two layers of fabric and bring it through to the right side of the front piece of fabric. Insert the needle horizontally a little further along to the right, then travel back and make a similar stitch just to the right of the first stitch, as shown in the second diagram. Continue working in this way to build up a plaited edge which completely covers the ground fabric. When the row of stitches has been completed, remove the tacking stitches and lightly press the join open from the wrong side. Press the join carefully over a well-padded surface to avoid flattening the embroidery.

# EDGING STITCHES

## ■ BRAID EDGING STITCH

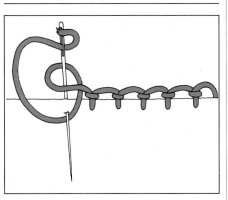

## ■ LOOPED EDGING STITCH

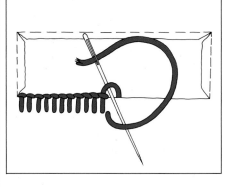

Braid edging stitch is used only on plain-weave fabric. It produces a durable edging and is often used to finish the edges of household linen such as pillowcases, tablecloths and napkins. This stitch is also used as a foundation for laced insertion stitch (page 168).

Unlike Armenian edging stitch (page 172) and Antwerp edging stitch (page 173), which produce a similar effect, braid edging stitch is rather difficult to work. Any type of embroidery thread can be used, but the most effective result is produced when the stitch is worked in a firm, round thread like pearl cotton or coton à broder. Keep the stitches quite small and arrange them at regular intervals along the row.

Work braid edging stitch from right to left along the edge, holding the edge of the fabric away from yourself. Bring the thread through from beneath the edge and loop it as shown. Take the needle through the loop and insert it into the back of the fabric, letting it emerge a short distance from the edge, as shown in the diagram. Pull the needle through over the working thread, leaving the resulting knot quite slack.

The secret of working this stitch neatly lies in adjusting the size of loop at this stage by pulling it gently away from the edge of the fabric with the needle. Try to keep all the loops of an identical size to achieve the correct appearance. After the loop has been adjusted, tighten the knot firmly by pulling the thread outwards at right angles to the edge of the fabric. This movement will produce a firm knot which lies neatly along the edge of the fabric. Some practice is usually required before braid edging stitch can be worked in an even manner, as the loops tend to vary in size at first.

Looped edging stitch is used on plain-weave and closely woven even-weave fabric. The stitch produces a neat, firm edging which is more durable than buttonhole edging stitch (page 172), although the appearance of the stitches is similar. Use looped edging stitch to cover a raw edge and for all types of cutwork when you need to make a strong anchoring foundation around a shape which is to be filled with one of the lacy detached filling stitches.

Any type of embroidery thread can be used to work looped edging stitch, but a round, smooth thread such as pearl cotton or coton à broder makes the stitch stand out from the background more effectively than a flat thread such as stranded cotton. However, a stranded thread should ideally be used when working the stitch on a lightweight fabric as it provides better fabric coverage. Work the stitches closely together around the edge of the shape so that none of the ground fabric shows through the stitching.

Work looped edging stitch over a tiny turned edge from left to right, snipping into the fabric at the corners to give a neat finish when working rectangular shapes. Secure the thread neatly as near to the edge as possible, then insert the needle upwards from behind, making the required length of stitch in from the edge. Before pulling the thread through, slip the needle under the loop, as shown in the diagram, and tighten the stitch by pulling the thread away from yourself.

*The handsome piece of cutwork shown opposite dates from the early part of this century. The motifs have been outlined with looped edging stitches to give a neat but strong finish.*

# EDGING STITCHES

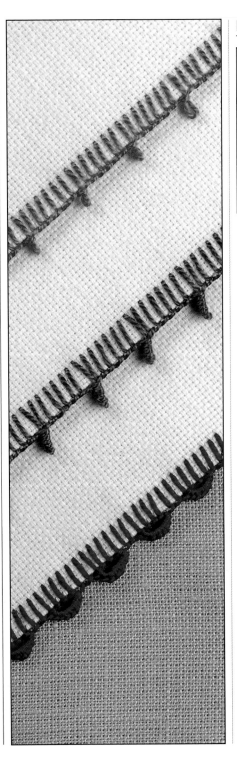

## ▌ LOOP PICOT

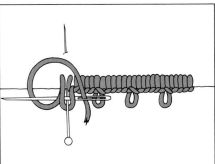

(Also known as pinned picot.)

Loop picots are worked on plain-weave fabric and are the simplest form of picots. Use them to decorate an ordinary buttonhole stitch edge (page 17) or a row of buttonhole stitches worked on the surface of the fabric. Loop picots are also frequently worked as an ornament on embroidered bars in cutwork and needle-made lace.

Work loop picots from right to left. (Working in this direction makes the buttonhole stitch edging a little tricky to execute, but the picots are much easier to work.) Work buttonhole stitches along the edge, positioning them close to each other to completely cover the fabric. When you reach the point where you wish to make the picot, insert a dressmaking pin into the fabric close to the last buttonhole stitch, as shown in the diagram. Loop the thread under the pin from right to left, then take a stitch into the fabric just to the left of the previous stitch. Adjust the loop to the required size, then secure it by slipping the needle under the loop, over the pin, under and then over the working thread, as shown in the diagram. Tighten the working thread, remove the pin and continue to stitch the edging.

## ▌ BUTTONHOLE PICOT

(Also known as Venetian picot.)

Buttonhole picots are larger than loop picots (above). Use them on plain-weave fabric to decorate an ordinary buttonhole stitch edge (page 17).

Work buttonhole picots from right to left. First, work buttonhole stitches along the edge until you reach the point where you wish to make the picot. Next, insert a dressmaking pin

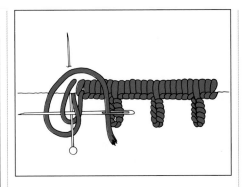

into the fabric close to the last stitch, as shown. Loop the thread under the pin from right to left, then take a stitch into the fabric to the left of the previous stitch. Adjust the loop to the required size and insert the needle through the loop and over the pin, making sure that the point of the needle goes over the working thread, as shown. Pull the needle through and tighten the resulting stitch to form the end of the picot. Work buttonhole stitches over the rest of the loop, then continue to work the edging.

## ▌ RING PICOT

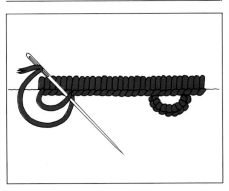

Ring picots are used on plain-weave fabric. The stitch is easy to work and makes a large, rather heavy picot which can be used to decorate an ordinary buttonhole stitch edge (page 17) or a row of buttonhole stitches worked on the surface of the fabric. Each ring picot is worked directly into the buttonhole stitch loops without entering the ground fabric. Any type of embroidery thread can be used, depending on the weight of the ground fabric, stitch size and effect required, but a flat, stranded cotton produces a flatter picot than a round thread such as pearl cotton or coton à broder.

Work ring picots from right to left. First, work buttonhole stitches along the edge until you reach the point where you wish to make the picot. Arrange the stitches closely together to completely cover the fabric. Next, make a loop with the working thread by taking the needle through a buttonhole loop three or four stitches back along the edging, without entering the ground fabric. Tighten the working thread to make a small loop as the subsequent buttonholing will greatly enlarge this space. Work closely spaced buttonhole stitches into the loop until the edge of the fabric is reached. Secure the ring of stitches by working the next stitch of the buttonhole stitch edging.

## ▌BULLION PICOT

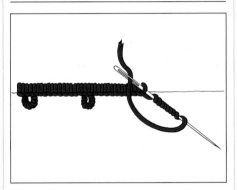

Bullion picots are used only on plain-weave fabric. The stitch is quick and easy to work and can be used to decorate an ordinary buttonhole stitch edge (page 17) or a row of buttonhole stitches worked on the surface of the fabric. Any type of embroidery thread can be used, depending on the effect required.

Work bullion picots from left to right in the usual manner. First, work buttonhole stitches along the edge until you reach the point where you wish to make the picot. Arrange the buttonhole stitches closely together to completely cover the fabric. Next, insert the needle behind the upright of the last buttonhole stitch, without entering the ground fabric. Hold the head of the needle down with the left thumb and twist the thread five or six times around the point of the needle in exactly the same way as when making a bullion knot (page 69). Place the left thumb over the coils, pull the needle right through and then tighten the coils. Secure the picot by working the next buttonhole stitch close to the previous one.

## ▌WOVEN PICOT

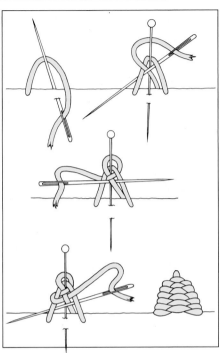

Woven picots are rather large and, unlike other picots, are worked directly into the fabric edge. Use woven picots to decorate the edge of both plain- and even-weave fabric. Any type of embroidery thread can be used, but a firm, rather stiff thread gives the best results.

Hold the edge of the fabric away from you when working woven picots. First, bring the thread through the fabric and make a loop, as shown in the first diagram, adjusting the loop to the required size. Next, insert a dressmaking pin over the loop and into the fabric to help keep the loop firm while the picot is being worked. Pass the working thread behind the top of the pin, then slip the needle through the loop, as shown in the second diagram. Tighten the stitch gently to form the top of the picot. Make a series of weaving stitches from side to side of the loop, as shown in the third and fourth diagrams. Pull each stitch tightly and continue weaving until the loop is filled and the edge of the fabric is reached. By this stage, the picot should be neatly worked and should stand out quite stiffly from the fabric. Secure the end of the thread as neatly as possible and remove the pin from the fabric.

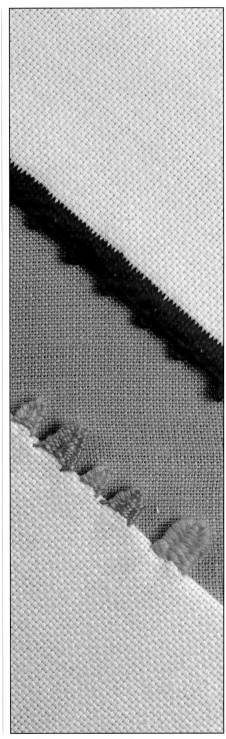

# CUT AND DRAWN STITCHES

This chapter contains three distinct groups of stitches, all of which are used in the many different types of openwork embroidery. The first group includes embroidered bars and eyelet holes. These are used in cutwork, either for joining motifs together to form an open background, or to produce a neat pattern of embroidered perforations across a plain-weave fabric. Hem stitches, which make up the second group, are used both to finish hems on even-weave fabric and to produce wide, ornamental borders of different kinds.

The third group of stitches contains three filling stitches which are worked on the lattice-work of threads left behind after alternate pairs of horizontal and vertical threads have been withdrawn from a square of fabric. Use these stitches on a loosely woven fabric with a regular weave to produce blocks of delicate, lacy embroidery.

# CUT AND DRAWN STITCHES

## ■ BUTTONHOLED BAR

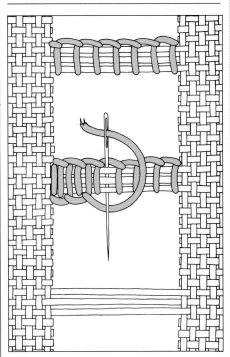

A buttonholed bar is used in all types of cutwork on both plain- and even-weave fabric.

On an even-weave fabric, make a foundation for the bar of three or more horizontal fabric threads which remain after a group of threads has been withdrawn and some of the short horizontal ones cut away. Work ordinary buttonhole stitches (page 17) closely together over the threads. Double buttonhole stitches (page 26) can alternatively be used to cover the bar. In this case, work the first row of stitches rather openly, as shown at the top of the diagram, and fit the second row into the spaces, as shown at the centre of the diagram.

To work a buttonholed bar on a plain-weave fabric, take the working thread three times between the motifs to make a foundation. Proceed to work the bar as described above.

## ■ OVERCAST BAR

(Also known as corded bar and twisted bar.)

An overcast bar is used as a joining device in all types of cutwork on both plain- and even-weave fabric. It is narrower and more rounded than a buttonholed bar (above). Work overcast

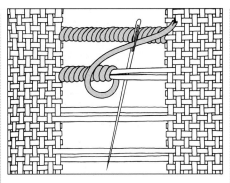

bars when you need to join together small, rather delicate motifs.

On an even-weave fabric, make a foundation for the bar of two or more horizontal fabric threads which remain after a group of threads has been withdrawn and some of the horizontal ones cut away, as shown at the bottom of the diagram. Work overcast stitches (page 15) closely together from left to right over the threads to make a firm, rounded bar.

To work an overcast bar on a plain-weave fabric, take the working thread three times between the motifs to make a foundation. Proceed to work the bar as described above.

## ■ WOVEN BAR

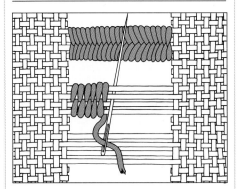

A woven bar is used in all types of cutwork on both plain- and even-weave fabric. The stitch produces a flat, firm bar which is much stronger than the two previous bars. Use woven bars when you need to join together motifs on a fairly heavy fabric.

On an even-weave fabric, make a foundation for the woven bar of an even number of horizontal fabric threads which remain after a group of threads has been withdrawn and some

of the short horizontal ones cut away, as shown at the bottom of the diagram. Work a weaving stitch from left to right over the threads, as shown by the needle in the diagram.

To work a woven bar on a plain-weave fabric, take the working thread an even number of times between the motifs to make the foundation, then proceed as above.

## ■ EYELET HOLE

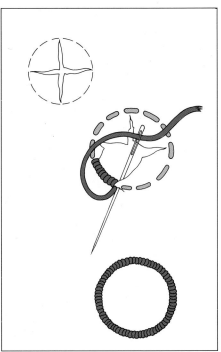

Eyelet holes are worked on finely woven plain-weave fabric. They are used mainly in Broderie Anglaise embroidery (otherwise known as eyelet or Swiss embroidery), which is traditionally worked in white thread on white fabric. In this type of embroidery, tiny perforations with embroidered edges are used to make pretty floral motifs across the fabric. Broderie Anglaise embroidery reached the height of popularity during the late eighteenth and early nineteenth centuries, when it was worked in elaborate patterns on dress sleeves, underwear and household linens.

To work a large eyelet hole, trace a circular outline on to the fabric. Cut across the centre of the circle, both vertically and horizontally, as shown in the first diagram. Outline the shape with tiny running stitches (page 12). Turn one of the cut points under with the needle and begin to work a row of closely packed overcast stitches (page 15) around the circle. Continue to turn the fabric under as you proceed around the circle. Work oval eyelets in the same manner, but for triangular eyelets, make the overcast stitches slightly longer at the points. After the eyelet holes have been completed, trim away the surplus fabric from the back of the work. Work tiny round eyelet holes in the same way, but pierce the fabric with a stiletto after working the outline of running stitches.

## ▌SHADOW EYELET

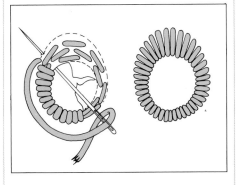

(Also known as shaded eyelet.)

Shadow eyelets are worked on finely woven plain-weave fabric. They are similar to ordinary eyelet holes (left), and are also used in Broderie Anglaise embroidery. This type of eyelet produces a much heavier effect and makes a round eyelet appear almost oval. Use this stitch when you need a circular or oval eyelet with a bold, rather solid effect.

To work a shadow eyelet, trace a circular outline on to the fabric to denote the hole. Mark a second, asymmetrical outline around the first outline to denote the outside of the eyelet. Pad the shape by working several rows of running stitches (page 12) in between the two lines. Cut across the centre of the circle, both vertically and horizontally, as you would if working an ordinary eyelet hole. Turn one of the cut points under with the needle and begin to work a row of closely packed overcast stitches (page 15) around the circle. Continue to turn the fabric under as you proceed. Follow the outside line carefully by gradually changing the length of the overcast stitches. When the stitching has been completed, trim away the surplus fabric.

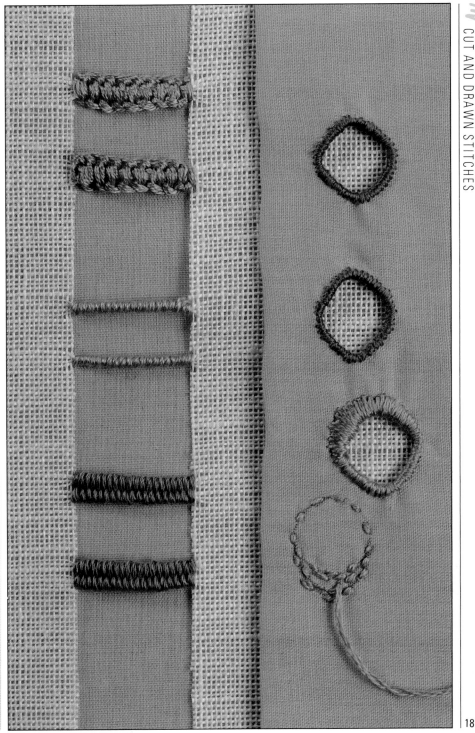

## HEM STITCH

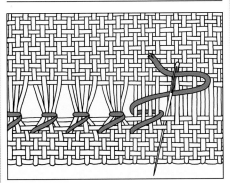

Hem stitching is a technique used to decorate and secure a hem on even-weave fabric. Use it on items of household linen and to make decorative hems and borders on garments. Hem stitches are traditionally worked in white thread on white fabric, but any type of fine cotton or linen embroidery thread can be used, depending on the weight of the fabric, stitch size and effect required. Ordinary hem stitch is extremely easy to work and should be used on fabric with a fairly loose, distinct weave like an even-weave linen.

Draw out the required number of fabric threads, two or three being usual when working this stitch. Turn the hem up just to the edge of the drawn threads and tack it in position. With the right side of the work facing towards you, bring the needle through at the left-hand side of the hem. Pick up the first three or four vertical fabric threads from right to left, as shown, then insert the needle so that it pierces the hem at the back and emerges on the front just to the right of the group of threads. Pull the working thread tight to gather the group of threads into a cluster at the bottom. Repeat along the row, always picking up the hem at the back when making the stitch shown in the diagram. Remove the tacking thread at the end of the row. Secure the embroidery thread as neatly as possible inside the hem at the beginning and end of each length.

## ANTIQUE HEM STITCH

Antique hem stitch is a variation of ordinary hem stitch (above) which is worked on the wrong side of the fabric. It produces a much neater finish than the previous stitch, because only the tiny horizontal stitches which secure

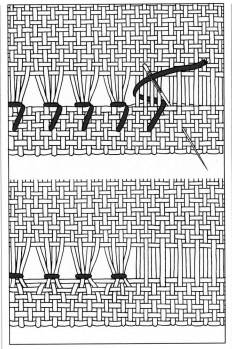

the clusters are visible on the right side of the work. Use the stitch to make decorative hems and borders on tablecloths, napkins and garments.

Antique hem stitch is traditionally worked in white thread on white fabric. Any type of fine cotton or linen embroidery thread can be used, depending on the weight of the fabric, stitch size and effect required. Always work the stitch on fabric with a loose, distinct weave such as an even-weave linen, as two or three horizontal threads are removed from the fabric before the embroidery takes place.

First, draw out the required number of fabric threads, two or three being usual when working antique hem stitch. Turn the hem up just to the edge of the drawn threads, then tack it in position. With the wrong side of the work facing towards you, bring the needle through at the left-hand side of the hem. Pick up the first three or four vertical fabric threads from right to left. Slip the needle in between the hem, as shown in the first diagram, letting it emerge to the right of the group of threads. Pull the working thread tight to gather the group of threads into a cluster at the bottom. Repeat along the row. The second diagram shows the effect produced on the right side of the fabric.

## LADDER HEM STITCH

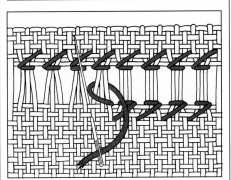

(Also known as ladder stitch.)

Ladder hem stitch is an attractive variation of ordinary hem stitch (left) which makes a border with a ladder pattern. It produces a wider border than either of the two previous stitches and unlike them is worked on both the upper and lower ends of the vertical fabric threads. Use the stitch to make decorative hems and borders on garments and on household linen such as tablecloths and napkins.

Ladder hem stitch is usually worked in white thread on white fabric. Any type of fine cotton or linen embroidery thread can be used, depending on the weight of the fabric, stitch size and effect required. Always work the stitch on fabric with a loose, distinct weave such as an even-weave linen.

First, draw out the required number of fabric threads, three or four being usual when working ladder hem stitch. Turn the hem up to the edge of the drawn threads, then tack it in position. With the right side of the work facing towards you, bring the needle through at the left-hand side of the hem and work a row of ordinary hem stitches in the usual way, grouping three vertical fabric threads with each stitch. Next, turn the work around and make a second row of ordinary hem stitches above the line of drawn threads. Arrange the stitches so that they group the same cluster of threads as those in the lower row. Use antique hem stitch instead to work the lower row if you prefer.

*All the various forms of hem stitch are popular for finishing the edges of tablecloths. The cloth on the left has three ornate borders with needlewoven motifs in each of the corners.*

183

# CUT AND DRAWN STITCHES

## ▌SERPENTINE HEM STITCH

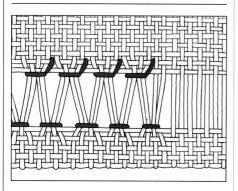

(Also known as trellis hem stitch.)

Serpentine hem stitch is a decorative variation of ladder hem stitch (page 183) which produces an attractive zigzag border. Any type of fine cotton or linen embroidery thread can be used to work the stitch, depending on the weight of the fabric, stitch size and effect required. Always work serpentine hem stitch on a fabric with a loose, distinct weave such as an even-weave linen.

First, draw out the fabric threads, three or four being usual when working serpentine hem stitch. Turn the hem up just to the edge of the drawn threads, then tack it in position. With the wrong side of the work facing towards you, bring the needle through at the left-hand side of the hem and work a row of antique hem stitches (page 183) in the usual way, grouping four or any other even number of vertical fabric threads with each stitch. Turn the work around so that the right side is facing towards you and work a row of ordinary hem stitches (page 183) above the line of drawn threads. Divide and regroup the vertical threads as shown in the diagram. Remove the tacking stitches. Use ordinary hem stitches to work both the upper and lower rows if you prefer.

## ▌ITALIAN HEM STITCH

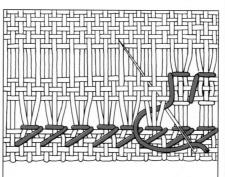

(Also known as double hem stitch, Roumanian hem stitch and double-rowed openwork.)

Italian hem stitch is a wide, decorative hem stitch worked in two journeys.

Draw out three or four fabric threads. Turn the hem up to the edge of the drawn threads, then tack it in position. With the wrong side of the work facing towards you, bring the needle through at the left-hand side and work a row of ordinary hem stitches (page 183), grouping three vertical threads into each cluster. Leave three or four horizontal threads intact and withdraw a second group of horizontal threads equal in number to those drawn out for the first row of stitching. Work a row of embroidery along the band of intact horizontal threads, as shown, grouping the vertical threads above and below the band into clusters.

## ▌WOVEN HEM STITCH

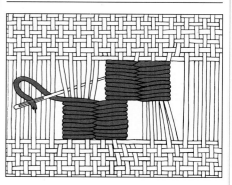

(Also known as needle weaving and openwork insertion stitch.)

Woven hem stitch is the strongest form of hem stitching and can be built up into elaborate borders.

Draw out four or five horizontal fabric threads. Bring the needle through at the right and weave over the first group of vertical threads (three, four or five according to the weight of the fabric) and under the second group of threads. Turn and weave over the second group of threads and under the first. Continue until the block of stitches covers half the depth of the border. Weave another block, this time covering the lower half of both the second group of threads and of a third new group. Repeat along the row.

## ▌RUSSIAN DRAWN FILLING

Russian drawn filling is worked on even-weave fabric with distinct, easily counted threads that are loose enough to be easily withdrawn. Any type of cotton or linen embroidery thread can be

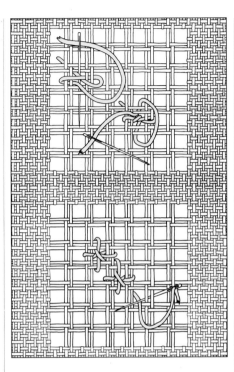

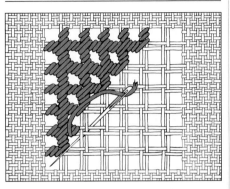

the correct effect. Work the stitch in diagonal rows from top left to bottom right. Arrange the twisted crosses to cover alternate squares for an open effect, or work them in each square to produce a solidly stitched surface.

## RUSSIAN OVERCAST FILLING

Russian overcast filling is worked on even-weave cotton or linen with easily counted, loosely woven threads.

To work this stitch, first prepare the fabric. Cut alternate pairs of horizontal and vertical fabric threads, as shown in the diagram, forming a lattice-work square of threads. Secure the working thread neatly on the back of the fabric and bring it through at the left of the shape. Work overcast stitches (page 15) over the lattice in a stepped formation, moving diagonally up to the top of the shape. Work the overcast stitches closely together so that they cover the fabric threads completely. The needle in the diagram shows the method of working an overcast stitch over an intersection, just before proceeding to the vertical bar above.

## WEAVING STITCH FILLING

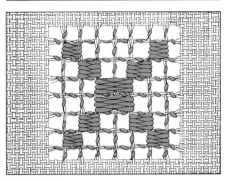

Weaving stitch filling is worked on even-weave cotton or linen with easily counted threads which are loosely woven and therefore easy to withdraw.

To work this stitch, first prepare the fabric. Cut alternate pairs of horizontal and vertical fabric threads, as shown in the diagram, forming a lattice-work square of fabric threads. Secure the working thread neatly on the back of the fabric and bring it through to the right side. Work overcast stitches (page 15) over all the vertical pairs of fabric threads, as shown, arranging one of the stitches in between each set of horizontal threads. Repeat the overcast stitches along the horizontal pairs of threads in the same way. Finally, work blocks of weaving in the square in exactly the same way as for woven hem stitch (left), securing the beginning and end of each length of thread as neatly as possible on the wrong side. Work the blocks in diagonal rows and arrange the weaving stitches to fall either vertically or horizontally across each block.

used, providing it is of a similar weight and texture to the ground fabric.

To work Russian drawn filling, first prepare the fabric. Cut alternate pairs of horizontal and vertical fabric threads, as shown in the diagram, to form a lattice-work square of fabric threads. Secure the working thread neatly on the back of the fabric and bring it through at the top left of the shape. Work a twisted cross over two vertical and two horizontal pairs of fabric threads, as shown. Follow the sequence of stitches carefully from the diagrams to achieve

# CHAPTER FOURTEEN

# PULLED FABRIC STITCHES

Pulled fabric stitches create attractive designs on even-weave fabric. These designs are achieved by pulling the fabric threads with a tightly worked stitch to make a regular pattern across the fabric. This type of embroidery is also known as drawn thread work and pulled work, and is traditionally worked in a self-coloured thread.

Use any type of embroidery thread to work these stitches, but make sure that it is strong enough to hold the pulled threads firmly in position and of a similar weight and texture to the fabric. Always work on fabric held in an embroidery hoop or frame, but do not stretch the fabric as tightly as you would when working a surface stitch. Instead, let the hoop or frame hold the fabric quite loosely, so that the horizontal and vertical fabric threads are kept just at right angles to each other. You may need to loosen the fabric from time to time to allow the threads to be pulled correctly.

# PULLED FABRIC STITCHES

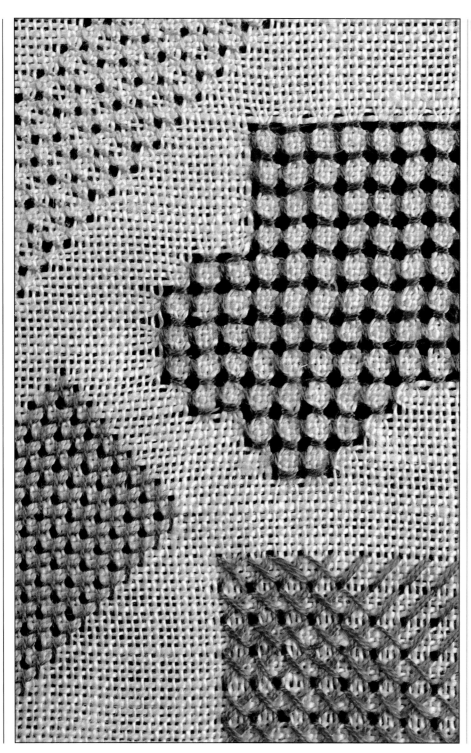

## NET FILLING

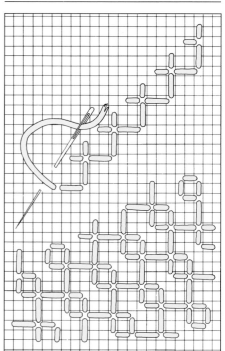

Net filling is used on even-weave cotton or linen fabric with well-defined, easily counted threads. It produces a neat, closely worked surface with a small pattern of holes. The stitches should be pulled tightly as they are being worked to emphasise the pattern. Any type of embroidery thread can be used, providing it is strong enough to hold the pulled threads securely in position and of a similar weight and texture to the ground fabric. Use a blunt-ended tapestry needle to avoid splitting the fabric threads and always work on fabric held in a hoop or frame. Adjust the fabric when necessary to allow the threads to be pulled correctly.

Work net filling in diagonal rows from top right to bottom left of the shape to be filled. Begin at the top right-hand corner and work a row of single faggot stitches (page 192) over three vertical and three horizontal fabric threads across to the left-hand corner. Secure the end of the thread neatly on the wrong side. Bring the needle through at the top right-hand corner again, letting it emerge at the top of the first stitch in the previous row. Work another row of single faggot stitches, but this time take the stitches over two threads, as shown in the first diagram. Turn the work upside-down and repeat the row of single faggot stitches, again working over two threads. Repeat these three rows until the shape is filled, arranging the rows as shown in the second diagram. Drawn faggot filling (page 204) is worked in a similar manner to this stitch.

## PUNCH STITCH

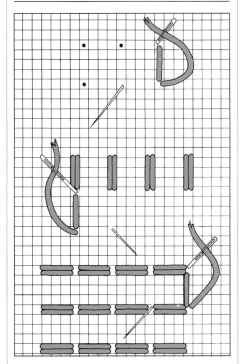

Punch stitch is used on even-weave fabric with well-defined, easily counted threads. It produces a regular pattern of large holes over the surface of the fabric. Work the rows of stitches alternately from right to left and left to right and pull the stitches tightly as they are being worked to accentuate the pattern. Any type of thread can be used, providing it is strong enough to hold the pulled threads securely and of a similar weight and texture to the ground fabric. Use a blunt-ended tapestry needle to avoid splitting the fabric threads.

Bring the needle through at the top right of the shape to be filled and insert it four fabric threads above, then bring it through at the base of the first stitch. Insert the needle at the top of the first stitch to finish the double upright stitch and pull the working thread tightly. Bring the

needle through four threads to the left and four threads down and make another double upright stitch over four threads.

Continue in this way along the row, working double upright stitches over four threads and leaving four threads in between each pair. At the end of the first row, turn and work a similar row, taking the tops of the stitches into the holes made in the row above. Cover the whole shape in this manner, pulling each stitch as tightly as possible as you work. To finish, turn the work around so that the top of the stitching becomes the left-hand side. Repeat the rows of double upright stitches to complete the squares, as shown in the diagram.

## RIDGE FILLING

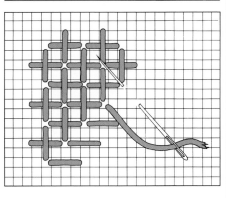

Ridge filling is a variation of diagonal raised band (page 204) which is worked on even-weave cotton or linen fabric with well-defined, easily counted threads. It produces a closely worked surface with a regular pattern of narrow ridges running diagonally in both directions across the fabric. Pull the stitches as tightly as possible as they are being worked to emphasise the ridges. Any type of embroidery thread can be used to work ridge filling, providing it is strong enough to hold the pulled threads securely and of a similar weight and texture to the ground fabric. Use a blunt-ended tapestry needle to avoid splitting the fabric threads when working the stitches and always work on fabric held in an embroidery hoop or frame.

Work rows of diagonal raised band over four fabric threads from top right to bottom left of the shape to be filled. Arrange the rows closely together, as shown in the diagram, and pull each stitch as tightly as possible. Work each row of stitches into the holes made in the previous row.

## RUSSIAN FILLING

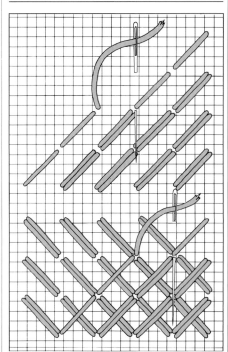

Russian filling is worked in two journeys on even-weave fabric with well-defined, easily counted threads. It produces a regular trellis pattern accentuated by large holes. Any type of embroidery thread can be used, providing it is strong enough to hold the pulled threads securely and of a similar weight and texture to the ground fabric.

Work the first journey in rows running from bottom left to top right of the shape to be filled. Working from the bottom, insert the needle four fabric threads to the right and four above, and bring it through four threads down, as shown in the first diagram. Insert the needle four threads to the right and four above, bringing it through at the top of the first stitch. Continue in this way along the row, pulling the stitches tightly.

Work the second row in the same direction, beginning four threads to the right of the previous row. Turn the work for the second journey, so that the top of the embroidery becomes the left-hand side. Work rows of stitches in exactly the same way and use the holes already made on the first journey, so that the two sets of stitches cross at right angles, as shown in the second diagram.

# PULLED FABRIC STITCHES

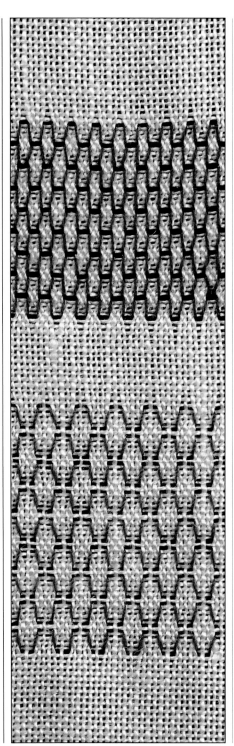

## WAVE STITCH FILLING

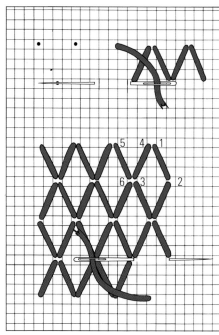

(Also known as straight line stitch.)

Wave stitch filling is used on even-weave fabric with well-defined, easily counted threads. It produces a regular trellis pattern emphasised by large holes. Pull the stitches as tightly as possible as they are being worked to create the large holes. Any type of embroidery thread can be used, providing it is strong enough to hold the pulled threads securely in position and of a similar weight and texture to the ground fabric. Use a blunt-ended tapestry needle to avoid splitting the fabric threads when working the stitches and always work on fabric held in an embroidery hoop or frame.

Work wave stitch filling in horizontal rows from right to left and left to right. First, bring the needle through at the top of the shape to be filled, two fabric threads in from the right-hand edge. Insert the needle two threads to the right and four threads down, then bring it through four threads to the left. Insert the needle at the top of the stitch just made, bring it through four threads to the left, then insert it at the base of the second stitch and bring it through four threads to the left. Continue in this way to the end of the row, pulling each stitch tightly. Make sure that the needle always enters the fabric in

a horizontal position, as shown in the diagram. At the end of the row, insert the needle into the top of the last stitch and bring the thread through eight threads below, ready to work the next row. To do this, turn the work upside-down and work the row in the same way as before.

## WINDOW FILLING

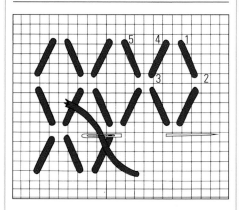

(Also known as straight line stitch.)

Window filling is used on even-weave cotton or linen with well-defined, easily counted threads. It produces a regular pattern of holes, each containing two cross threads of fabric.

Window filling is worked from right to left in a similar way to the previous stitch, but in this case one fabric thread is left in between the stitches and the rows, as shown. First, bring the needle through at the top of the shape to be filled, two fabric threads in from the right. Insert the needle two threads to the right and four threads down, then bring it through five threads to the left. Insert the needle two threads to the right and four threads above, then bring it through five threads to the left. Continue in this way to the end of the row, pulling each stitch tightly. Make sure that the needle enters the fabric only in a horizontal position, as shown. At the end of the row, insert the needle into the top of the last stitch and bring the thread through nine threads below, then turn the work upside-down and work the next row as before.

## DOUBLE WINDOW FILLING

(Also known as open window filling.)

Double window filling is a widely spaced variation of ordinary window filling (above) which is worked on even-weave fabric with well-defined, easily counted threads. It

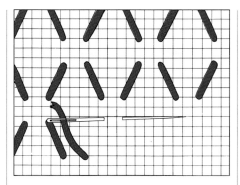

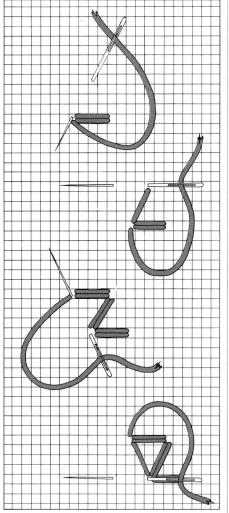

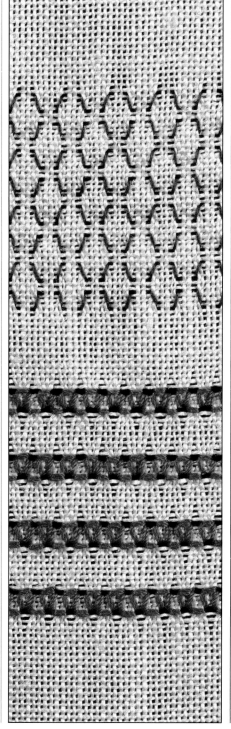

produces a neat, rather delicate pattern. The
stitches should be pulled as tightly as possible
as they are being worked to emphasise this
pattern. Any type of embroidery thread can be
used, providing it is strong enough to hold the
pulled threads securely in position and of a
similar weight and texture to the ground fabric.
Use a blunt-ended tapestry needle to avoid
splitting the fabric threads.

Work this stitch from right to left in the same
way as window filling, but in this case arrange
the stitches across the fabric slightly differently,
as shown in the diagram. Leave two fabric
threads unworked at the top of the pairs of
stitches, and six threads unworked at the base;
separate the rows by two threads.

## ▌ THREE-SIDED STITCH

(Also known as Bermuda faggoting, lace stitch,
point turc and Turkish stitch.)

Three-sided stitch is both a pulled fabric
stitch worked on even-weave cotton or linen, and an
openwork stitch used on finely woven plain-
weave fabric. It produces a pretty, triangular
trellis pattern and can be used either as a border
or in multiple rows to fill a shape. Pull the
stitches as tightly as possible as they are being
worked to accentuate the trellis pattern. When
using this stitch on a plain-weave fabric, work
the stitches in the same sequence, but do not
count the threads. Instead, work the stitches
evenly across the fabric in a fine thread and use
a thick needle which will punch a small hole
each time it enters the fabric.

Work this stitch in horizontal rows from right
to left. First, bring the needle through four fabric
threads from the edge of the shape to be filled.
Insert the needle four threads to the right, then
bring it out where it first emerged. Insert the
needle again four threads to the right and bring

it through at the left side of the stitch just
worked, as shown in the diagram. This makes a
pair of back stitches (page 13) worked one over
the other. Next, insert the needle two threads
to the right and four threads up and make
another pair of back stitches in the same way,
bringing the needle through four threads to the
left. Make a third pair of back stitches from this
point to the top of the second pair. Work a
fourth pair of stitches as shown, and repeat the
sequence from the beginning along the row.

To work three-sided stitch in multiple rows,
arrange the rows underneath each other so that
the stitches in each row share some of the
holes made by the stitches in the previous row.

# PULLED FABRIC STITCHES

## ■ SINGLE FAGGOT STITCH

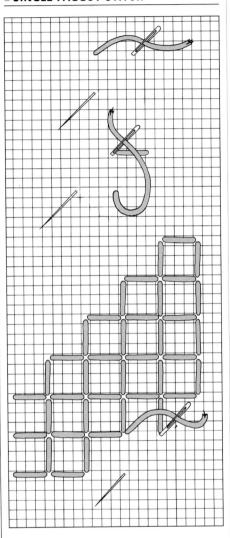

(Also known as diagonal line stitch and diagonal square stitch.)

Single faggot stitch is used on even-weave fabric with easily counted threads. It produces a regular pattern of holes across the fabric. The stitches should be pulled tightly as they are being worked to enhance the pattern. Use a blunt-ended tapestry needle to avoid splitting the fabric threads.

Bring the needle through at the top right of the shape to be filled, four fabric threads from the edge. Insert the needle four threads to the right and bring it through four threads to the left

and four threads down. Next, insert the needle where it first emerged, bringing it through four threads to the left and four threads down. Insert the needle at the base of the second stitch and continue in this way to the end of the row, pulling each stitch tightly. To work the second row, turn the work upside-down and repeat the sequence of stitches, using some of the holes made by the stitches in the first row. Repeat until the shape is covered

## ■ FESTOON FILLING STITCH

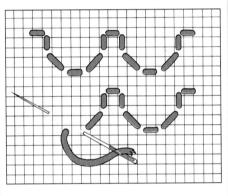

Festoon filling stitch is worked in back stitches (page 13) on even-weave cotton or linen with well-defined, easily counted threads. It produces a pattern of regular, wavy lines. The stitches should be pulled tightly as they are being worked to emphasise the pattern. Any type of embroidery thread can be used, providing it is strong enough to hold the pulled threads securely in position and of a similar weight and texture to the ground fabric.

Bring the needle through at the top right of the shape to be filled, two fabric threads from the edge. Insert the needle two threads to the right, bring it through two threads to the left and two threads down, and insert it where it first emerged. Bring the needle out two threads to the left and four threads down. Continue working back stitches in this way, following the outline shown. Position each row six threads below the previous row, as shown.

## ■ FOUR-SIDED STITCH

(Also known as square openwork stitch and four-sided openwork stitch.)

Four-sided stitch produces an effect similar to hem stitching (page 183) and makes an attractive border for any embroidered item

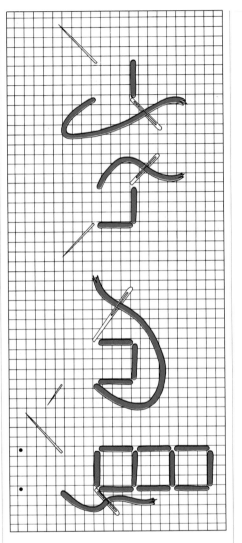

made of loosely woven, even-weave cotton or linen. It is worked in single rows from right to left, and the stitches should be pulled tightly as they are being worked. Any type of embroidery thread can be used, providing it is strong enough to hold the pulled threads securely in position and of a similar weight and texture to the ground fabric.

Bring the needle through at the right, and insert it four fabric threads above, then bring it through four threads to the left and four threads down. Next, insert the needle where it first emerged, and bring it through four threads to the left and four threads up. Insert it at the top of the first stitch and bring it through at the left of the second stitch, as shown. Insert the needle at the left of the third stitch and bring it through four threads to the left and four threads down, ready to work the next stitch.

## GOBELIN FILLING STITCH

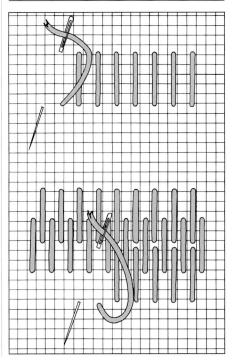

Gobelin filling stitch is used on even-weave fabric with well-defined, easily counted threads. It produces a solidly stitched surface which is quick and easy to execute. The stitches should not be pulled as tightly as most other pulled fabric stitches. Any type of thread can be used, providing it is strong enough to hold the pulled threads securely and of a similar weight to the ground fabric. Use a blunt-ended tapestry needle to avoid splitting the fabric threads.

Work this stitch from right to left in horizontal rows. Begin at the top of the shape to be filled and work a row of vertical straight stitches over six fabric threads, leaving two threads in between each stitch, as shown. Work the second row underneath, arranging the stitches three threads lower than the first row of stitches, and filling in the gaps left in the first row, as shown in the second diagram. Repeat to fill the shape.

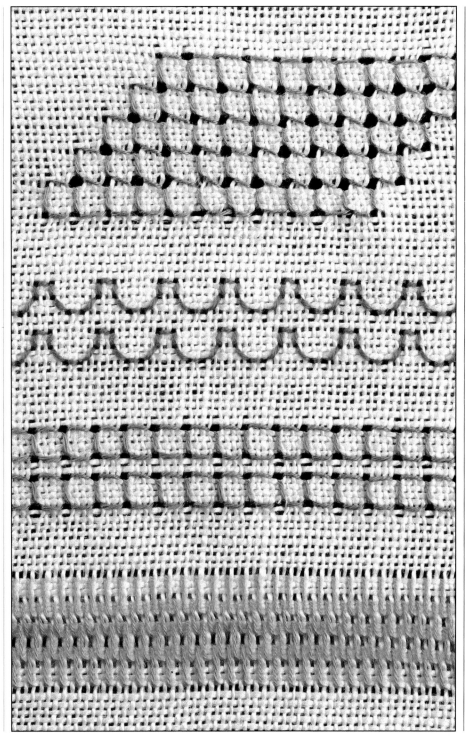

# PULLED FABRIC STITCHES

## DIAMOND FILLING STITCH

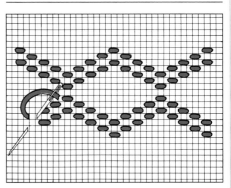

Diamond filling stitch is worked in double back stitches (page 47) on even-weave fabric with easily counted threads. It produces a bold pattern of raised diamonds. The stitches should be pulled tightly as they are being worked to enhance the diamond pattern. Any type of thread can be used, providing it is strong enough to hold the pulled threads securely.

Work in horizontal rows from right to left. Bring the needle through two fabric threads from the edge of the shape to be filled, then insert it two threads to the right. Bring the needle through two threads to the left and two threads down; insert the needle two threads to the right and bring it through four threads to the left and one thread above. Continue in this way, arranging each pair of back stitches one thread lower than the preceding pair, as shown in the diagram. After five pairs of stitches have been made, work the next four to rise by one thread, and so on. Complete the diamond shapes by arranging subsequent rows as shown.

## LOZENGE FILLING

Lozenge filling is worked in horizontal rows on even-weave fabric with easily counted threads. It produces a bold, lozenge-shaped pattern across the fabric and is quick and easy to work. The stitches should not be pulled as tightly as most other pulled fabric stitches. Any type of embroidery thread can be used to work lozenge filling, providing it is strong enough to hold the pulled threads securely in position and of a similar weight and texture to the ground fabric. Use a blunt-ended tapestry needle to avoid splitting the fabric threads when working the stitches and always work on fabric held in an embroidery hoop or frame.

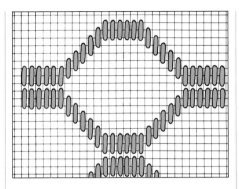

Work lozenge filling in rows from left to right. Bring the needle through at the left of the shape to be filled and a little distance from the top. Work a row of vertical ordinary satin stitches (page 102) over three fabric threads, arranging them to form a regular, stepped line, as shown. Complete the lozenge shapes by arranging subsequent rows as shown.

## STEP STITCH FILLING

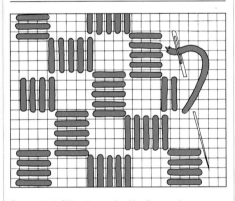

Step stitch filling is worked in diagonal rows on even-weave cotton or linen with easily counted threads. It creates a closely worked texture across the fabric. The stitches should not be pulled as tightly as most other pulled fabric stitches. Any type of embroidery thread can be used, providing it is strong enough to hold the pulled threads securely in place and of a similar weight and texture to the ground fabric. Use a blunt-ended tapestry needle to avoid splitting the fabric threads when working the stitches and always work on fabric held in an embroidery hoop or frame.

Begin at the top left of the shape to be filled and work blocks of five ordinary satin stitches (page 102) over four fabric threads. Work the

blocks of stitches vertically and horizontally in a diagonal row, as shown in the diagram, arranging them in a stepped formation so that all of the blocks in subsequent rows touch at one corner.

## CHESSBOARD FILLING STITCH

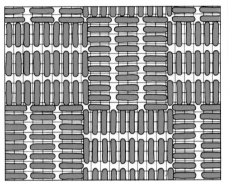

Chessboard filling stitch is worked in blocks of vertical and horizontal stitches on even-weave fabric with well-defined, easily counted threads. It produces an attractive, raised basketweave pattern across the fabric. The stitch is simple and quick to execute, but should not be pulled as tightly as most other pulled fabric stitches. Any type of embroidery thread can be used, providing it is strong enough to hold the pulled threads securely in place and of a similar weight and texture to the ground fabric. Use a blunt-ended tapestry needle to avoid splitting the fabric threads and always work on fabric held in an embroidery hoop or frame.

Begin at the top left of the shape to be filled and work a rectangular block of ordinary satin stitches (page 102) over three fabric threads. Work ten satin stitches in each block and arrange the blocks directly underneath one another in three horizontal rows. Make a second block, this time working vertical rows of ten satin stitches, as shown in the diagram. Alternate the two types of blocks over the shape to make a chessboard pattern.

## RIPPLE STITCH

Ripple stitch is worked in double back stitches (page 47) on even-weave fabric with easily counted threads. It produces a delicate, wavy pattern across the fabric. The stitches should be pulled tightly as they are being worked. Any type of strong embroidery thread can be used.

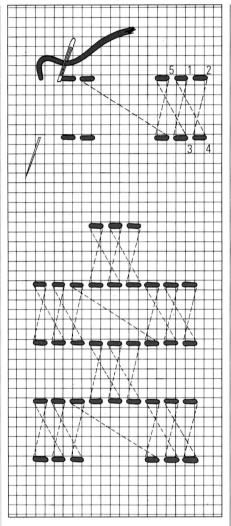

Work this stitch in horizontal rows from right to left. Bring the needle through at the top right of the shape, two fabric threads to the left. Insert the needle two threads to the right, and bring it through two threads to the left and six threads down; insert the needle two threads to the right and bring it through four threads to the left and six threads above. Continue in this way until three pairs of double back stitches have been worked, then carry the working thread behind ten vertical fabric threads and work another set of three double back stitches. Arrange the rows underneath each other, as shown, working each row of stitches in the spaces left in the preceding row.

# PULLED FABRIC STITCHES

## ▌ALGERIAN EYE STITCH

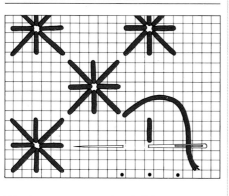

(Also known as star eyelet stitch.)

Algerian eye stitch is used on even-weave fabric with well-defined, easily counted threads. It produces a regular chessboard pattern of large eyelets over the surface of the fabric. Work the eyelets in diagonal rows, arranging them as shown, or position them closely together to create a solidly stitched surface punctuated by regular holes. Pull the stitches tightly as they are being worked to accentuate the pattern made by the holes.

Any type of embroidery thread can be used, providing it is strong enough to hold the pulled threads securely in position and of a similar weight and texture to the ground fabric. Use a blunt-ended tapestry needle to avoid splitting the fabric threads and always work on fabric held in an embroidery hoop or frame.

Bring the needle through at the top right of the shape to be filled. Work eight straight stitches radiating from the same central hole, as shown in the diagram. Arrange the stitches in a square consisting of six vertical and six horizontal fabric threads, and pull the stitches as tightly as possible. Position the eyelets in diagonal rows, working subsequent rows so that the corner stitches share the same holes and making a chessboard pattern across the fabric, as shown in the diagram.

## ▌DIAGONAL OVERCAST GROUND

Diagonal overcast ground is used on even-weave fabric with easily counted threads.

Work from the top of the shape in horizontal zigzag rows of overcast stitches (page 15). Do not attempt to work this stitch in diagonal lines, in spite of its appearance, as the pull on the fabric will be incorrect. Bring the needle through

at the top left of the shape, and insert it two threads above and two threads to the right. Work a diagonal group of six overcast stitches, as shown, pulling the stitches as tightly as possible. After inserting the needle to make the last stitch in the group, bring it through two threads to the right and two threads down; insert the needle two threads to the left and two threads up and work a group of six overcast stitches upwards, at right angles to the first group.

Continue in this way to the end of the row. Work subsequent rows underneath the first row, arranging them to make a diamond-shaped lattice, as shown in the diagram. Leave a tiny square of unworked fabric at the point where the rows touch. You can leave the stitch at this stage, or decorate it by working a detached eyelet (page 203) in the centre of each diamond shape, as shown in the diagram.

## ▌OBLIQUE FILLING

Oblique filling is used on even-weave fabric with easily counted threads. Each stitch is made up of a large central hole surrounded by smaller holes and the stitch creates an attractive filling of large eyelets arranged in

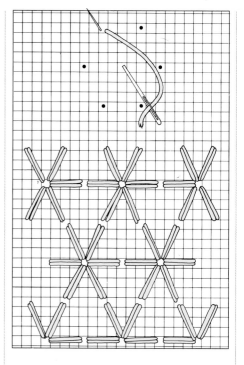

oblique rows across the fabric. Pull the stitches as tightly as possible as they are being worked to emphasise the pattern. Any type of embroidery thread can be used, providing it is strong enough to hold the pulled threads securely and of a similar weight and texture to the ground fabric.

Work this stitch in horizontal rows from right to left. Bring the needle through at the top of the shape to be filled and a little way from the right-hand edge. Insert the needle in the centre, as shown, two threads to the right and four threads down. Repeat, working the needle through the same holes to form a double stitch. Bring the thread through four threads to the right and repeat the double stitch from this point to the centre. Work the star all round in this way, pulling the double stitches very tightly, then proceed to make the next star at the left. Arrange subsequent rows of the stitch as shown in the diagram.

*This effective example of pulled fabric work on linen has been worked in coloured silk and metal threads. The embroidery is from Turkey and dates from the Ottoman period.*

# PULLED FABRIC STITCHES

## ALGERIAN FILLING STITCH

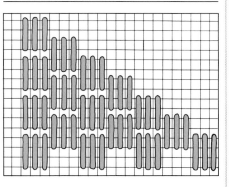

Algerian filling stitch produces a solidly stitched pattern of squares on even-weave fabric with easily counted threads. It should not be pulled as tightly as other pulled fabric stitches. Any type of embroidery thread can be used, providing it is strong enough to hold the pulled threads in place and of a similar weight and texture to the ground fabric. Use a blunt-ended tapestry needle to avoid splitting the fabric threads and always work on fabric held in an embroidery hoop or frame.

To execute this stitch, work blocks of three ordinary satin stitches (page 102) over four horizontal fabric threads. Work the blocks in diagonal rows, beginning at the top left corner of the shape to be filled, and arrange them in a stepped formation, as shown.

## FRAMED CROSS FILLING

Framed cross filling produces a small, all-over pattern on even-weave fabric with easily counted threads.

Work this stitch in horizontal rows. Bring the needle through at the top left and insert it four fabric threads above. Bring the needle through four threads to the right and four threads down, and insert it four threads above; bring the needle through one thread to the right and four threads down and insert it four threads above. Repeat along the row.

Work the second row from right to left, leaving one fabric thread unworked in between the rows and arranging the stitches underneath each other as shown. When the required

number of horizontal rows has been worked, turn the fabric so that the top of the embroidery becomes the left side. Repeat the process from the beginning, positioning the stitches in the way shown in the second diagram.

## COBBLER FILLING STITCH

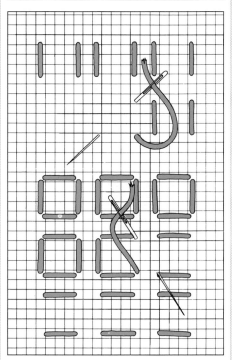

Cobbler filling stitch is similar to the previous stitch and is worked on even-weave fabric with easily counted threads. Pull the stitches tightly as they are being worked to emphasise the

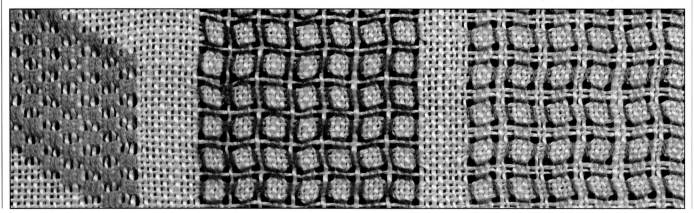

MARY THOMAS'S DICTIONARY OF EMBROIDERY STITCHES

open pattern produced by the stitch. Work this stitch in horizontal rows. First, bring the needle through at the top left and insert it four fabric threads above. Next, bring the needle through four threads to the right and four threads down, and insert it four threads above; bring the needle through two threads to the right and four threads down, then insert it four threads above. Continue in this way, spacing the upright stitches alternately four fabric threads and two fabric threads apart.

Work the second row from right to left, leaving two fabric threads unworked in between the rows and arranging the stitches underneath each other as shown. When the required number of horizontal rows has been worked, turn the fabric so that the top of the embroidery becomes the left side. Repeat the process from the beginning, positioning the stitches as shown in the second diagram.

## ▌ DIAGONAL CHEVRON STITCH

Diagonal chevron stitch produces a pattern of diagonal ridges on even-weave fabric with easily counted threads. Pull each stitch tightly to form the ridges.

Work in diagonal rows in two journeys. Bring the needle through at the top right and fill the shape to be covered with rows of single faggot stitches (page 192). Set the rows three fabric threads apart, as shown. Next, make the set of stitches shown in the second diagram, which shows one row complete and the second in progress. Bring the needle through at the bottom of the row, as shown, insert it three threads to the right and three threads above, and bring it through three threads down; insert the needle three threads to the right and three

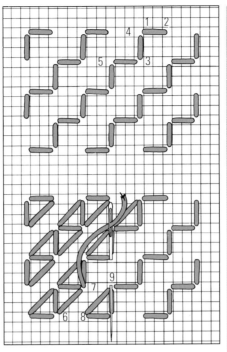

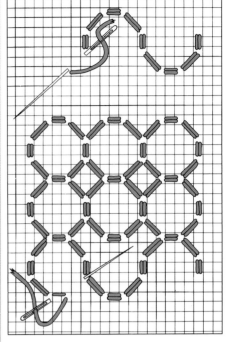

threads above, then bring it through at the top of the first stitch and repeat the two stitches. Continue in this way, working the stitches into the holes made on the first journey.

## ▌ RINGED BACK STITCH FILLING

Ringed back stitch filling is worked on even-weave fabric with easily counted threads.

Work the stitch in two journeys. Bring the needle through at the right and make a pair of back stitches (page 13), inserting the needle

two fabric threads to the right and two threads above. Next, bring the thread through four threads to the left and two threads down, and make a second pair of back stitches as shown. Repeat along the row, pulling each stitch tightly. Turn the work upside-down and repeat the first journey. The two journeys meet at the vertical stitches, which means that there will be four back stitches to each vertical group. Arrange each row so that it meets the previous row along the lower horizontal stitches and work four back stitches in each horizontal group.

# PULLED FABRIC STITCHES

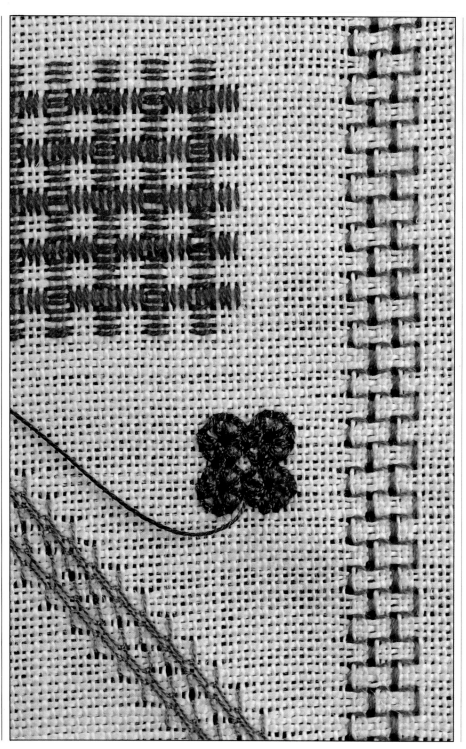

## OPEN BASKET FILLING

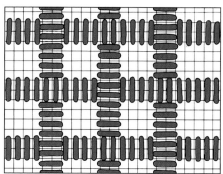

Open basket filling is worked in vertical and horizontal rows on even-weave fabric with easily counted threads. It produces an attractive basketweave pattern across the fabric. To make it easier to work the stitches where the rows intersect, avoid pulling the stitches as tightly as you would most other pulled fabric stitches. Any type of embroidery thread can be used to work open basket filling, providing it is strong enough to hold the pulled threads securely and of a similar weight and texture to the ground fabric. Use a blunt-ended tapestry needle to avoid splitting the fabric threads when working the stitches and always work on fabric held in an embroidery hoop or frame.

First, work all the vertical rows in ordinary satin stitches (page 102). Work groups of ten stitches over three fabric threads, as shown in the diagram, spacing the groups three threads apart. Take the thread behind the fabric when passing from group to group. Work the horizontal rows in the same way, arranging them to fill the gaps left in the vertical rows.

## DRAWN BUTTONHOLE STITCH

Drawn buttonhole stitch is a variation of ordinary buttonhole stitch (page 17) worked on even-weave cotton or linen with easily counted threads. It produces a striking diagonal pattern. The stitches should be pulled as tightly as possible as they are being worked to emphasise the pattern. Any type of thread can be used, providing it is strong enough to hold the pulled threads firmly and of a similar weight and texture to the ground fabric. Use a blunt-ended tapestry needle to avoid splitting the fabric threads and always work on fabric held in an embroidery hoop or frame.

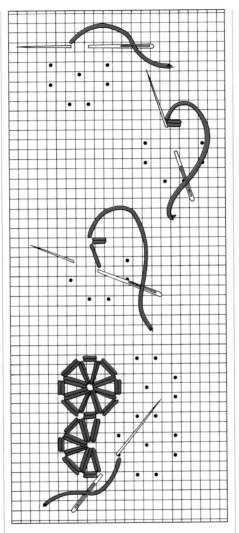

Work drawn buttonhole stitch in diagonal rows from top left to bottom right of the shape to be filled, arranging the rows back to back in pairs. First, bring the needle through and hold the working thread down on the surface of the fabric with your left thumb. Next, insert the needle three fabric threads to the right and bring it out three threads down. Draw the needle through the fabric over the working thread. Repeat along the row, working the stitches three threads to the right and three threads down to form a diagonal line. Pull each stitch as tightly as possible as it is being worked. At the end of the row, turn the fabric upside-down and work a second row one fabric thread above the first. Arrange subsequent rows of drawn buttonhole stitches to fill the shape as shown in the diagram.

## EYELET STITCH FILLING

Eyelet stitch filling is used on even-weave fabric with easily counted threads. It produces a solidly stitched surface of tiny eyelets which can be arranged in either straight or diagonal rows to fill a shape. Any type of embroidery thread can be used, providing it is strong enough to hold the pulled threads securely and

of a similar weight and texture to the ground fabric, but a fine thread provides the best result.

First, bring the needle through and insert it two fabric threads to the right. Bring the needle through where it first emerged, making a back stitch (page 13). Work a second back stitch directly over the top. Next, insert the needle three threads down and one thread to the right and make a back stitch, as shown in the second diagram. Work a second back stitch in the same place, then bring the needle through three threads to the left and one thread up ready to work the next pair of back stitches. Work each eyelet in this way, forming the pairs of back stitches alternately around the circumference

and into the centre, as shown, and pulling the thread tightly. Arrange the eyelets in straight rows across the fabric, as shown in the fourth diagram, or work the rows so that the eyelets touch diagonally.

## HONEYCOMB FILLING STITCH

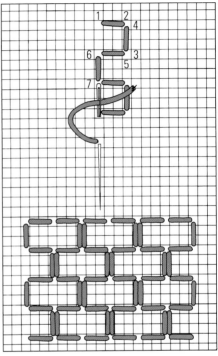

Honeycomb filling stitch is quick and easy to work and makes a pretty honeycomb pattern on even-weave fabric with easily counted threads. The stitches should be pulled as tightly as possible as they are being worked.

Work this stitch up and down in vertical rows. Begin at the top left and bring the needle through, inserting it three fabric threads to the right. Bring the needle through three threads down, insert it at the end of the first stitch and bring it through at the base of the stitch just made. Insert the needle three threads to the left, and bring it through three threads down; insert the needle at the end of the third stitch and bring it through at the base of the stitch just made. Continue in this way along the row, pulling each stitch tightly. Work the next row upwards. The inside vertical stitches in each pair of rows should be worked into the same holes in the fabric.

# PULLED FABRIC STITCHES

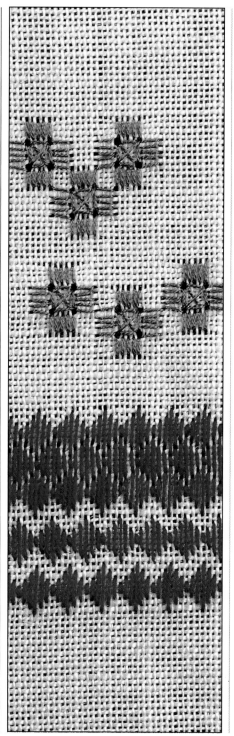

## MOSAIC FILLING

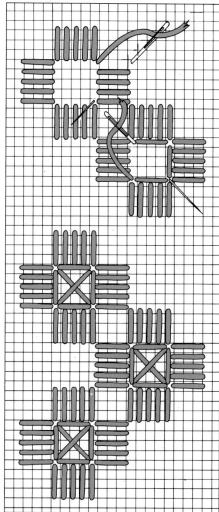

two more blocks to complete the square, as shown in the first diagram. Next, bring the needle through at the bottom right-hand corner of the unworked square at the centre, and work a four-sided stitch (page 192), as shown in the second diagram.

To finish, bring the needle through again at the bottom right-hand corner and work an ordinary cross stitch (page 34) to share the same holes as the four-sided stitch. Arrange the blocks alternately, as shown, or work them solidly. In this case, the right-hand side of one block will form the left-hand side of the next block, and so on.

## MOSAIC DIAMOND FILLING

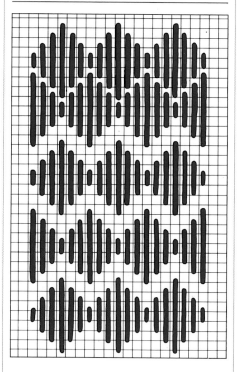

Mosaic filling makes a strong, heavily worked pattern of square blocks which are usually arranged to make a chessboard pattern. Work it on an even-weave fabric with easily counted threads. Any type of embroidery thread can be used, providing it is strong enough to hold the pulled threads securely and of a similar weight and texture to the ground fabric.

First, work a block of five vertical ordinary satin stitches (page 102) from right to left over four fabric threads. Work a block of five horizontal satin stitches at right angles to the first block and touching it at one corner. Work

Mosaic diamond filling is worked on even-weave cotton or linen with easily counted threads. It produces a solidly stitched pattern of diamonds and is quick and easy to execute. To prevent distortion of the diamond pattern, avoid pulling the stitches as tightly as you would most other pulled fabric stitches. Any type of embroidery thread can be used, providing it is strong enough to hold the pulled threads securely and of a similar weight and texture to the ground fabric. Use a blunt-ended tapestry needle to avoid splitting the fabric threads when working the stitches.

Work horizontal rows of vertical ordinary satin stitches (page 102) from left to right and right to left of the shape to be filled. Form the satin stitches into diamond shapes by working them over two, four, six, eight, six, four and two fabric threads, as shown in the diagram. The shortest stitch in each subsequent row should always be worked directly under the longest stitch in the preceding row. Arrange the rows closely together so that the diamond shapes interlock, as shown in the first diagram. Alternatively, leave two or more fabric threads in between each row, as shown in the second diagram, to give an open finish.

## DRAWN SQUARE

Drawn square is worked on even-weave fabric with easily counted threads. It produces a large, decorative square block which can be used alone or worked in equally spaced groups to fill a shape. Pull the stitches as tightly as possible to accentuate the heavy outline. Any type of embroidery thread can be used, providing it is strong enough to hold the pulled threads securely and of a similar weight and texture to the ground fabric. Use a blunt-ended tapestry needle to avoid splitting the fabric threads.

Work each drawn square over twelve vertical and twelve horizontal fabric threads, pulling all the stitches as tightly as possible. Form the outside of the square in ordinary satin stitches (page 102) worked over two threads, as shown in the diagram. At each corner, work five stitches into the same hole. At the centre of the square, work sixteen stitches radiating from the same central hole. To make a larger, more raised square, work the outer stitches over three threads instead of two.

## DETACHED EYELETS

Detached eyelets can be worked individually as isolated stitches, arranged in a straight line to make a border, or used to produce a pretty open filling. They are worked in two sizes: the eyelet shown in the first diagram is small and rounded, while the one in the second diagram is larger and square in shape. Any type of embroidery thread can be used, providing it is strong enough to hold the pulled threads securely and of a similar weight and texture to the fabric.

Work the rounded eyelet over four vertical and four horizontal fabric threads. Work sixteen ordinary satin stitches (page 102) over two threads, arranging the stitches so that they all radiate from the same central hole. Pull the stitches tightly to achieve a well-shaped, rounded eyelet.

Work the larger eyelet over six vertical and six horizontal fabric threads. Work twenty-four satin stitches over two threads, as shown, pulling the stitches tightly. In this case, leave two vertical and two horizontal threads unworked at the centre of the eyelet. Three stitches at each corner and three at each side should be worked into the same holes on the inside edge of the stitch, as shown.

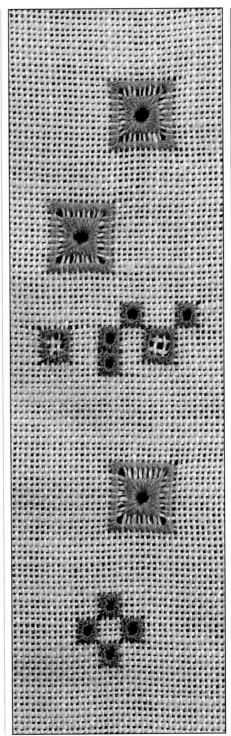

# PULLED FABRIC STITCHES

## ▋DIAGONAL DRAWN FILLING

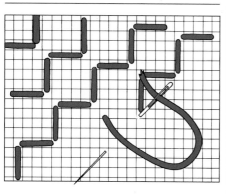

Diagonal drawn filling is a simple, open variation of single faggot stitch (page 192) which is worked on even-weave cotton or linen with well-defined, easily counted threads. It produces an attractive, lacy filling with a strong diagonal feel. The stitches should be pulled tightly as they are being worked to emphasise the characteristic lacy appearance of the filling. Any type of embroidery thread can be used, providing it is strong enough to hold the pulled threads securely in position and of a similar weight and texture to the ground fabric. Use a blunt-ended tapestry needle to avoid splitting the fabric threads when working the stitches and always work on fabric held in an embroidery hoop or frame.

First, work a row of single faggot stitches from top right to bottom left of the shape to be filled. Secure the end of the thread neatly on the wrong side of the fabric, then work another row of single faggot stitches from the top. Set this row one thread below the first row and one thread to the right, as shown in the diagram. Repeat the rows until the shape is filled. For a more open effect, arrange the rows of single faggot stitches either two or three fabric threads apart.

## ▋DIAGONAL RAISED BAND

Diagonal raised band is used on even-weave fabric with easily counted threads. It produces diagonal rows of raised ridges separated by rows of holes across the fabric. Pull the stitches tightly to accentuate the ridges and holes. Any type of embroidery thread can be used, providing it is strong enough to hold the pulled threads securely and of a similar weight and texture to the ground fabric.

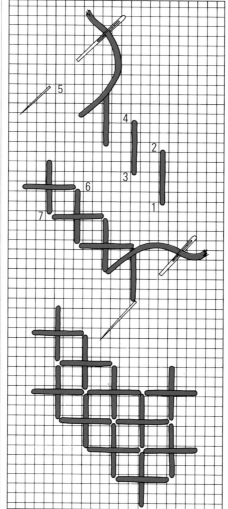

Work from bottom right to top left of the shape to be filled. First, bring the needle through and insert it six fabric threads above, bringing it through three threads to the left and three threads down. Insert the needle six threads above. Continue in this way, ending the row as shown in the first diagram. Work back down the row, inserting the needle six threads to the right and bringing it through three threads to the left and three threads down. Continue in this way, working the stitches into the holes made in the previous row and pulling the stitches tightly to form ridges across the fabric.

Arrange the rows closely together, as shown in the third diagram, or leave two or more fabric threads in between each row for a more open appearance. An attractive effect can be produced if two rows of single faggot stitches (page 192) are worked in between each row of diagonal raised band.

## ▋DRAWN FAGGOT FILLING

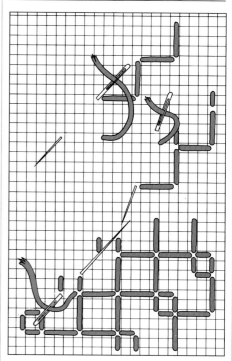

Drawn faggot filling is worked in diagonal rows on even-weave cotton or linen with easily counted threads. It produces an all-over pattern of lacy holes across the fabric.

Begin at the top right of the shape to be filled and work a row of single faggot stitches (page 192) over four fabric threads, as shown in the first diagram. Return to the top corner, and bring the thread through at the top of the first stitch. Insert the needle two threads above, and bring it through two threads to the left and two threads down; insert the needle two threads above, then bring it through two threads to the left and six threads down. Continue in this way to the bottom of the row, then turn the work upside-down and work pairs of similar stitches back along the row to complete the small squares, as shown in the third diagram. Repeat the three rows until the shape is filled, pulling each stitch tightly.

## ▌DOUBLE FAGGOT FILLING

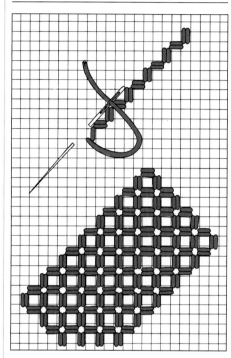

Double faggot filling is used on loosely woven, even-weave cotton or linen with easily counted threads. It produces a solidly stitched filling with a small, regular pattern. Any type of thread can be used, providing it is strong enough to hold the pulled threads securely and of a similar weight and texture to the fabric.

Work double faggot filling in a similar way to single faggot stitch (page 192). Beginning at the top right of the shape to be filled, bring the needle through, and insert it two fabric threads above; bring the needle through where it first emerged, and insert it at the top of the stitch just worked. Bring the needle through two threads to the left and two threads down, and insert it at the base of the first two stitches; bring the needle through at the end of the stitch just worked, and insert it at the base of the first stitch. Next, bring the needle through two threads to the left and work another pair of stitches as before. Repeat along the row, pulling each stitch tightly. Turn the fabric and work the second row in the same way, taking the needle into some of the holes made in the first row, as shown in the diagram. Repeat the two rows until the shape is filled.

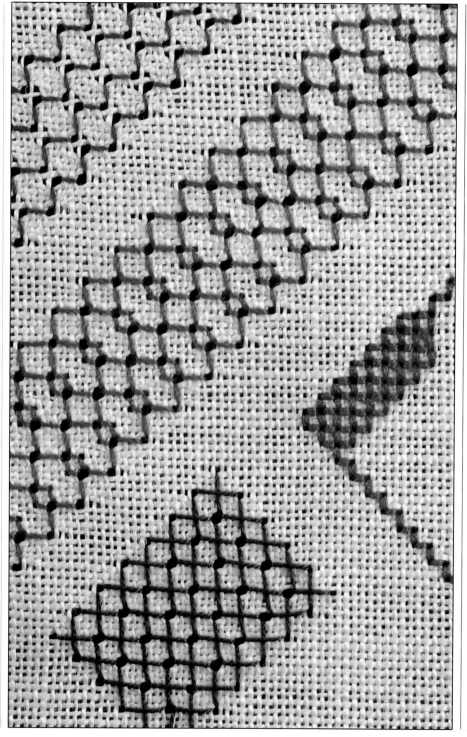

# INDEX

# INDEX

## ACKNOWLEDGMENTS

The publishers would like to thank the following for supplying the embroideries featured in this book:

Wendy Bailey, Barbara Baran, Jan Eaton, Eve's Lace at Antiquarius, Gavin Fry, Mrs Irena Mayer, Paul McAlinden, Amy Speak.